PRAISE FOR *UNTIL I AM FREE*

"Dr. Keisha Blain's beautiful prose and infectious passion for uncovering our historical roots tell Hamer's amazing life story. If America truly respected its own roots, it would see a 'Fannie Lou Hamer' defending the US Constitution to include 'We the People.' Dr. Blain unveils Hamer's leadership in this historical documentation, once again demonstrating that when Black women sit down and demand a seat on the bus or simply get let into the room, we spend the next generation demanding a seat at the table. *Until I Am Free* allows the reader to see a long part of the political and cultural lines from Fannie Lou Hamer to Vice President Kamala Harris."

—DONNA BRAZILE, former chair
of the Democratic National Committee

"What if our nation had taken Fannie Lou Hamer seriously? This is the motivating question of Keisha Blain's insightful new book, *Until I Am Free: Fannie Lou Hamer's Enduring Message to America*. Blain leaves us yearning to live in an America guided by Hamer's unyielding commitment to justice, her full embrace of community, her creative spirit of collective problem-solving, and her unreserved love for Black people. This is a book for everyone who doesn't know the legacy of Fannie Lou Hamer and for everyone who thinks they do, because Blain recovers and uncovers a Hamer who is an activist, an organizer, and a thinker far more exceptional and fully human than most will expect to encounter."

—MELISSA HARRIS-PERRY, author, media host, and the Maya
Angelou Presidential Chair of Politics at Wake Forest University

"We all know Fannie Lou Hamer, the courageous civil rights icon who survived white violence and stood up to Lyndon B. Johnson and the Democratic Party. Keisha Blain's magnificent *Until I Am Free* introduces us to Hamer the political thinker, the strategist and theorist, the internationalist whose expansive vision of freedom embraced the oppressed everywhere. A pathbreaking contribution to our history and a precious guide for today's activists fighting for the world Hamer envisioned."

—ROBIN D. G. KELLEY, author of *Freedom Dreams:
The Black Radical Imagination*

"With elegant, passionate, and powerful prose, award-winning historian Keisha Blain weaves together the political and intellectual legacy of Mississippi sharecropper and visionary political leader Fannie Lou Hamer with the contemporary struggle for racial justice and human freedom. With 'boldness and radical honesty,' Hamer confronted in her own time many of the issues that Black activists are confronting today: state violence, sexism and white supremacy, political disenfranchisement, and economic exploitation. Grounded in the material conditions of her lived experience, Hamer crafted a worldview and a politics of radical inclusivity that guided her actions and inspired others. This book expands the boundaries of the Black radical political and intellectual tradition and re-centers a voice that is too prescient to be ignored."

—BARBARA RANSBY, author of *Making All Black Lives Matter: Reimagining Freedom in the Twenty-First Century*

"In *Until I Am Free*, Dr. Keisha N. Blain has written a rich, detailed, and moving portrait of a woman who was one of the most important civil rights activists in American history. In this meticulous biography of Fannie Lou Hamer, Dr. Blain puts her life and work in conversation with the world around us. In doing so, she gives the reader a profound sense of how Hamer's too-often-ignored contributions helped shape and lay the groundwork for so much of the work that activists continue to do today. This incredibly important book provides new ways of understanding a woman who saw this country for what it was and demanded that it be better."

—CLINT SMITH, author of *How the Word Is Passed: A Reckoning with the History of Slavery Across America*

"Keisha Blain brings Fannie Lou Hamer and her fight for liberation to life in the exhilarating *Until I Am Free*. Alight with curiosity and passion, Blain's view of Hamer is both intimate and political, exquisitely sensitive to the challenges faced by a Black woman sharecropper whose body was too often the site of white supremacist, misogynist violence, and whose revolutionary story has too rarely been framed as such. *Until I Am Free* corrects that omission and will be an invaluable resource for generations to come."

—REBECCA TRAISTER, author of *Good and Mad: The Revolutionary Power of Women's Anger*

UNTIL
I AM FREE

Fannie Lou Hamer, Mississippi, 1960s.

UNTIL
I AM FREE

Fannie Lou Hamer's Enduring
Message to America

KEISHA N. BLAIN

Beacon Press, Boston

BEACON PRESS
Boston, Massachusetts
www.beacon.org

Beacon Press books are published under the auspices
of the Unitarian Universalist Association of Congregations.

24 23 22 21   8 7 6 5 4 3 2 1

This book is printed on acid-free paper that meets the uncoated paper
ANSI/NISO specifications for permanence as revised in 1992.

Jacket image: Photo by Ken Thompson, © The General Board of
Global Ministries of the United Methodist Church, Inc. Used with
permission of Global Ministries.

Text design and composition by Kim Arney

Library of Congress Cataloging-in-Publication Data

Names Blain, Keisha N., author.
Title: Until I am free : Fannie Lou Hamer's enduring message
to America / Keisha N. Blain.
Other titles: Fannie Lou Hamer's enduring message to America
Description: Boston : Beacon Press, [2021] | Includes bibliographical
references and index.
Identifiers: LCCN 2021019372 (print) | LCCN 2021019373 (ebook) |
ISBN 9780807061503 (hardcover) | ISBN 9780807061527 (ebook)
Subjects: LCSH: Hamer, Fannie Lou. | Hamer, Fannie Lou—Influence. |
African American women civil rights workers—Biography. | Civil rights
workers—United States—Biography. | African Americans—Civil
rights—History. | Civil rights movements—United States—History. |
African Americans—Civil rights—Mississippi.
Classification: LCC E185.97.H35 B53 2021 (print) | LCC E185.97.H35
(ebook) | DDC 323.092 [B]—dc23
LC record available at https://lccn.loc.gov/2021019372
LC ebook record available at https://lccn.loc.gov/2021019373

*To Jay and "Little Jay,"
with love*

CONTENTS

A LONG FIGHT AHEAD

We have a long fight and this fight is not mine alone. But you are not free whether you are white or black, until I am free. Because no man is an island to himself. And until I'm free in Mississippi, you are not free in Washington; you are not free in New York.

—FANNIE LOU HAMER[1]

I still remember the very first time I heard about Fannie Lou Hamer. It was in spring 2008, when I was a senior at Binghamton University, and I was taking a course on the American civil rights movement. The professor had assigned readings on Hamer, including interviews and a speech Hamer delivered in the 1960s. I was blown away by what I read and couldn't help wondering why it had taken me so long to encounter this fearless and extraordinary Black woman. The more I learned about Hamer's life and her political vision, however, it became clear to me why she hadn't received the same level of attention and acclaim as so many others: she didn't reflect the public's memory of the civil rights movement. Mainstream historical narratives on Black social movements, then and now, privilege the ideas and political activities of men. Most Americans connect the civil rights movement and Black Power era with Black men such as Martin Luther King Jr., John Lewis, and Malcolm X, to mention a few. And when Black women leaders enter the conversation, the focus tends to be on the same prominent figures, such as Rosa Parks, Coretta Scott

King, and Angela Davis. Needless to say, these trailblazing leaders have all fundamentally shaped American society; their work and lives should be deeply studied. However, the historical record is far richer and more interesting than many realize, including a diverse array of activists and leaders from different classes and all walks of life.

Fannie Lou Hamer's story captures the contributions of a Black woman sharecropper with limited formal education and limited material resources—but an all-consuming passion for social justice. Born in Mississippi on October 6, 1917, Hamer was the youngest of twenty children. The granddaughter of enslaved people, Hamer worked as a sharecropper for much of her life—a brutal practice, closely mirroring the rhythms of slavery in the United States. From sunup to sundown, Hamer and her family cultivated cotton on a local plantation, expanding the fortunes of the white landowners as the Hamer family sank deeper and deeper into debt. At the tender age of twelve, she concluded her studies at a local schoolhouse so she could help her family meet their growing financial pressures. Still, they remained trapped in poverty—the result of the exploitative nature of the sharecropping system and the violence used to maintain it. The difficulties of Hamer's childhood extended well into adulthood when she struggled to make ends meet. Despite her limited material resources and the various challenges she endured as a Black woman living in poverty in Mississippi, Hamer committed herself to making a difference in the lives of others.

Her life changed dramatically in 1962. At age forty-four, she attended a mass meeting at a local church in Sunflower County, Mississippi, organized by activists in the Student Nonviolent Coordinating Committee (SNCC), an interracial civil rights organization. The meeting started her on the path to becoming a voting rights activist. Deeply moved by the words of the young SNCC activists that evening, Hamer learned of her constitutional rights as a citizen of the United States—she later said it was the first time she learned she had the right to vote. That year, Hamer became a field secretary for SNCC and worked to assist Black residents in Mississippi with voter registration. Activists in SNCC later praised Hamer for the role she played in amplifying their work and keeping them focused on accomplishing their goals. "As for the SNCC part of her continuing movement life, she kept us on track," members of the SNCC legacy project noted. "It was not difficult for a group of young people, like we were then, to sometimes stumble off course; she kept us focused on doing what was right. She commanded our respect as well as our love."[2]

When she joined the civil rights movement in 1962, Hamer decided to dedicate her time and talents to the betterment of Black people and other marginalized groups. In the years to follow, she launched a number of initiatives aimed at expanding voting rights as well as addressing racism and inequality in her community and across the nation. Working alongside SNCC activists, Hamer spearheaded voter education workshops in the South, facilitated voter registration drives, and participated in marches and sit-ins throughout the region.[3] Her efforts to expand voting rights for Black people in the South drew the ire of many, especially local white supremacists who attempted to impede her political work at every turn. From the moment she joined the civil rights movement, Hamer became a target of violence, harassment, and intimidation. By extension, her loved ones also became the targets of local law enforcement. In one instance, Hamer's husband, Perry ("Pap"), was arrested and jailed. Local police also targeted one of Hamer's daughters, who was arrested in 1963.[4] Hamer was also harassed for a water bill in the amount of $9,000, even though the Hamers had no running water at the time. And on one occasion, local police officers barged into her home—all the way to her and Pap's bedroom—in the wee hours of the morning, waving guns and flashlights, with a litany of questions about her personal affairs.

These incidents went beyond intimidation when Hamer endured a brutal beating in Winona, Mississippi, in 1963. In June of that year, Hamer was traveling back home with fellow activists after attending a voters' workshop in South Carolina. They decided to stop in Winona to grab a bite to eat. What was supposed to be a quick rest stop became one of the most harrowing experiences of Hamer's life. The owners of the restaurant refused to serve Black patrons. Then, from the bus, Hamer noticed police officers shoving her friends into their patrol cars. Within minutes of exiting the bus, Hamer was grabbed by an officer who began violently kicking her. Later at the police station, officers, aided by prisoners, unleashed a brutal beating on Hamer, which left her with permanent scars and physically disabled.

Despite the painful and traumatic experiences, Hamer refused to be thrown off her mission. As activist Dorothy Height, president of the National Council of Negro Women (NCNW), once remarked, Hamer "turned all of her own suffering into freedom and justice for her people."[5] In the aftermath of the 1963 Winona beating, Hamer amplified her political work, determined to transform American society through an expansion of Black voting rights. Hamer not only helped to register voters but also empowered others by entering the realm of electoral politics. In 1964, one year after she successfully registered to vote for the first time, Hamer ran for a seat in the US House of Representatives to challenge white Mississippi Democrat Jamie Whitten, who was seeking a thirteenth term. Although her chances of winning were slim, she explained to a reporter, "I'm showing people that a Negro can run for office."[6] With a limited budget, Hamer ran a spirited campaign backed by a coalition of civil rights organizations, promising to tackle the issues of poverty and hunger. Unsuccessful in her first bid for Congress that year, Hamer went on to run for office twice more—ever committed to the idea that electoral politics and public service could help overturn decades of unjust laws and policies in the United States.

One of the things that stood out to me when I first learned about Hamer was her unique ability to speak to the heart of any issue. Her demeanor and approach cut directly to the core of the problems facing Americans, without ever tiptoeing around an issue or worrying about anyone's feelings or comfort level. Those who had the great fortune to hear Hamer speak left her presence completely transformed. Civil rights activist Eleanor Holmes Norton, with whom Hamer organized during the 1960s, described Hamer as "an unbelievably brilliant orator and conceptualizer. . . . [Y]ou've never heard a room flying [like one] Fannie Lou set afire," Norton explained.[7] After Hamer spoke, Norton added, those who were listening "never needed to hear anyone else speak [on the issue] again."[8]

Hamer's passion and candidness forced those around her to look deep within themselves—to acknowledge their failings and often their own prejudices. She was unafraid to publicly condemn those who perpetuated injustice and did not shy away from acknowledging societal ills and demanding more from public officials. She even challenged civil rights leaders and allies in the struggle, pointing out their inconsistencies and the moments when they were too complacent. Responding to those who insisted on gradualism—waiting for the "right" moment to secure Black rights and liberation—Hamer looked to history as her guide. "For three hundred years," she explained, "we've given them [white people] time. And I've been tired so long," she continued, "now I am sick and tired of being sick and tired. We want a change in this society in America," she added.[9]

Hamer's political work was motivated by her Christian faith. She believed that God was on her side and favored everyone fighting for the rights and equality of Black people. But she also understood that faith alone could not bring an end to racial injustice in this country. And faith alone could not dismantle white supremacy.[10] Combining faith with action, Hamer fought to secure the rights and liberation of Black people and all oppressed groups. Hamer's fiery resolve to improve American society left a lasting, positive mark on all who crossed her path. Heather Booth, a young white volunteer who met Hamer in Ruleville, Mississippi, during the 1960s, recalled the impact Hamer had on her life: "While I was a very young volunteer, and so inexperienced in the reality of Mississippi, she treated me and the other volunteers on an equal footing—neither above nor below her in respect. And by doing so, modeled how we each can treat each other. And showed us how to center ourselves in morality to do the right thing."[11]

Hamer's boldness and radical honesty were on full display in August 1964, when she spoke before a televised audience at the Democratic National Convention in Atlantic City, New Jersey. She had traveled all the way from Mississippi on behalf of the Mississippi Freedom Democratic Party (MFDP)—an organization she helped establish in April 1964 to challenge the all-white Mississippi delegation. Hamer's televised speech, delivered before millions, addressed two central issues that remain relevant in contemporary Black political discourse: voter suppression and state-sanctioned violence. First, she addressed the issue of Black voting rights. She told the story of how when she went down to the courthouse in Indianola, Mississippi, to attempt to register to vote in 1962, she was confronted by one roadblock after another. When she returned home that evening, the owner of the plantation where she worked as a sharecropper gave her an ultimatum: "If you don't go down and withdraw your registration, you will have to leave." And leave she did.

In her speech before the Democratic National Convention, Hamer went on to describe the persistent acts of racist violence Black people faced on a daily basis in the Jim Crow South. She told the stories of shots being fired at the homes of those who supported her stance on voting. And then she told the story of her own experiences with state-sanctioned violence—she recounted the details of the severe beating she received in that Winona jail cell in 1963.[12] As she reflected on her own painful experiences and the experiences of other Black people in the South, Hamer could not help but to "question America." "Is this America," she asked as tears welled up in her eyes, "the land of the free and the home of the brave, where we have to sleep with our telephones off of the hooks because our lives be threatened daily, because we want to live as decent human beings, in America?" These crucial words shook the nation to its core. Hamer had asked a poignant question that all Americans were forced to ponder. If Americans claimed to be committed to the ideals of "liberty and justice for all," then Hamer's testimony laid bare the full extent of American hypocrisy.

Those who heard the speech, either in person or on television, were transformed by its power. Although the speech made Hamer an instant celebrity, it was but one of the many moving and dynamic speeches she delivered during the 1960s and '70s. Those who worked alongside her on a daily basis and those who lived in her community witnessed the full extent of Hamer's work, extending far beyond that one televised speech. Indeed, Hamer set out to touch the lives of everyone she encountered, never turning away a person in need—regardless of their race. She loved people, and that love propelled Hamer to dedicate her life and her resources, no matter how small, to improving the lives of the people in Sunflower County. And she connected the fight on the ground in the Mississippi Delta with the struggle of people all over the world who sought to overcome the politics of hate with love.

Love for others guided her political activism and provided the impetus for her decision to undertake several initiatives during her lifetime. As she once explained, "Freedom is in my soul and love is in my heart."[13] During the late 1960s, she launched the Freedom Farm Cooperative, a community-based rural project, to tackle poverty in Mississippi and advance economic empowerment. As someone whose life had been deeply affected by hunger and poverty, Hamer envisioned Freedom Farm as a response to the hunger and poverty that ran rampant in Sunflower County. Hamer also continued her national advocacy, including her valuable contributions to the women's rights movement. A victim of sexual and medical abuse, Hamer turned her pain into political action, becoming the first civil rights activist to publicly speak out against forced sterilizations. Although she did not identify as a feminist, Hamer firmly believed in women's empowerment and advocated for women's representation in electoral politics. In 1971, she joined forces with a diverse group of women, including feminist leader Gloria Steinem and US congresswoman Shirley Chisholm, to establish the National Women's Political Caucus (NWPC), with whom she worked to expand women's political participation at the local, state, and national levels.

Although Hamer was deeply committed to securing political rights for Black people in the United States, she was also a vocal champion in the struggle for human rights. She recognized that the challenges Black Americans encountered were inextricably linked to freedom struggles abroad. Throughout her political career, she also saw how global developments shaped American life and culture. She supported African liberation movements, and long before many other civil rights activists addressed the issue, Hamer boldly condemned American involvement in the Vietnam War. Her position on Vietnam, and her overall critique of American foreign policy during the 1960s and '70s, underscored her expansive vision of freedom. By linking national concerns to global ones, Hamer compelled others to see the value of forging transnational political collaborations in order to effectively build a more just and equal society.

These are just some of the highlights of Fannie Lou Hamer's extraordinary life and activism. Her political career was comparatively short—only fifteen years—but immensely impactful. From the moment she joined the civil rights movement at age forty-four to her passing at the age of fifty-nine, Hamer accomplished more than most people manage to accomplish in a lifetime—and she did so with few material resources. Despite humble beginnings and limited formal education, Hamer refused to be sidelined in the movement and refused to be intimidated by those of higher social status and with better jobs and education. She knew her leadership and intellectual contributions were valuable, and she lived with a clear sense of purpose—to make a better life for herself and others. Yet her life experiences grounded her in reality—she never imagined a better future without a clear plan of action. And she maintained hope that America could one day live up to its promise and its ideals.

Even those who never met Hamer in person were transformed by her words as well as her deeds. This is certainly true for me. My intellectual encounter with Hamer during my early twenties changed the course of my life. Though I had already resolved to become a historian of the Black experience—with plans to one day write books that would center the diverse voices of individuals from all walks of life—I constantly battled self-doubt. As a first-generation college student from a family of modest means, I questioned the quality of what I had to offer. My desire to make a difference in society seemed completely displaced from the reality of my material circumstances. Hamer's powerful example bolstered my sense of purpose and desire to make a meaningful difference in the lives of others. And through her example, I learned to think less about what I don't have and instead focus on what I *do* have and how it can best be of use in the service of others. Hamer also taught me the value of straightforward dialogue—the need to always be direct about the challenges we're facing as a nation, especially about issues of race and racism. Above all, she taught me the importance of using my voice as a Black woman in America to call out injustice wherever I see it. Her story and the lessons she taught through her words and example provide a model for how I approach the ongoing fight for human rights.

Since I first encountered Hamer in a college course on the civil rights movement, I have thought often about how she would respond to many of the challenges we're facing in the United States. In truth, there has been little change since the 1960s and '70s. While there is much to celebrate about the achievements we have made as a nation—including the dismantling of Jim Crow and the expansion of Black voting rights—many of the roadblocks Hamer encountered in her lifetime continue to shape the lives of Black people in the United States today. Economic inequality remains a challenge in Hamer's hometown of Ruleville, Mississippi, with more than 40 percent of the population living below the poverty line—the majority of whom are Black and Latinx residents.[14] And despite the expansion of voting rights in the state, no African American candidate has been elected to statewide office since 1890.[15] Hamer's fight lives on today as Black people in the United States continue to face many of the same challenges she fought so vigorously to correct.

Despite the many political gains and triumphs over the years, racism and white supremacy persist in all aspects of American life and culture. Since the passage of the 1965 Voting Rights Act, which upheld Black Americans' right to vote as guaranteed by the Fifteenth Amendment of the US Constitution, a number of state and local laws have worked in tandem to curtail these rights. Moreover, the systemic problem of police violence and brutality in Black communities across the nation mirrors the pervasive lynchings of the Jim Crow era. These realities, combined with other social problems such as hunger, poverty, and economic inequality, continue to plague American society, and in so doing, threaten American democracy. The defining feature of Hamer's political vision was her belief that the United States could indeed live up to its ideals. Even as she held some amount of skepticism, Hamer never lost hope that the nation could in fact one day be transformed—it would require a lot of work and it would take some time, but it was possible. Through individual and collective effort, Americans committed to social justice could build an inclusive democracy that lived up to the promises of the US Constitution.

This was the message she passionately conveyed in a 1967 speech before members of a local NCNW chapter in Mississippi. "We have a long fight and this fight is not mine alone," she explained. "But you are not free whether you are white or black, until I am free. Because no man is an island to himself. And until I'm free in Mississippi, you are not free in Washington; you are not free in New York."[16] Her remarks underscored how the fate of Black people in the United States was—and still is—connected to all Americans, regardless of race, class, or even location. America's mistreatment of and disregard for Black people in Mississippi, Hamer argued, signaled the nation's failure to live up to its promises. And this failure was one that fundamentally shaped the lives of everyone on US soil. The societal problems that hampered Black life were concerns that all Americans had to face—whether they wanted to confront those issues or not.

In Hamer's framing, no one could truly experience freedom if others in that society were constrained. She reiterated this message on a number of occasions, underscoring the danger of being complicit in the face of injustice. "Until I am free," she boldly told the mostly white audience members at the University of Wisconsin in 1971, "you are not either."[17] In so many ways, Hamer's words are timeless. They speak to the current moment and offer hope and guidance for those of us who are committed to social justice today, as they did for freedom fighters during the 1960s and '70s.

That's why I decided to write this book. *Until I Am Free* centers Hamer's ideas and political philosophies to demonstrate how they speak to our current moment. It posits that Hamer's insights and political strategies during the 1960s and '70s provide a blueprint for tackling a range of contemporary social issues. A blend of social commentary, biography, and intellectual history, *Until I Am Free* draws from an array of sources—including Hamer's speeches and oral and written interviews, films, historical newspapers, and archival material—to illuminate Hamer's perspectives on several prescient and interconnected themes: race and racism; social justice; voting rights and voter suppression; internationalism and human rights; state-sanctioned violence; leadership and activism; economic inequality; and women's rights. *Until I Am Free* builds on a rich and ever-growing body of research and writing on Hamer to highlight some—but certainly not all—aspects of her life's story to understand the influences, forces, and developments that shaped her thinking and political vision.[18] In these pages, Hamer's words and ideas take center stage, allowing us all to hear the activist's voice and deeply engage with her words as though we had the privilege to sit right beside her.

What might we learn, and how might our society change, if we simply listened to Fannie Lou Hamer? *Until I Am Free* grapples with this question. It is a manifesto, deeply rooted in history, for anyone committed to social justice. The book challenges us all to listen to a working-poor and disabled Black woman activist and intellectual from the past as we confront contemporary concerns, many of which consumed Hamer's mind during her lifetime. More than forty years since Hamer's death, her words still speak truth to power, laying bare the faults in American society and offering valuable insights on how we might yet continue the fight to help the nation live up to its core ideals of "equality and justice for all." In the spirit of Hamer, *Until I Am Free* takes as its premise that our histories and experiences may be different, but our fates are deeply intertwined. Try as we might, we cannot disentangle ourselves from the concerns of others who make up this diverse nation. The work of democracy is incomplete, but the fight is certainly not over. As Hamer reiterated time and time again, we still have the power to make these ideals a reality. Our individual futures, as well as our collective future, in the United States depend on it. We must keep pushing for change. We have a long fight ahead.

UNTIL
I AM FREE

CHAPTER ONE

LET YOUR LIGHT SHINE

"A city that's set on a hill cannot be hid." And I don't mind my light shining. I don't hide that I'm fighting for freedom.

—FANNIE LOU HAMER[1]

O n August 27, 1962, Fannie Lou Hamer found her calling. That evening, the forty-four-year-old Black sharecropper attended a mass meeting arranged by the Student Nonviolent Coordinating Committee (SNCC), an interracial civil rights group that played a central role in organizing and encouraging Black residents in the South to register to vote.[2] Held at the William Chapel Missionary Baptist Church in Ruleville, the SNCC meeting brought together activists and local residents interested in learning more about the group's voting registration efforts in the community.[3] The meeting transformed Hamer, who learned for the first time that she had a right to vote as a citizen of the United States: "I didn't know anything about voting; I didn't know anything about registering to vote."[4]

"They were talking about [how] we could vote out people that we didn't want in office," she later recalled. "That sounded interesting enough to me that I wanted to try it."[5] Hamer realized in that moment that she had the ability to transform American society—access to the ballot gave her the power to shape local, state, and national politics. The 1962 mass meeting in Mississippi marked the beginning of Hamer's entry into civil rights activism. From that day forward, she chose to devote her life to expanding Black political rights—emboldened by the belief that Black people, through the formal political process, held the power to overturn centuries of unjust laws.

It was especially fitting that Hamer came to realize her life's purpose while sitting in the pews of a local church. A woman of faith, Hamer was grounded by the teachings of the Bible. She believed that God had ordained her calling—to passionately advocate for Black people and other marginalized groups. It was a spiritual calling as much as a political one. Hamer herself captured this dual purpose and vision during a 1963 speech at the Freedom Vote rally in Greenwood, Mississippi. Citing the mission of Jesus, as recounted in Luke 4:18, Hamer emphasized the importance of knowing one's calling. She cautioned attendees not to focus on the challenges ahead or on those who schemed against Black people: "Pits have been dug for us for ages. But they didn't know, when they was digging pits for us, they had some pits dug for themselves."[6] Emboldened by her belief that God was on the side of all those seeking freedom and justice, Hamer told those in attendance to embrace their life's purpose.

Accepting one's life's calling, Hamer argued, was akin to shining a light into a world of darkness. "That's why I love the song 'This Little Light of Mine,'" she explained. "From the fifth chapter of Matthew, [Jesus] said, 'A city that's set on a hill cannot be hid.' And I don't mind my light shining," Hamer continued. "I don't hide that I'm fighting for freedom because Christ died to set us free."[7] For Hamer, her calling was made clear in August 1962 when she learned of the power of the vote. She set out to live a life deeply devoted to the cause of freedom. This was not the life she could have imagined only a few years prior, but it was the path she firmly believed God had placed before her. The experiences in her past had empowered her to recognize this moment.

"LIFE WAS VERY HARD."

Hamer, the granddaughter of enslaved African Americans, was born Fannie Alma Louise Du Bois Townsend on October 6, 1917, into a family of sharecroppers in Webster County, Mississippi.[8] Both her parents, James Lee and Lou Ella Townsend, were natives of Mississippi, and she was the youngest of their twenty children.[9] While James and Lou Ella worked as sharecroppers on a local plantation, they also held various positions on the side. According to Hamer, her father was a Baptist preacher and her mother was a domestic. At the age of two, Hamer and her family relocated to Sunflower County, Mississippi, where she would spend the rest of her life.[10] Their move coincided with the first wave of the Great Migration. While millions of Black Southerners relocated to Northern and Western Cities, some Black families, like Hamer's, remained in the region but moved to other towns in search of better job opportunities. The Townsend family found work on the plantation of E. W. Brandon, a white landowner near the town of Ruleville.[11] Like most Black people living in Mississippi, the Townsend family worked the cotton crops—clearing, planting, chopping, and picking. Since the late eighteenth century, the United States relied heavily on the growing institution of slavery to maintain the production of cotton—the first mass consumer commodity. During the nineteenth century, cotton was the primary American export, which fundamentally shaped the American economy.[12] In the aftermath of the Civil War, cotton continued to play a central role in the United States, especially in Southern states. White landowners in the South relied on cotton production—and the exploited labor of Black people—to maintain their economic power.

Hamer's family joined countless other Black families in the region, where oppressive plantation work shaped everyday life. Reflecting on her life many years later, Hamer emphasized the challenges her family endured as Black people living in the Jim Crow South during the early twentieth century. "Life was very hard," Hamer explained. "We never hardly had enough to eat; we didn't have clothes to wear. We had to work real hard," she continued "because I started working when I was about six years old."[13] Despite long days of backbreaking work, the Townsend family did not have enough resources to meet the family's needs. "So many times for dinner we would have greens with no seasonin' . . . and flour gravy," Hamer recalled. "My mother would mix flour with a little grease and try to make gravy out of it."[14]

Like so many other Black children growing up in the South during this period, few educational opportunities existed for Hamer and her siblings. Following the end of slavery with the passage of the Thirteenth Amendment in 1865, white Southerners worked to keep Black people from having access to formal education.[15] Black Southerners devised a range of strategies after the Civil War to resist white supremacist policies and practices. The rise of Black educational spaces, including church schools and historically Black colleges and universities (HBCUs), aimed to counter local resistance to Black education. Yet the few schools that did exist in the Mississippi Delta had limited resources and financial support. The vast disparities in quality between white and Black schools in the South, fueled by white supremacist tactics and ideology, created a difficult atmosphere for Black parents in Mississippi and across the South.

The dire financial need of Southern Black families further compounded these challenges. In the aftermath of slavery, sharecropping emerged as the primary means by which Southern Black farmers could earn a living. This system—designed by white landowners—created a cycle of unending dependency, debt, and debt peonage for Black Americans, with little prospect for landownership or the accumulation of wealth.[16] In a typical family of sharecroppers, each member was expected to contribute to the cultivation of crops, and children were no exception. Each hour devoted to educational instruction was one hour removed from work on the plantation. Black parents struggled to support the educational development of their children while confronting the painful reality that their livelihood depended on their children as a labor force. In an effort to respond to this dual concern, Black schools in the Mississippi Delta largely operated around the production season. On local plantations, therefore, schools were open for sharecropping children when the workload was light.[17] In Hamer's case, she generally attended school only after the harvest was complete.[18]

The truncated school calendar allowed greater flexibility for Black sharecropping families, but it also meant that Black children had far less instruction—and were therefore less formally educated—than their white counterparts. Hamer attended school when she could, on and off, for a period of six years. As she explained, "I didn't have a chance to go to school too much, because school would only last about four months at the time when I was a kid going to school. Most of the time we didn't have clothes to wear to that [school]," she continued, "and then if any work would come up that we would have to do, the parents would take us out of the school to cut stalks and burn stalks or work in dead lands or things like that. It was just really tough as a kid."[19]

Despite the challenges she endured as a child, Hamer deeply valued the limited formal education she received. "I loved reading when I was in school," she later recalled. In addition to reading the Bible, Hamer read an array of children's books—often filled with stories that reinforced ideas of white superiority and Black inferiority.[20] While she did not always grasp the covert messages in what appeared to be lighthearted children's books, Hamer took advantage of every opportunity to learn as much as she could. "I learned to read real well when I was going to school," she explained. "I never had a chance to go to school too long—about six years—but I believe I can compete today with a kid now that's twelfth grade at least."[21]

Hamer was only six years old when she began working in the cotton fields. Like the majority of white landowners in Mississippi whose success depended on the deliberate inequity of the sharecropping system, E. W. Brandon exploited the labor of Black tenants to grow cotton. Brandon had no qualms about manipulating Black children if it meant he would be able to bolster his wealth, a position he made clear when he approached a young Hamer to trick her into picking cotton on the plantation. In a 1965 interview with *Freedomways,* Hamer recounted the moment Brandon prematurely lured her into a life of sharecropping:

> I would like to talk about some of the things that happened that made me know that there was something wrong in the South from a child. My parents moved to Sunflower County when I was two years old. I remember, and I will never forget, one day—I was six years old and I was playing beside the road and this plantation owner drove up to me and stopped and asked me "could I pick some cotton." I told him I didn't know and he said, "Yes, you can. I will give you things that you want from the commissary store," and he named things like crackerjacks and sardines—and it was a huge list that he called off. So I picked the 30 pounds of cotton that week, but I found out what actually happened was he was trapping me into beginning the work I was to keep doing. And I never did get out of his debt again.[22]

The incident, forever etched in Hamer's mind, illuminates the lengths to which white landowners went to maintain their wealth and preserve white supremacy. Indeed, the expansion of landowner-ship and wealth for white people—at the expense of Black people—helped to keep white supremacy firmly in place. It was a lesson Hamer learned at a tender age and one she would carry for the rest of her life.

The lack of access to quality health care and other social resources further exacerbated the harsh conditions of cotton production in Mississippi. With a lack of access to medical care, African Americans in the South had to devise their own strategies to address ailments and illnesses as best they could.[23] No home remedy, however, could curb the devastating effects of the polio epidemic that swept the nation during the early twentieth century. Polio—a diagnosis that led to per-manent disability and, in many cases, death—hit African American communities especially hard, though the cases of polio in the Black South generally went underreported.[24] Like many African Americans in the region, Hamer contracted the virus as a child, leaving her with a persistent limp.[25]

Despite everything "wrong in the South," as Hamer put it, her parents tried to create a supportive atmosphere at home. Her father, James, worked diligently on the farm and did whatever he could—even bootlegging—to help make ends meet.[26] A sharecropper by day, James was also a Baptist minister who raised his children surrounded by the teachings of the Bible.[27] Hamer's experiences in her father's ser-vices—which drew a small group of faithful parishioners who met in the cramped Townsend home—were transformative. A young Hamer drew strength from the teachings of the Bible, listening carefully to the verses her father shared week after week. In this setting, among close friends and family, Hamer began to use her voice to sing the church songs she had come to learn on the farm.[28]

As a child, Hamer attended a Baptist church called Stranger's Home, a small gathering of believers with few material resources but an abundance of faith. "Stranger's Home, it was called, and that's just what it was," Hamer later remarked.[29] At the age of twelve, she was baptized in the Quiver River—a rite of passage that marked her pub-lic entry into the faith.[30] Hamer's exposure to Christian teachings at a young age left a lasting mark on her life.[31] In the years to follow, she became a practical theologian, living out her faith and beliefs through concrete steps and actions.[32] She proposed real-life practical solutions to the challenges in her community and across the nation. Her faith propelled her to find ways to transform those around her, and she creatively used the lessons from the Bible to guide her civic and political engagement.[33] Although Hamer said very little about her father, the few recollections from her siblings revealed that James could be a strict parent—especially so with Fannie. As the youngest child in the family, Hamer often delved into mischief on the plantation, wreaking havoc for her older siblings. In one instance, later described by her sister, Laura Ratliff, a young Hamer made a mess in the kitchen and quickly ran away when her father arrived to witness the scene.[34] "Papa would want to whip Fannie Lou because she was just too bad, but Mama wouldn't let anyone touch her," Ratliff recalled.[35]

The revelations from Ratliff exemplify the close relationship Hamer had with her mother, Lou Ella. According to Hamer, Lou Ella taught her how to live a life of courage and dignity.[36] Hamer's recounting of her mother's decision to gift her with a Black doll exemplifies Lou Ella's commitment to instilling a sense of race pride in her children and empowering them in an environment that tried to strip them of their personhood. "I was the only Black child with a Black doll," Hamer recalled. "This gift came when I asked my mother one day why I wasn't white. She was a woman who believed deeply that black was beautiful and not a shade less than beautiful," she said firmly.[37] Hamer elaborated on this point years later, emphasizing that her mother worked to cultivate Black pride in her children. "So my mother told me," Hamer recalled, "number one, she wanted me to remember to respect myself as a black child and as I got older she told me to respect myself as a black woman. And she said, 'Maybe you don't understand what I am talking about now, but one day if you respect yourself other people will have to respect you.'"[38] Lou Ella's prophetic words would form the core of Hamer's philosophy. Though she could not have known it then, Hamer would revisit her mother's advice time and time again as she navigated the difficulties of life in the Mississippi Delta, where racism and white supremacy shaped every aspect of Black life. Hamer would come to understand racism's powerful hold as she came of age working on the Brandon plantation.

Once Hamer stopped attending school, she devoted the majority of her time to chopping and picking cotton with her parents and siblings.[39] The work was grueling, and it yielded little in result. "We'd make fifty and sixty bales and wouldn't clear enough money to live on in the winter months," Hamer explained.[40] It took several years before her parents managed to earn enough money in the harvesting season one year to get by during the winter. With the money they earned that year, James purchased "some wagons and cultivators, plow tools and mules in the hopes that he could rent the next year."[41] His hopes were quickly dashed, however, when a white neighbor poisoned the recently purchased livestock. The white man's vindictive actions served a greater purpose in the community. Similar to the act of lynching, the poisoning kept an aspiring Black family "in their place" by crippling their finances, thereby reinforcing the broader system of white supremacy that defined the Jim Crow South.

The act permanently damaged the Townsend family's finances. "That poisoning knocked us right back down flat. We never did get back up again," Hamer admitted.[42] "White people never like to see Negroes get a little success. All of this stuff is no secret in the state of Mississippi."[43] In the aftermath of the devastating poisoning, Hamer's father drew strength from the book of Psalms, reminding his faithful parishioners that "evildoers . . . shall be cut down like the green grass and wither away as the green herb."[44] At the conclusion of the sermon, Hamer's father encouraged her to sing her favorite song. In this moment of darkness, as the family was reeling from an act of vandalism and violence, Hamer's rendition of "This Little Light of Mine" no doubt soothed hearts and minds: "This little light of mine, I'm gonna let it shine / This little light of mine, I'm gonna let it shine / Let it shine, let it shine, let it shine."[45] Those words became a guiding mantra in Hamer's life and came to embody her life's mission long before she entered the national spotlight.

Despite their best efforts, the family's circumstances only became more difficult with time.[46] Already elderly by the time of the poisoning, James Lee and Lou Ella struggled to keep up the grueling hours of sharecropping and, even with their children's help on the plantation, found themselves in a never-ending cycle of poverty. During the winter months, Lou Ella devised a range of creative strategies to ensure that her family would have something to eat—no matter how small. Hamer would later reflect on her mother's efforts to keep the family afloat during the direst of circumstances:

> My parents were getting up in age and weren't young when I was born. I used to watch my mother try and keep her family going after we didn't get enough money out of the cotton crop. To feed us during the winter months mama would go 'round from plantation to plantation and would ask landowners if she could have the cotton that had been left, which was called scrappin' cotton. When they would tell her that we could have that cotton, we would walk for miles and miles in the run of the week. We wouldn't have on shoes or anything because we didn't have them. She would always tie our feet up with rags because the ground would be froze real hard. We would walk from field to field until we had scrapped a bale of cotton. Then she'd take that bale of cotton and sell it and that would give us some of the food that we would need.[47]

Hamer's description captured the strength and determination of her mother, who tried to improve the circumstances for her children as best as she could. As Hamer later emphasized, her mother was as resourceful as she was fiercely protective of her children.[48] When a white supervisor on the plantation raised his fist to strike one of Hamer's brothers, Lou Ella quickly moved into action and grabbed the overseer's arm.[49] Her defiant warning let the overseer know that no one could touch her children—a bold act of defiance, one that could have easily cost Lou Ella her life. Yet Lou Ella stood steadfast to defend her children and showed her willingness to place her life on the line to protect those she loved. No doubt Lou Ella was guided by the same instinct when she chose to carry a 9-millimeter pistol, carefully tucked away in her cast-iron pot, as she worked on the plantation.[50]

Through her example, Lou Ella taught Hamer the importance of Black pride and self-respect—and a commitment to defending one's principles at any cost. Still, as Hamer came to understand, Black people living in the Jim Crow South could never escape a life of pain and hardship. Hamer watched on helplessly as her parents' health deteriorated as they worked from "sunup to sundown" on the farm.

In 1930, while "clearing new ground" on the plantation, Hamer's mother was struck in the eye with a splinter as she chopped wood. With no means of seeking medical care, Lou Ella's eyesight diminished over time and eventually led to permanent blindness.[51] The tragic accident would be one of many catastrophic experiences Fannie endured during this period. In 1939, her father, James, passed away shortly after having a stroke.[52] His passing dealt another significant blow to Hamer, who had developed her Christian faith under his teaching and spiritual mentoring. The gradual dismantling of her close-knit family further intensified the pain of losing her father. In only a matter of years, Hamer watched on in disappointment as each of her nineteen siblings left the Brandon plantation to pursue new opportunities.[53]

Sometime around 1944, Hamer followed suit. After working on the Brandon plantation since the age of six, Hamer left around the age of twenty-seven to begin working for W. D. Marlow, a white landowner in Ruleville.[54] Her departure coincided with her growing relationship with Perry "Pap" Hamer, a local sharecropper who was already employed on the Marlow plantation. The circumstances surrounding Hamer's relationship with Pap are shrouded in mystery—perhaps because Hamer was already married when the two fell in love. Though Hamer never discussed her love life during these years or later, extant court records reveal that at the age of twenty, Hamer married a man by the name of Charlie Gray, a farm laborer from Ruleville.[55] If Gray's petition for divorce from Fannie Lou tells the full story of their union, then it appears that Hamer abandoned her marriage to begin a life with Pap.[56] In Hamer's close-knit Christian community, the mere accusation of adultery—let alone the act—would have certainly raised some eyebrows. During an era in which ideas of "respectable" behavior informed Black life and culture, charges of adultery would have tainted Hamer's public image.[57] Perhaps this is why she carefully concealed this information from others. Those who were aware of the circumstances refused to publicly discuss it—likely for the same reasons Hamer kept the details to herself.[58]

What was recorded publicly—and celebrated widely—was the union that took place between Fannie Lou and Perry "Pap" Hamer in July 1944.[59] A farmer and skilled tractor driver, Pap was five years older than Fannie Lou and was originally from the small town of Kilmichael, Mississippi.[60] He made the trek to Ruleville, Mississippi—perhaps in search of new job opportunities—sometime around 1932 and began working on the Marlow plantation. It's unclear when he and Fannie Lou first crossed paths, but there is no doubt that the two fell madly in love. The affection and admiration between the two were undeniable, and this love sustained Hamer during difficult moments of her life. "I love all 225 pounds of him," Hamer once noted. "I just like to look at him, do things for him."[61] Together, Fannie Lou and Pap started their new life, working as sharecroppers on the Marlow plantation in Ruleville during the 1940s and '50s. In the early 1950s, Lou Ella—then in her eighties—moved in with Hamer and her husband. Pap, who had lost his mother at a young age, embraced Lou Ella as his own mother, and the two maintained a close relationship until her passing in 1961.[62]

Even in death, Lou Ella's words and experiences loomed large in Hamer's life. "My life has been almost like my mother's was, because I married a man who sharecropped," Hamer explained in her auto-biography.[63] While she had some access to resources Lou Ella did not have during her life—such as a more modern home with running water—Hamer spent her days much as her mother did, toiling on the farm from dawn to dusk.[64] When the plantation owner caught wind of the fact that Hamer could read and write, he expanded her responsibilities on the farm—promoting her to the position of timekeeper and relying on her to keep a record of the cotton production.[65] These new duties gave her a window into the extent to which white land-owners were exploiting Black sharecroppers. Hamer later described some of these tactics and her efforts to resist:

> So, as I was in charge with keeping up with the cotton weights on this plantation, this landowner not only would rob us economically through the cotton, but I would have to weigh the cotton and keep up with the weight and this man had to have a "p" [a device used to weigh the cotton lower. So I would always carry my p to the field and I would use my unloaded p until I would see him coming. And when I would see him coming at us, I'd switch p's and use his loaded p, but it would always, you know, give us a few pounds.[66]

Hamer's descriptions underscore how white landowners worked to ensure that Black sharecroppers remained in a constant state of need—even as they worked tirelessly on the plantation. While she could do little to overturn the system of exploitation, Hamer used her position as time- and recordkeeper to resist, rigging the scale in an effort to help others in need. It was a dangerous act—one that could have easily led to her dismissal or worse. Yet the act of defiance illuminated Hamer's willingness to take personal risks if they would benefit others.

Despite the pivotal role she played as time- and recordkeeper on the plantation, Hamer still encountered the same disregard as other Black farmers. Recounting her experiences, she pointed to how the white landowner relied on her help to keep track of his cotton production and yet would remind her that she was not allowed to sit at his table. Deeply troubled by her treatment on the plantation, Hamer covertly resisted—skillfully finding ways to assert her authority in a space that stifled Black freedom and autonomy. In response to being told that she could not eat at the table, Hamer defied the order by eating at the family's table when they were away, intentionally using the dishes, silverware, and other items they deemed too sacred to be shared with Black people:

Now one thing that would really bug me was when they would tell me that I couldn't eat at the table with them; I would have to wait for all them [to be] finished. So, what I would do was eat first. I would just eat and have myself a time. And maybe some of the things I'd done wasn't right because I would eat out all of the spoons and watch them eat behind me. And then whenever they would leave home, I would get in that bathtub, because I didn't have one. I would get in that bathtub and I would take me a bubble bath. And I would put some of everything on me that they had been using because—one thing about it, you know, just like a man who drinks whiskey: if you drink, you can't smell mine because you already got some in you. So I had to wash the clothes; I had to iron the clothes—I wore them clothes, too. I would wear them clothes, you know, if they was having a party in ten miles I would show off one of them dresses because I had them at my house. I would wear it and

I would look at them, you know, the next day wearing something that I had been wearing. And you just don't know. And that's why it's so, it's so funny to see people today saying what we can't do, when we've already done it.[67]

Hamer's descriptions were reminiscent of the diverse ways Black women resisted slavery.[68] Similar to enslaved Black women during the nineteenth century, Hamer recognized the power of her individual acts of resistance to slowly chip away at systems of oppression. By wearing the white women's clothing, using their personal items, and inhabiting their private spaces, Hamer expressed her own autonomy and defiance to rules and regulations meant to uphold racism and white supremacy. In the years to follow, she would continue in this path of resistance, viewing her fight for Black rights and freedom as expressions of her divine calling to be a light in a dark world.

"HANDS THAT PICK COTTON NOW PICK PUBLIC OFFICIALS."

During the summer of 1962, Fannie Lou Hamer's life changed forever. That summer, the Student Nonviolent Coordinating Committee (SNCC) arrived in Ruleville, Mississippi. Originally established in April 1960 at Shaw University, an HBCU in North Carolina, SNCC—led by young activists—emerged as one of the more radical groups of the civil rights movement. Unlike Martin Luther King Jr.'s organization, the Southern Christian Leadership Conference (SCLC), SNCC adopted a model of group-centered leadership. Under the mentorship of activist Ella Baker, SNCC activists resisted the top-down, charismatic leadership model on which SCLC and many other organizations were based.[69] During the early 1960s, SNCC drew hundreds of activists of diverse races and backgrounds, who worked to coordinate nonviolent, direct-action campaigns against segregation and racism. They played an integral role in organizing sit-ins, Freedom Rides, and voter education projects.[70] Their work around voter registration in Mississippi brought them to Ruleville, along with a coalition of civil rights groups under the banner of the Council of Federated Organizations (COFO). On Saturday, August 26, 1962, Hamer's pastor,

Rev. J. D. Story, had announced plans for a mass meeting to be held at the church the next day.[71] Although Hamer was at first reluctant to attend, the prodding of her close friend Mary Tucker convinced Hamer to reconsider her decision to skip the meeting.[72]

That decision proved to be a transformative one. The activists at William Chapel Missionary Baptist Church that evening, including SNCC executive secretary James Forman, delivered a series of speeches aimed at convincing local residents to register to vote. Forman and the others underscored the power of the vote for ordinary Black people in the United States. "I'd never heard that," Hamer recalled. Emphasizing the remote nature of Ruleville, Mississippi, as well as how the demands of sharecropping left little time for broader concerns, Hamer explained why she had not previously heard of voting rights: "We hadn't heard anything about registering to vote, because when you see this flat land in here, when the people would get out of the fields if they had a radio, they'd be too tired to play it. So we didn't know what was going on in the rest of the state, even, much less in other places."[73]

Notwithstanding the challenges that Hamer identified in her interview, her emphasis on having no knowledge of voting rights alludes to the lengths to which white supremacists went to keep Black people shut out of the formal political process. The exclusion of Black Americans from the ballot was a decades-long process. Despite the passage of the Fourteenth and Fifteenth Amendments during the nineteenth century, only 5 percent of Mississippi's 450,000 Black residents were registered voters during the 1960s.[74] In order to ensure that Black Americans did not uproot decades of restrictive and unconstitutional laws and practices, white Southerners diligently worked to block African Americans from the vote. Those who dared to defy them met the barrel of a gun. The violent force that white Americans used to prevent the Black vote only served to underscore its immense power. As Hamer later acknowledged, "America is divided against itself because they don't want us [Black people] to have even the ballot here in Mississippi. If we had been treated right all these years, they wouldn't be afraid for us to get the ballot."[75]

Hamer immediately grasped the power of the vote when she became aware of her constitutional rights in August 1962. Despite humble beginnings and her limited access to formal education, the right to vote meant that she would be empowered as a citizen of the United States. To have the ability to shape local, state, and national politics was no small matter. Reflecting on the service that evening, Hamer narrowed in on James Forman's speech, which had a particular appeal above all the others:

> James Bevel preached that night from the twelfth chapter of St. Luke, and the fifty-fourth verse: "Discerning the Signs of Time." And after he preached this sermon, he talked about how a man could look at a cloud and predict the rain and it would become so. And today men cannot discern this time; it was a beautiful sermon. After James Bevel had preached, Mr. Moore, Dave Dennis and some of the others talked, and then Jim Forman from SNCC got up and talked about how it was our constitutional right, that we have a right to register and vote. And he talked about, you know, what we could do if we had the power of the vote. And during the time Jim Forman was talking about how it was our right and how they'd passed the Fifteenth Amendment that I'd never heard of, I was one of the persons that made up my mind that this was something important to me. And it seemed like it was something that I wanted to take a chance on.[76]

Hamer's recollection captured the powerful fusion of the sacred and the secular that evening—the call to action from activist James Forman following the biblical pronouncements of Rev. James Bevel. As Hamer listened to the speakers at the mass meeting that evening, she could see the possibilities before her. Through voting rights, ordinary citizens like Hamer could transform American society. Perhaps Hamer caught a glimpse of what she later articulated during a 1971 speech: "Hands that pick cotton now pick public officials."[77] It was a message that captured the transformative power of voting rights—to empower Black Americans and others operating at the margins of society.

In the weeks following the mass meeting, Hamer embarked on a lifelong mission to help Black Americans secure voting rights. For Hamer, this was a divine mission. The words of her favorite song, therefore, took on a new meaning: "This little light of mine, I'm gonna let it shine / This little light of mine, I'm gonna let it shine / Let it shine, let it shine, let it shine." At the age of forty-four, Hamer set out to let her light shine when she became a member of SNCC, working alongside many of the activists who had played such a pivotal role in her entrance into the civil rights movement. Within a year, she became a field secretary for SNCC, the oldest in the organization's history.[78] It was a position that opened up an opportunity for Hamer to speak about the significance of voting rights and to help register Black Americans to vote. Her work with SNCC allowed her to shine a light into the darkness of racism and white supremacy.[79]

During the 1960s, Hamer set out to inform Black residents in Mississippi and beyond about the transformative power of the vote. Building on the rich legacy of Black women suffragists, including women like Frances Ellen Watkins Harper and Ida B. Wells-Barnett, Hamer worked to help others understand how the act of voting could not only change their lives but could also improve the lives of every Black American.[80] This calling involved filling in the knowledge gaps many Black people had about their rights in the United States as well as eradicating the deliberate misinformation spread by white Southerners. Through the voting education classes Hamer taught for SNCC, she emphasized the "duties of citizenship under a constitutional form of government."[81]

The US Constitution was Hamer's focal point. Perhaps guided by her own experiences—and her prior lack of knowledge on the topic—Hamer spoke at length about the legal protections the US Constitution provided for American citizens and how the Thirteenth, Fourteenth, and Fifteenth Amendments reaffirmed that those rights could not be denied to Black people. This was certainly a recurring theme that ran throughout history. For decades, Black activists and intellectuals in the United States invoked the Constitution to make demands of the state and all Americans. During the early twentieth century, for example, anti-lynching crusader Ida B. Wells-Barnett invoked the US Constitution to make a case for why African Americans should be protected from acts of violence and intimidation.[82] In a 1910 essay titled "How Enfranchisement Stops Lynchings," she decried states' refusal to enforce laws meant to protect all citizens of the United States: "Although the Constitution specifically says, no state shall do so, they *do* deprive persons of life, liberty and property without due process of law, and *do* deny equal protection of the laws to persons of Negro descent."[83] Like Wells-Barnett, Hamer took hold of the US Constitution—its significance, its stated values, and, above all, its symbolism—to lay out a vision of freedom for Black people.[84] Addressing a packed audience of African Americans in Indianola, Mississippi, in 1964, for example, Hamer asked a pointed question, alluding to the significance of the US Constitution in shaping American politics: "We want ours and we want ours now. I question sometime, actually, has any of these people that hate so—which is the white [American]—read anything about the Constitution? Eighteen hundred and seventy, the Fifteenth Amendment was added on to the Constitution of the United States that gave every man a chance to vote for what he think to be the right way," she further explained. "And now this is '64 and they still trying to keep us away from the ballot."[85]

Hamer's repeated emphasis on the US Constitution and its guarantees served a dual rhetorical purpose. On the one hand, she attempted to empower Black people by suggesting that federal law was on their side. Although local laws and policies attempted to curtail the Black vote, Hamer aimed to shine a light on how the power of the US Constitution superseded all local and state laws. On the other hand, Hamer was not oblivious to its limitations. She also evoked the Constitution to underscore the gravity—and even the absurdity—of the circumstances. Black Americans during the 1960s were fighting to obtain rights already promised to them during the era of Reconstruction. "My mind goes back to the problems that we have had in the past," she noted. "And I think about the Constitution of the United States that says, 'With the people, for the people, and by the people.' And every time I hear it now I just double over laughing because it's not true; it hasn't been true."[86] In another instance, during a 1964 speech Hamer boldly questioned if the "Constitution is really going to be of any help in this American society. . . . We want to see is democracy real?" she asked.[87] "We want to see this because the challenge is based upon the violation of the Thirteenth, Fourteenth, and Fifteenth Amendments to the United States Constitution, which hadn't done anything for us yet."[88] A sober reality grounded her skepticism; she knew from personal experience the difficulties of Black life in the South and across the nation. And she knew that what was written on paper had little effect on the day-to-day lives of Black Americans.

Still, Hamer adopted an optimistic posture that was informed by the belief that Black people held the power to change society in their hands. The limitations of the Constitution notwithstanding, Hamer emphasized the power of the vote—the basic right of citizenship in the United States. "We're tired of being mistreated. We are tired of dying for nothing. And God wants us to take a stand," Hamer argued. "And the only way that we can change the system in the State of Mississippi is by going to the courthouse, registering to vote, but you got to stand up. Freedom is not something that's put in your lap. You will have to go to the courthouse and say I want to register. This is a protest to show them that I am not satisfied."[89] Indeed, she implored audiences that even if the United States failed to live up to the promises of freedom and democracy, Black people could move the nation forward through the transformative act of voting. "We are going to make [democracy] true," she insisted, "with a handful, for a handful, by a handful."[90]

Hamer's speeches during the 1960s aimed to remind her audiences of the ideals of American democracy—an inclusive vision that embraced, in theory, all Americans, regardless of their race and socioeconomic background. White Southerners' actions revealed that they had long abandoned those ideals. However, Hamer was determined to shed light on the principles of American democracy and insist that Americans attempt to live up to these ideals. "We have a grave problem that's facing us today in the country," she argued, "and if we're going to make democracy a reality, we better start working now."[91] She would, at times, criticize the national anthem, pointing to its inherent hypocrisy:

I cannot stand when people stand to sing the national anthem, "O say can you see, by the dawn's early light, what so proudly we hail . . ." I ask myself the question, "What do we have to hail?" When actually, "the land of the free and the home of the brave" means "the land of the tree and the home of the grave" in Mississippi. It's time for us to wake, and if we going to make democracy a reality, we have to work to eliminate some of the problems with not only blacks but the poor whites as well.[92]

For Hamer, the national anthem held little meaning for Black Americans who lived under the constant threat of violence and terror—in the "land of the tree and the home of the grave." Hamer's question—"What do we have to hail?"—originated from a place of pain as she reflected on the daily mistreatment of Black people in the South. For Black people, deemed second-class citizens in the United States, Hamer posited that there was not much to celebrate.

At the very moment she uttered those words, Black people were facing rampant acts of white supremacist violence and terror. From the period of 1882 to 1968, an estimated 4,743 lynchings occurred in the United States, with Black people accounting for more than 70 percent of the victims.[93] Most of these crimes occurred in the South. And as Hamer emphasized, Mississippi had a long history of white supremacist violence, earning her designation of the state as "the land of the tree and the home of the grave."[94] The 1955 lynching of fourteen-year-old Emmett Till, the most infamous lynching of the twentieth century, took place in or near Sunflower County.[95] Born to Mamie and Louis Till in Chicago, Illinois, in 1941, Emmett had traveled to Money, Mississippi, in August 1955 to visit the family of his great-aunt and great-uncle, Elizabeth and Moses Wright. During his visit, Emmett joined several teenagers on a trip to Bryant's Grocery and Meat Market to purchase candy. While in the store, Emmett had a brief exchange with Carolyn Bryant, one of the store's owners, who falsely accused the fourteen-year-old boy of making a sexual remark toward her.[96] On August 28, 1955, in the wee hours of the morning, Roy Bryant, Carolyn's husband, and his half-brother J. W. Milam, with the help of several others, kidnapped Emmett from his great-uncle's home. Three days later, Emmett's decomposed body was pulled from Mississippi's Tallahatchie River. Despite the overwhelming evidence of the defendants' guilt and widespread pleas for justice, an all-white jury later acquitted Milam and Bryant of murdering Emmett.[97] In 1973, eighteen years after the lynching, Bryant and his family found refuge in Hamer's hometown of Ruleville after living for several years in Louisiana and Texas.[98]

Hamer therefore understood the danger associated with simply living as a Black person in the US South. And she was well aware of the violence Black Southerners endured simply because they desired to exercise their constitutional rights. "All we want is a chance to participate in the government of Mississippi, and all of the violence, all of the bombings, all of the people that have been murdered in Mississippi because they wanted to vote. . . . This is the price we pay in the state of Mississippi," Hamer said, "for just wanting to have a chance, as American citizens, to exercise our constitutional right that we were insured by the Fifteenth Amendment."[99] By shedding light on the conditions of Black life in the South, Hamer underscored the source of her ambivalence with the national anthem and the ideals it upheld.

Yet Hamer never lost sight of the need to keep fighting to realize the ideals of American democracy. "Now, we've got to make some changes in this country," she argued. "The changes we have to have in this country are going to be for the liberation of all people—because nobody's free until everybody's free."[100] In Hamer's vision, it was the onus of all Americans committed to social justice to address the unfinished work of democracy. "We need people to work for freedom, now! Not freedom tomorrow, but we want freedom now," she declared.[101] And in Hamer's view, the work of freedom was a righteous cause. Speaking in the prophetic tradition, Hamer issued an urgent warning to all Americans during a 1964 speech in Indianola, Mississippi. Drawing inspiration from the Bible—and also alluding to Abraham Lincoln's famous 1858 speech—Hamer argued, "A house divided against itself cannot stand; America is divided against itself and without their considering us [African Americans] human beings, one day America will crumble. Because God is not pleased," she continued.[102] "God is not pleased at all the murdering, and all of the brutality, and all the killings for no reason at all. God is not pleased at the Negro children in the state of Mississippi suffering from malnutrition. God is not pleased because we have to go raggedy each day. God is not pleased because we have to go to the field and work from ten to eleven hours for three lousy dollars."[103]

Embracing her divine calling as a freedom fighter, Hamer set out to bring light into a world of darkness. Though she firmly believed that God would use her life—and her powerful voice—to bring moral clarity to America, she could not have imagined the widespread impact she would have in her lifetime. The light Hamer began to shine when she walked out of the mass meeting on August 27, 1962, illuminated the way for millions of people, from all walks of life, in the decades to follow.

CHAPTER TWO

TELL IT LIKE IT IS

I'm going to tell you just like it is. . . . There's so much hypocrisy in this society and if we want America to be a free society, we have to stop telling lies.

—FANNIE LOU HAMER[1]

On July 10, 2015, Sandra Bland, a twenty-eight-year-old Black woman from Illinois, was driving alone in Prairie View, Texas. She was on her way to Prairie View A&M University, where she had recently secured a new position. According to Brian Encinia, the white Texas state trooper who stopped her that afternoon, Bland failed to signal as she moved from one lane to the next. What began as a routine traffic stop quickly escalated when Encinia asked Bland to extinguish her cigarette and immediately exit her car.[2] In only a matter of minutes, Encinia tried to force Bland from the car as he called for backup. He then drew a Taser and pointed it directly at Bland. "I will light you up! Get out—now!" As Bland exited the car, tensions continued to escalate. Within an hour of driving down a quiet street in Prairie View, Bland was stopped, arrested, and later taken to a jail in Waller County, Texas. When she was found hanging in her cell three days later, the encounter, which had been recorded on the officer's dashcam, circulated widely across the nation.[3] Thousands decried the circumstances that led to Bland's tragic death, questioning the stop, the detainment, and the officer's repeated threats. Although Bland's death was officially ruled a suicide, many rejected the pronouncement—and rightfully so. In addition to the many questions that still remain unanswered concerning Bland's short time in a Waller County jail cell, there is no denying that Encinia played a role in her death. Encinia's racial profiling, which motivated his decision to stop Bland in the first place, and his failure to de-escalate what should have been a routine traffic stop led to an unlawful arrest and created the environment that led to Bland's untimely death.[4]

Sandra Bland's life and the circumstances of her death cast a spotlight on one of the social issues that has dominated public discourse during the twenty-first century: state-sanctioned violence. Bland's encounter with Encinia was recorded and as a result garnered nationwide attention. Yet thousands of Black people in the United States have had similar experiences—tense exchanges with police officers that often amount to a death sentence. In a 2019 *Los Angeles Times* article, a group of researchers identified police violence as one of the leading causes of death for Black American men.[5] While their research emphasized the experiences of Black men and boys, it also revealed that state-sanctioned violence imperiled Black women and girls to a greater degree than white women.[6] In the years before Bland's confrontation with law enforcement, countless Black women died in police custody, with many of their stories going unnoticed. For example, in December 2002, Nizah Morris, a Black transgender woman, sustained a fatal head injury while being transported by three Philadelphia police officers. Although local activists worked to shed light on the tragic events of that evening, Morris's case, like so many cases of police violence against Black transgender people, failed to garner much national attention.[7] In July 2015, the same month of Bland's death, several other Black women died in police custody, including Raynette Turner of Mount Vernon, New York, and eighteen-year-old Kindra Chapman of Homewood, Alabama.[8] Weeks later, officers killed Mya Hall, a young Black transgender woman in Baltimore, after she made a wrong turn while driving on a parkway in Fort Meade.[9] These are just a few of the recent cases of Black women whose lives were cut short by the police in the United States.[10]

The threat of violence Black Americans face each time they encounter a police officer today is no different from the fear of lynching

Black people felt during each confrontation with a white officer during the Jim Crow era. And this violence was—and is—not limited to encounters with the police. Black Americans today also face violence at the hands of other agents of the state, including white medical professionals who continue to treat their Black patients differently from patients of other racial groups.[11] Fannie Lou Hamer lived with this fear of everyday public and private acts of violence while navigating the South. During the early 1960s, she used her growing visibility and national platform to share those experiences and denounce the actions of the police as well as the white doctors who committed acts of violence against Black women through forced sterilizations. For Hamer, one of the strategies for addressing the persistent problem of state-sanctioned violence was the use of public testimony as a mode of resistance and revelation. In this way, the act was driven by both personal and political motivations. A source of empowerment and healing, public testimony also provided a vehicle for Hamer to make her audience "co-owners of trauma."[12] Those who listened to Hamer's testimony bore witness to the pain and violence and were therefore transformed by the experience.

If the violence Black women endured from the state at the hands of police officers, white physicians, and others was designed to silence them, Hamer refused to capitulate. As Hamer recognized in her day-to-day organizing in the US South, acts of police violence and white mob violence often occurred in secret, behind closed doors and far from the gaze of others. For every public and documented act of racist violence, dozens more had taken place in secret, never to be counted or documented. In Hamer's view, those who managed to survive these brazen acts of violence needed to serve as public witnesses—speaking truthfully and openly about their personal experiences in an effort to bear witness to the pain and suffering of racial and sexual violence; bringing greater awareness to others; and initiating radical changes. "I'm going to tell it like it is," Hamer often warned before her public speeches, as a way to boldly alert listeners to the eye-opening accounts that would follow. The mantra "tell it like it is" is a political strategy that Hamer employed in her lifetime and one that remains a powerful feature of African American culture today.

"THEY BEAT ME TILL MY BODY WAS HARD."

Fannie Lou Hamer's perspective on policing and state-sanctioned violence emerged from painful personal experiences.[13] According to Hamer, her first recollection of state-endorsed racist violence took place in the Mississippi Delta around 1923, when she was only six years old.[14] Like the vast majority of Black people living in the Delta during the early twentieth century, Hamer's parents were sharecroppers, working tirelessly on a local plantation to be able to provide for their children. Another sharecropper in the community named Joe Pullum was violently murdered by local whites following a dispute involving $150.[15] In all likelihood, Hamer did not witness the actual lynching, but her knowledge of the story—which had circulated widely in the Mississippi Delta—had a lasting effect. The lynching became part of Hamer's memory about growing up in the Jim Crow South. Throughout her lifetime, she repeatedly told the story of Pullum's death to underscore the circumstances of Black life in Mississippi.[16]

In an interview with Black communist Jack O'Dell, then an editor of *Freedomways*, Hamer reflected on Pullum's life, the circumstances leading up to his death, and the challenges he faced as a Black man living in Mississippi at the time:

> There was a man named Joe [Pullum]. He was a great Christian man; but one time, he was living with a white family and this white family robbed him of what he earned. They didn't pay him anything. This white man gave him $150 to go to the hill . . . to get another Negro family. Joe knew what this white man had been doing to him so he kept the $150 and didn't go. This white man talked with him, then shot him in the shoulder and Joe went back into the house and got a Winchester and killed this white man. The other white fellow that was with him he "outrun the word of God" back to town. That gave this Negro a chance to go down on the bayou that was called Powers Bayou and he got in a hollowed-out stump where there was enough room for a person. He got in there and he stayed and was tracked there, but they couldn't see him and every time a white man would peep out, he busted him. He killed 13 white men and wounded 26 and Mississippi was a quiet place for a long time.[17]

Hamer's account of Pullum's life offers a glimpse into how the sharecropping system exploited Black Americans, creating a cycle of dependency and debt.[18] Like countless other Black Southerners at the time, Pullum's fate was directly tied to the whims of his white boss, who in 1923 decided to withhold money from Pullum even after he had completed the necessary work. With no available recourse or protection from the state, Pullum decided to take matters into his own hands. But as Hamer's account reveals, Pullum had already lost the fight long before his death—not for lack of trying but because of a rigged system that empowered whites and marginalized Black people. The Jim Crow laws and culture of the US South worked to maintain white supremacy, leaving African Americans completely unprotected.

Pullum's attempts to resist the racist Jim Crow system and insist on his right to receive wages for his work resulted in his death. Similar to countless other Black people in the US South and other parts of the nation, Pullum was lynched by a white mob. From 1889 to 1945, an estimated 476 people were lynched in the state of Mississippi, representing 13 percent of the lynchings taking place nationally.[19] Even as lynchings began to gradually decline in other states during the postwar era, Mississippi witnessed a significant increase.[20] For a Black person, living in Mississippi during the early twentieth century meant enduring a constant state of fear. Hamer came to this realization at a very young age, and Pullum's tragic death provided one of her earliest memories of state-sanctioned violence. Although local white residents killed Pullum, the tacit support of the state government ensured they could commit the violent act and get away with it.

As Ida B. Wells-Barnett, anti-lynching crusader and cofounder of the National Association for the Advancement of Colored People (NAACP), revealed in her writings and speeches decades earlier, the role of police forces in protecting white perpetrators was directly tied to the rise of lynchings.[21] Born in 1862, Wells worked as a journalist and teacher in Memphis during the late nineteenth century. In 1892, white supremacists lynched her three friends—local business owners Calvin McDowell, Thomas Moss, and William "Henry" Stewart—representing a pattern of white mob violence that targeted Black people across the South. In 1895, Wells-Barnett released her landmark study *The Red Record*, which denounced lynching and urged readers to call for a federal investigation into white mob violence.[22] The findings of Wells-Barnett's study, as well as her subsequent writings and speeches, underscored how law enforcement often failed to use their "great power to protect the victim" from white mob violence.[23]

The aftermath of Pullum's murder revealed the complicity of law enforcement in Hamer's hometown. In a painful scene that has played out in Black communities over and over again, white vigilantes paraded Pullum's body—tied to the back of a truck—for all to see. And when they were done, they cut off Pullum's ear, which they proudly displayed in the window of a local store.[24] It was an act of intimidation and a clear message meant to terrorize Black people—all in the public eye and certainly with the full knowledge and support of law enforcement. It was, without question, state-sanctioned violence.

Hamer's early experiences left a lasting imprint on her life. As she admitted in the 1965 interview with O'Dell, "I remember that [lynching] until this day and I won't forget it."[25] Throughout her lifetime, Hamer witnessed similar acts of violence against Black people in Mississippi. "All of those things, when they would happen," Hamer explained, "would make me sick in the pit of my stomach and year after year, every time something would happen it would make me more and more aware of what would have to be done in the state of Mississippi."[26] Hamer spoke often about how white supremacist violence shaped Black life in the state. From the everyday acts of violence at the hands of individual citizens to the coordinated lynch mobs and campaigns of terror led by the Ku Klux Klan (KKK), Black Southerners lived in a state of constant fear. They could not escape the unrelenting violence aimed at keeping them in subordinate positions and preventing them from exercising their citizenship rights. "We're tired of all this beatin,' we're tired of takin' this," Hamer explained. "It's been a hundred years and we're still being beaten and shot at, crosses are still being burned, because we want to vote."[27] Despite the violence meant to curb Black political rights, Hamer determinedly pushed forward. "I'm goin' to stay in Mississippi and if they shoot me down, I'll be buried here," she boldly declared.[28]

As she traveled across the state to help organize local residents and encourage them to register to vote, Hamer would put those words to the test. Her first known encounter with the police was in August

1962—not long after she had joined the civil rights movement. She was among a group of eighteen Black residents from Sunflower County, Mississippi, who had volunteered to register to vote.[29] The Student Nonviolent Coordinating Committee (SNCC) organized the group as part of its grassroots effort to help enfranchise Black Mississippians.[30] On Friday, August 31, 1962, Hamer boarded the bus with this group of activists on their way to Indianola, approximately twenty-six miles away from Ruleville.[31] Their journey was a historic one, marked with their determination to register Black people to vote in a state that had disenfranchised its Black citizens through an array of legal and extralegal measures, including poll taxes and violence.

Given these realities, Hamer and the other activists who boarded the bus to Indianola anticipated encountering roadblocks on their trip. Hamer later recalled the worry that crossed her mind as she prepared for the trip: "I just had a feeling because the morning I left home to go down to register I carried some extra shoes and a bag because I said, 'If I'm arrested or anything, I'll have some extra shoes to put on.' So I had a feeling something might happen; I just didn't know. I didn't know it was going to be as much involved as it finally was."[32]

The first challenge Hamer and her associates faced was at the front doors of the courthouse in Indianola, where armed guards greeted them as they attempted to enter. Describing the scene, Hamer later noted, "I saw more policemens with guns than I'd ever seen in my life at one time. They were standing around and I will never forget that day."[33] After making it through the door of the courthouse, poll workers informed the activists that they would be required to take literacy tests in order to register to vote. These discriminatory literacy tests were yet another strategy employed by white supremacists in an effort to disenfranchise Black people. With limited formal education, Hamer did the best she could, later recalling that she struggled with parts of the test on the function of de facto laws and the state constitution.[34] "The registrar brought out a huge black book and he pointed out a section to me with the sixteenth section of the constitution of Mississippi and he told me to copy that section, and it was dealing with de facto laws," Hamer explained.[35] "And I knowed about as much about a de facto law as a horse knows about New Year's," she remarked with honesty and humor. "He told me to tell the meanings of the section that I had just copied. Quite naturally, I flunked the test."[36]

As Hamer and her associates prepared to leave, they saw that police officers had surrounded the old school bus in which they had traveled to the courthouse. Hamer later described the scene in vivid detail: "By the time the eighteen of us going in two by two had finished taking the literacy test—now there's people, mind you, there that day with guns, dogs, and rifles. Some of them looking exactly like Jed Clampett with the *Beverly Hillbillies,* only they wasn't kidding."[37] The group of activists managed to leave the courthouse without incident. However, on the journey back home, police stopped them, and an officer ordered them off the bus. While the activists were not surprised to be stopped by the police, they were certainly bewildered when the officer fined them for driving a bus of the "wrong color."[38]

In a startling scene that underscores the absurdity of white supremacist practices, the police officer charged the driver for driving a bus that was "too yellow." The officer's "reasoning" was that the bus was deceptive—too closely resembling a school bus. In reality, the stop had nothing to do with the color of the bus. Given the visibility of Hamer and her colleagues—the notoriety associated with their attempts to register to vote—the police officer knew why the activists were traveling from Indianola. Hamer later pointed out that she had seen the officer earlier in the day while attempting to register.[39] Yet he used his power as an agent of the state to remind the activists they were living in the Jim Crow South, with all of its insulting indignities that could quickly escalate to state-sanctioned violence. After forcing Hamer and her colleagues to return to the courthouse in Indianola, the officer arrested the driver, civil rights activist Lawrence Guyot, and initially charged him a fine of $100—close to $850 in today's currency.[40] Hamer and the other passengers convinced the officer to reduce the fine since there was no way they could pay it. The fee was ultimately reduced to $30 and paid by the group, who pooled their resources together.

The 1962 incident in Indianola was a frightening one for Hamer and her associates. Yet they were grateful to return home unscathed and were further united in their efforts to combat voter suppression. Hamer recounted this story in her speeches on a number of occasions, illuminating some of the challenges Black people encountered while trying to exercise their constitutional rights. She also told the story to shed light on the function of state-sanctioned violence in the South during the 1960s: to intimidate and terrorize Black people. The white intimidation Hamer experienced in Indianola only continued when she returned home later that evening and would follow her for the rest of her life. Although she was unsuccessful in her first attempt to register to vote in Indianola, Hamer took great pride in the fact that she had tried. As she once noted, "If we think about the things that have happened to us in the past, if we think about the lynchings, the mobbings, and all of the things that have happened throughout the state of Mississippi, and we don't have enough dignity to walk up and vote for our own people, there's something wrong with us."[41] As Hamer emphasized, voting and registering to vote were acts of defiance to the system of white supremacy that shaped Black life in Mississippi and across the nation.

Hamer's defiance came at a cost. That evening, when she returned to the plantation where she worked, Hamer was forced to leave. The owner, who was displeased that Hamer had traveled to Indianola to register, gave her an ultimatum: "If you don't go down and withdraw your registration, you will have to leave. . . . We're not ready for that in Mississippi."[42] Hamer left the plantation that evening and never returned. She had no choice but to leave her husband, Perry "Pap" Hamer, behind to continue working on the plantation so they would not lose their one remaining source of income. It was a painful personal sacrifice but one she would have to make time and time again for the sake of her family's safety and security. Despite losing her job that evening, Hamer praised the development for opening up new avenues for her to advance the cause of social justice. "[When] they kicked me off the plantation," Hamer reportedly told a fellow worker, "they set me free." She added, "It's the best thing that could happen. Now I can work for my people."[43]

Several days after Hamer was forced off the plantation, white supremacists sprayed sixteen bullets into the home where she had been staying with her friends Mr. and Mrs. Robert Tucker.[44] They also shot up several surrounding homes. Hamer knew the bullets, which resulted in the injury of two young girls, had been meant for her, yet she was undeterred. "The only thing they could do to me was to kill me," she later said in an interview, "and it seemed like they'd been trying to do that a little bit at a time ever since I could remember."[45] To add insult to injury, W. D. Marlow, the owner of the plantation on which Hamer had worked, refused to fully compensate the Hamer family for their labor. Within weeks of Hamer's ejection from the plantation, Marlow fired Pap and took the couple's car, leaving them without a place to stay or a means of transportation.[46]

Hamer's confrontation with the police in 1962 paled in comparison with the Winona incident that took place a year later. In June 1963, Hamer was traveling with a group of other activists on the way to Mississippi after attending a voters' workshop in South Carolina. Several of them got off a bus in Winona, Mississippi, to grab a bite to eat.[47] To their dismay, but not to their surprise, Hamer's colleagues encountered resistance from the owners of Staley's Café, who made it clear that Black people were not welcomed. Hamer initially remained on the bus but decided to exit when she noticed police officers shoving her friends into police cars. She later admitted that she had abandoned all reason when she saw her friends in distress. At the moment, all she wanted to do was help.[48] When a white officer grabbed her and started kicking her, fear rose within her—knowing full well that this encounter would not end well.[49] In her televised speech before the 1964 Democratic National Convention, Hamer spoke candidly about her violent interaction with the police. She explained how the Winona beating left her with kidney damage, a blood clot in her eye, and a worsened physical limp from childhood she would carry for the rest of her life. According to Hamer, "They beat me till my body was hard, till I couldn't bend my fingers or get up when they told me to. That's how I got this blood clot in my left eye—the sight's nearly gone now. And my kidney was injured from the blows they gave me in the back."[50]

Unlike so many others, Hamer lived to tell her story. And she certainly told that story—over and over again to anyone who would listen. For Hamer, directly confronting racial and gendered inequalities was a key strategy to eradicate them. As she carefully explained in her

1965 *Freedomways* interview, exposing injustice was the only way to begin to dismantle systems of oppression:

> The only thing I really feel is necessary is that the black people, not only in Mississippi, will have to actually upset this apple-cart. What I mean by that is, so many things are under the covers that will have to be swept out and shown to this whole world, not just to America. There is so much hypocrisy in America. This thing they say of "the land of the free and the home of the brave" is all on paper. It doesn't mean anything to us. The only way we can make this thing a reality in America is to do all we can to destroy this system and bring this thing out to the light that has been under the cover all these years. That's why I believe in Christianity because the Scriptures said: "The things that have been done in the dark will be known on the house tops."[51]

Hamer's remarks emphasized the power of public testimony in the context of confronting state-sanctioned violence.[52] Oftentimes these acts of violence, especially when directed at Black women and girls, are hidden "under the covers"—a phrase that implies the act of secrecy but may also allude to sexual assault.

Hamer's account and experiences capture the interconnection between racial and sexual violence. Although she did not often address it publicly, Hamer later recalled the sexual nature of the assault she experienced in the Winona jailhouse.[53] In 1970, seven years after the Winona incident, Hamer disclosed that she was sexually assaulted in the jailhouse—a fact that she had not previously shared in public settings. Though she had alluded to it, Hamer waited for several years before she would reveal the details of the sexual assault that took place on June 9, 1963.[54] Speaking before a packed audience at Chicago's Loop College on May 27, 1970, Hamer recounted the police officers' sexual assaults as they unleashed the brutal beating. "I had taken my hands and smoothed my clothes down," she told the audience, "because I had never been exposed to five mens in one room in my life . . . [D]uring the time [of the beating], my dress worked up and I smoothed my dress down, one of the white men walked over and pulled my dress up."[55] As the beating continued, Hamer explained that another officer in the room tried "to feel under my clothes."[56] The assaults Hamer endured during the Winona jailhouse beating reflected the long history of racial and sexual violence that victimized Black women's lives.[57] Sexualized violence, much like lynchings and police intimidation, helped to maintain white supremacy in the Jim Crow South.

In another incident, shortly after Hamer had registered to vote, police officers barged into her home in the wee hours of the morning in February 1963. Hamer later recalled the officers' complete disregard for her privacy as they searched through the home with flashlights, questioning Hamer, who was in her nightgown. "I was in the bed," she later recalled, "[and] they didn't know how they would find me as a woman, in my house. . . . They flashed their lights around, and they had the guns in their hand, and then they backed out . . . like, you know, we were some kind of criminals."[58] The experience exemplified the persistent police harassment Hamer and her family endured. Yet it remained etched in her mind not only because of the personal intrusion but also because of the actors involved. In several speeches, including the one at Loop College in Chicago in 1970, Hamer disclosed that one of the officers present that morning was S. L. Milam, the brother of one of the men who lynched fourteen-year-old Emmett Till in 1955.[59] His presence at her home that morning was meant to terrify Hamer, sending a warning that her efforts to expand voting rights in the state could result in the same fate. The intrusion served as a reminder that violence and the threat of violence were at the heart of white supremacy.

In Hamer's view, public testimony was one powerful response to challenge this system. She believed that those who had the ability to tell their stories should tell them. Hamer's frequent recounting of the painful Winona incident was an effort to shine light on the pervasive daily acts of racist violence Black people endured in the Jim Crow South. In telling the story about how the state sanctioned such violence, Hamer was able to raise public awareness and help others understand that Black women were not protected from physical assault on account of their gender.[60] Hamer's narration of the painful and horrific experience with the police in Winona represented her attempt to sweep out some of the dirt that was hidden "under the covers" and show it to the world. By telling her story, repeatedly, Hamer hoped to empower others and to send the message that silence when confronting everyday degradation and violence was simply not an option.

"WHY HAD HE DONE THAT TO ME?"

Hamer's refusal to be silent in the face of injustice extended to every aspect of her life, including another form of state-sanctioned violence she endured at the hands of white doctors in Mississippi. Similar to police officers, many white doctors functioned as agents of the state—maintaining white supremacy and utilizing violence to control Black people's lives. Hamer's painful experiences in 1961 offer a glimpse of the kinds of challenges impoverished Black women faced. Despite the financial struggles she and Pap underwent while living in the Jim Crow South, Hamer was determined to have a child. After two failed pregnancies during her forties, Hamer was hospitalized in 1961 to remove a noncancerous "small uterine tumor."[61] Without Hamer's knowledge or consent, the white doctor conducting what was supposed to be a minor procedure decided to remove Hamer's uterus, rendering the activist infertile. This physical act of violence had lasting emotional and physiological effects too. Hamer "lost not only her capacity to reproduce, but everything that it symbolized for women, especially Black women living in a desperately poor, rural environment and possessing nothing that was truly theirs, save faith and their own bodies."[62]

To add insult to injury, Hamer learned about the violent act through gossip on the plantation on which she worked. The wife of the plantation owner, Vera Marlow, was a relative of the doctor who had completed the procedure. When Hamer returned home to rest, she heard the rumblings of others on the plantation, suggesting that she had been sterilized while unconscious. In an act of spite, Marlow had begun circulating the story to the cook, who relayed the sensitive information to other workers. Hamer would therefore be one of the last people to learn about this act of shocking violence committed on her body.[63] Though she was angry to find out what had been done to her, Hamer had little recourse as a Black woman in the Jim Crow South. She managed to confront the doctor, asking him to explain his reasoning for doing the procedure and not informing her. "Why? Why had he done that to me? He didn't have to say nothing—and he didn't," Hamer later explained.[64]

The doctor's silence when confronted with Hamer's anger spoke volumes. As a white doctor whose actions the state supported and protected, he owed Hamer no explanation—and he knew there was nothing she could do about it. As Hamer herself painfully admitted, she could not even seek out legal actions against the doctor if she hoped to live to see another day: "I would have been taking my hands and screwing tacks into my own casket." Moreover, she pointed to the rigged legal system, which made it impossible for white lawyers and prosecutors to convict white people for their crimes: "Getting a white lawyer to go against a white doctor?"[65] As a resident of Mississippi, Hamer had witnessed high-profiles cases like Emmett Till's in 1955 and watched in horror, along with the rest of the nation, as Till's killers walked free and later confessed to the crime in *Look* magazine.[66] The Emmett Till case, along with countless others, provided the evidence Hamer needed to know: she would have to find some other way to challenge the forced sterilization. In the aftermath of the forced hysterectomy, Hamer and Pap adopted two local Black girls— first Dorothy Jean, then ten years later Vergie Ree, who had sustained serious burn injuries as a baby.[67] The Hamers showered both girls with love and affection, grateful that they were able to expand their family through adoption despite the painful experience Hamer had endured years earlier.

If she could not obtain justice for the act of medical violence, Hamer decided she would use her voice to shine light on the practice, which was all too common in Mississippi and beyond. Indeed, the act of medical abuse of power and the violence against Hamer's body was something many poor Black women suffered through in the Jim Crow South. With few material resources, impoverished Black women and other women of color were most vulnerable to the exploitations of state agencies that worked to uphold racism and white supremacy.[68] The birth control movement of the late twentieth century was deeply tied to the work of white eugenicists who justified the sterilization of Black women. White eugenicists presumed that the "multiplication of the unfit posed a threat to the political stability of the nation."[69] This practice took place across the South during the twentieth century. For example, between 1929 and 1974 in North Carolina, doctors sterilized 7,600 people. Out of those sterilized, 85 percent were women and girls and 40 percent were women of color—most of whom were African American.[70] During the Jim Crow era, impoverished Black women in the Deep South were frequently subjected to hysterectomies or tubal ligations against their will and without their knowledge.[71] In Sunflower County, where Hamer had been sterilized, at least 60 percent of the Black women experienced forced sterilizations following pregnancy.[72] Deemed "unfit" to reproduce by white physicians and other state officials, Black women who entered hospitals for routine procedures ran the risk of being sterilized—and with little recourse to challenge the act.

Hamer was therefore one of many Black women who experienced the medical violence and violation of forced sterilization during this period.[73] Although few publicly discussed this deeply private and intimate trauma, Hamer was the first civil rights activist during the 1960s to openly address it.[74] In 1964, only three years after the painful incident, Hamer called attention to the racist and violent practice of forced sterilization at a conference on racism organized by the Council of Federated Organizations (COFO), a coalition of civil rights groups organizing in Mississippi at the time. Established in 1961, COFO was an umbrella organization that brought together activists in various statewide and national groups, including the SNCC, the Congress of Racial Equality (CORE), and the National Association for the Advancement of Colored People (NAACP).[75]

Members of COFO had organized a hearing to address the social climate of Mississippi as part of an effort to prepare Northern activists planning to travel to the state during Freedom Summer. Held in Washington, DC, on June 8, 1964, the hearing brought together twenty-four speakers who delivered testimonies before a group of distinguished panelists, including Congressman William Fitts Ryan of New York; Harold Taylor, former president of Sarah Lawrence College; and Harvard professor and psychiatrist Robert Coles. After Hamer briefly recounted an exchange with a long-distance telephone operator—who confirmed that her phone calls were being monitored—Coles raised doubts about her account, noting that "no telephone operator ever talked to me like this." "Well, it was the first time for me," Hamer responded, "but it did happen."[76]

Perhaps contemplating Coles's background in the medical field, Hamer quickly pointed out that Black women's experiences with forced sterilizations in Mississippi hospitals were yet another example of something that might seem unbelievable but that were in fact common practice. In a brief but poignant account, Hamer used the opportunity to illuminate the medical abuses and acts of violence Black women endured in local hospitals that were supposed to be spaces of healing and care:

> One of the other things that happened in Sunflower County, the North Sunflower County Hospital, I would say about six out of the ten Negro women that go to the hospital are sterilized with the tubes tied. They are getting up a law that said if a woman has an illegitimate baby and then a second one, they could draw time for six months or a five-hundred-dollar fine. What they didn't tell is that they are already doing these things, not only to single women but to married women.[77]

Reminiscent of earlier Black women activists and intellectuals who harnessed the power of their voices to condemn racism and white supremacy, Hamer used the opportunity to call attention to the practice of forced sterilizations. She decried the local attempts in Mississippi to pass HB 180, a law that would limit women's reproductive rights—and would almost certainly be used disproportionately against Black women. And drawing on her own observations, she centered the frequency of the practice, which had devastated the lives of countless Black women in the South. In 1965 alone, an estimated sixty Black women were forcefully sterilized at the hospital in Sunflower County immediately after giving birth.[78]

What is also striking about Hamer's recollection is how it exposed the hypocrisy of white doctors and revealed the limits of respectability politics.[79] By narrowing in on the fact that forced sterilizations were happening to married women and not solely single women, Hamer made it clear that even when Black women in the South operated within the bounds of white heteronormativity—in this case, becoming pregnant while married—they could not escape the pain and trauma of forced sterilizations. In the end, regardless of a Black woman's marriage status or the specific circumstances surrounding her pregnancy, they were vulnerable to state-sanctioned violence at the hands of racist white doctors and complicit hospital workers who deemed impoverished Black women "unfit" for reproduction.

Those who supported forced sterilization devalued Black life, but they also hoped to profit from Black women's suffering in whatever form it took. White medical professionals and staff stood to financially profit when completing forced sterilizations. By one estimate, Fannie Lou Hamer's initial procedure to remove a small tumor would have grossed the hospital $200.[80] Yet they could bill an estimated $800 for completing a forced sterilization. The financial incentive, combined with the racist beliefs that Black women were unsuitable for motherhood, fueled the unconscionable practice in the Mississippi Delta.[81] And while the act of forced sterilizations was pervasive in the US South, it was not limited to the region. During the 1960s, Black women were subjected to the violence of forced sterilizations in hospitals across the nation, with cases being reported in cities such as Boston, New York, and San Francisco.[82]

For Hamer, the issue of involuntary sterilization was as urgent as that of police brutality and other manifestations of state-sanctioned violence. All were acts of violence meted out on the bodies of Black people—and in this case, she called specific attention to the vulnerability of Black women. From Hamer's perspective, these acts of violence needed to be directly confronted if Black people ever hoped their circumstances would change. This perspective led the activist to boldly address medical violence—despite the private and intimate nature of the issue. And her courage left a lasting mark. Indeed, Hamer's work to bring attention to the problem of forced sterilization played a central role in dismantling Mississippi's HB 180. The Mississippi Senate eventually dropped the bill, motivated in part by the public outcry fueled by Hamer's testimony at the 1964 COFO hearing. Hamer's remarks would be one of the first documented occasions when an activist addressed the topic publicly, and it would certainly not be the last. In 1969, for example, Hamer discussed the practice before members of a feminist committee discussing abortion in Seattle, Washington.[83]

She shared her own painful personal experiences and denounced the common practice of forced sterilizations, which she and others often referred to as a "Mississippi appendectomy."[84]

Holding fast to her mantra—"tell it like it is"—Hamer refused to sugarcoat the problems impoverished Black women were facing throughout the United States. She publicly foregrounded the physical, psychological, and emotional abuse Black women endured at the hands of white doctors and police officers. She also highlighted how the state fully endorsed and protected these violent acts. In bringing these issues to the center of civil rights concerns, Hamer sent a powerful message to activists—then and now—about the enduring power of public testimony to transform American society. Much like earlier activists Frederick Douglass, who boldly confronted the sin of slavery, and Ida B. Wells-Barnett, who risked her life to confront and condemn lynchings, Fannie Lou Hamer used her voice to shed light on the injustices Black people endured.[85] Through her courageous words, she revealed how exposing the acts of violence that often happen in the dark or outside the purview of those who choose not to see is a crucial part of the struggle to dismantle racism and gendered violence. "The wrongs and the sickness of this country have been swept under the rug," she told audience members at Harvard University in 1968, "but I've come out from under the rug, and I'm going to tell it like it is."[86]

CHAPTER THREE

WE WANT LEADERS

We want people over us that's concerned about the people because we are human beings. . . . And we can no longer ignore the fact that we can't sit down and wait for things to change because as long as they can keep their feet on our neck, they will always do it. But it's time for us to stand up and be women and men.

—FANNIE LOU HAMER[1]

Just after midnight on March 13, 2020, Breonna Taylor, an EMT in Louisville, Kentucky, was shot and killed by police officers raiding her home. The officers had forcibly entered without warning, acting on a no-knock warrant as part of a drug investigation. The suspect they were seeking was not a resident of Taylor's home, and no drugs were ever found. But when they came through the door unexpectedly in plain clothes, Taylor's boyfriend, startled by the presence of intruders, fired his weapon. In only a matter of minutes, Taylor was dead—shot six times by police officers.[2] In the weeks following Taylor's death, a network of Black women activists—including Taylor's mother, Tamika Parker, and Taylor's sister, Ju'Niyah Palmer—rallied together to bring greater awareness to this senseless act of state violence. In April 2020, Taylor's mother sued the three police officers who fired shots into her daughter's apartment, pointing to the officers' use of excessive force and gross negligence.[3]

As protests erupted on the streets of Louisville, one activist launched a powerful digital campaign that significantly catapulted the case to the national spotlight. In June 2020, Cate Young, a twenty-nine-year-old Los Angeles–based writer originally from Trinidad and Tobago, introduced #BirthdayForBreonna as a call to action on what would have been Taylor's twenty-seventh birthday (June 5).[4] "I just wanted to do *something*," Young said. "I was like, I'm going to drive myself insane with worry and panic if I don't do something."[5] Young was deeply frustrated with the lack of national media attention the case was receiving despite the growth of local protests.[6] "It's important not to leave Black women out of the fight for Black lives because they are instrumental to that fight," Young argued.[7] Intent on mobilizing activists across the country, she launched the campaign by first appealing to her followers on Twitter and others within her social media and personal networks. She created a page with a list of actionable steps others could take on June 5 to fight for justice for Taylor's family. Young's campaign urged supporters to make donations to an online fund for Taylor's family and sign petitions to demand criminal charges for the police officers responsible for Taylor's death. The campaign also called upon supporters to send emails and birthday cards to Kentucky attorney general Daniel Cameron and Louisville metro mayor Greg Fischer, reiterating the same message.[8]

After only twenty-four hours, Young's #BirthdayForBreonna initiative spread like wildfire. "It has just been growing and growing," Young explained on June 6. "People really stepped up."[9] Indeed, the campaign captured the attention of millions of Americans that summer, who were deeply moved by Young's act of resistance and her affirmation of Black life. The hashtag began trending on Twitter, and supporters across the nation and the globe began to flood Instagram with Taylor's name. Young's creative idea quickly blossomed into a powerful act of protest, providing a way for countless Americans to challenge state violence from their homes as the coronavirus pandemic spread across the nation and globe. The hashtag #BirthdayForBreonna also drew supporters from diverse racial and social backgrounds. Business owners across the country backed the online campaign, with several bakers deciding to make cakes in Taylor's honor and one greeting card company even designing specialized cards in her memory.

Celebrities such as actresses Kerry Washington, Busy Philipps, and Charlize Theron joined the campaign, using their massive social media platforms to share the hashtag and encourage their followers to join the movement to seek justice for Taylor's relatives. By the afternoon of June 6, the online fund for Taylor's family had raised more than $5 million, significantly exceeding the original goal of $500,000.[10] The donations made it possible for the family to establish a fund in Taylor's name, dedicated to police reform and creating "better police officers, reasonable rules of engagement, more accountability and a focus on law enforcement."[11] Within two weeks of the #BirthdayForBreonna campaign launch, the Louisville Metro Council unanimously passed Breonna's Law to outlaw no-knock warrants and require the use of body cameras during searches. The Louisville Metro Police Department also fired the three officers involved in Taylor's killing.[12] In the ensuing months, the three officers appeared before a Kentucky grand jury, which ultimately failed to return manslaughter or homicide charges.

Despite the lack of legal accountability for the three officers involved in the Breonna Taylor case, the organizing efforts of Cate Young illuminate the extraordinary power of community leaders. Deeply moved by the painful circumstances of Taylor's death, Young worked to transform her concern into concrete steps that could make a difference in the lives of Taylor's loved ones. With clear vision and passion, Young developed a creative strategy to bring greater visibility to Taylor's killing. Although she had few resources and initially lacked the backing of any organizations or well-known figures, Young devised and launched a digital campaign that increased awareness, united millions of people, and raised millions of dollars for the Taylor family.

Decades before Young memorialized Breonna Taylor's murder as a tool to galvanize people into action, Fannie Lou Hamer emphasized how empowering people on the grassroots level was an important tactic for social and political change. And like Young, Hamer worked to shed light on issues most Americans tried to ignore. She carved out a space to advocate for social justice and forged innovative strategies to galvanize activists across the nation during the 1960s and '70s. Hamer emphasized the need for more leaders to engage with the grassroots and common folk—empowering these individuals to emerge as leaders—in order to challenge all forms of social injustices. She knew from past experience that leaders could come from all backgrounds—even those who lacked financial resources and formal education or had a marginalized social status. As she traveled across the nation, she recognized that the true test of leadership was the ability to empower others to *act*. This kind of work often took place behind the scenes, outside of the public limelight. Black communities needed this type of leader to ensure the vitality and the longevity of the civil rights movement. "We want leaders in our community," Hamer explained. "People will say . . . , 'Well, if we can get rid of Fannie Lou, [then] we can get rid of the trouble.' But what they don't know, freedom is like an eating cancer, if you kill me, it will break out all over the place."[13] For Hamer, galvanizing others to take action represented the most powerful expression of leadership. Far more than gaining visibility, she argued, the core aspect of effective leadership was to provide people with the necessary tools and resources to expand the fight for social justice.

"LET SOME OF THE GRASSROOT[S] PEOPLE HAVE A CHANCE."

Fannie Lou Hamer's ideas on leadership—especially the qualities that made a good leader versus an ineffective one—grew from personal experience. As a member of the Student Nonviolent Coordinating Committee (SNCC), one of the organizations that worked under the banner of the Council of Federated Organizations (COFO), Hamer worked closely with a diverse group of activists, including women leaders who served as role models.[14] Ella Baker's example of a Black woman's leadership style arguably had the most influence on Hamer, who openly admired Baker after their paths crossed in the early 1960s. Hamer admitted as much during a 1973 interview with historian Neil McMillen. When asked to identify "the most important Black leader in the United States today," Hamer focused specifically on Baker: "A woman that I really respect more than I do any other living woman at this time for her role in civil rights and activity is a woman in New York City named Miss Ella Baker. . . . She's a beautiful human being."[15]

Born in Norfolk, Virginia, in 1903, Baker grew up in North Carolina and went on to play an instrumental role in the growth of the civil rights movement.[16] After graduating from Shaw University, she joined the National Association for the Advancement of Colored People (NAACP), becoming a field secretary during the early 1940s. In 1957, she worked alongside Martin Luther King Jr. to help organize the Southern Christian Leadership Conference (SCLC) but parted ways with the group in 1960 over their leadership model. SCLC, like many civil rights organizations of the period, built the organization around one central (male) leader, mirroring the leadership structure of Black churches. Moreover, the organization's leaders were especially interested in planning large-scale and short-term public events known as *mobilizing*, as opposed to *grassroots organizing*—the bottom-up, community-based political activism that was vital to the development of local leaders. Whereas mobilizing drew national and sometimes international attention to specific events, grassroots organizing continued long after the media attention was gone.[17]

Baker embraced the organizing tradition, resisted the emphasis on one charismatic leader, and called on activists to adopt a group-centered model. Baker's inclusive vision—one that created space for leaders regardless of age, gender, class, education, or race—informed her efforts to help launch SNCC with student activists at Shaw University.[18] Indeed, she was the driving force behind the organization, having more influence in its development than any other activist in the movement.[19] As Baker explained, SNCC was "an opportunity for adult and youth to work together and provide genuine leadership—the development of the individual to his highest potential for the benefit of the group."[20] SNCC's reach and impact would extend far beyond Shaw, however. Hamer, like many other activists, experienced the transformative power of SNCC in the Deep South, which opened a world of possibilities for the sharecropper. Baker's mentoring and vision of leadership played an integral part in the development of Hamer's organizational philosophy.

Ella Baker's vision of group-centered leadership hinged on her belief in the power of grassroots political organizing. She understood local organizing as a necessary component of Black self-determination—the principle that people of African descent must take full control of their lives and future and determine the terms of their resistance.[21] This viewpoint provided the framework for SNCC's organizational efforts in the South during the 1960s. Indeed, SNCC's organizing work in Mississippi followed the activists' impulse to "advance the right of poor Black Mississippians to determine their own future."[22] A group-centered model of leadership, which tipped the scales of power from one or two celebrity-like leaders to a vast number of individuals, opened up a critical space for ordinary Black women—especially those who were impoverished and living in rural areas—to publicly shape the ideas and direction of the civil rights movement.[23]

In a 1966 interview, Hamer praised SNCC for providing a platform for local people to seek out their own destiny. "If SNCC hadn't of come into Mississippi," she insisted, "there never would have been a Fannie Lou Hamer."[24] She credited the organization for igniting the spark in her political activism simply by granting her the opportunity to lead. According to Hamer, her encounter with SNCC was the "first time" she had been "treated as a human being" by activists of any race.[25] In her telling, this meant that the youth in SNCC carefully listened to her and allowed her to share her thoughts and grievances. Throughout Hamer's life, she often credited SNCC activists for taking her ideas seriously.[26] For Hamer, the most powerful aspect of SNCC's work was their commitment to allowing local people to lead on their own terms, rather than dictating their every step. Along these lines, Hamer drew a stark contrast between SNCC's efforts and those of the NAACP:

> [SNCC] worked with the people. NAACP didn't work with the people. You know, I used to write membership for the [NAACP] and they don't care. They care about folk. You see I'm not particular about working with nobody that don't say "yes, sir" to everything to Mr. Charlie, and that's all the [NAACP] does. There ain't nothing that I respect less than the NAACP. It's awful. Now the legal affairs. I don't fight the legal affairs because they have some good attorneys. But I don't respect no man that as I said is a traitor to their own race. I don't respect no man for that.[27]

Hamer's remarks failed to account for the NAACP's diverse approaches to and engagement in local politics, which varied from chapter to chapter. They also failed to account for the crucial role local NAACP activists such as Amzie Moore and C. C. Bryant played in bringing SNCC into Mississippi.[28] However, Hamer's critiques did represent the perspective of a rural Mississippian on the limitations of the NAACP's approach, especially at the national level. They also capture the varied leadership styles, visions, and approaches undertaken by civil rights activists. Hamer denounced what she viewed as a paternalistic impulse among certain NAACP leaders who often attempted to dictate instructions that followed the line of respectability rather than allowing local people to carve out their own paths to achieving civil rights. While NAACP leaders like Roy Wilkins attempted to instruct Hamer on how best to accomplish her political goals, the leaders of SNCC such as Baker, Bob Moses, and James Forman listened to Hamer and encouraged her to pursue the path that best represented the interests of Black people in Mississippi.[29]

In Hamer's political vision, the most effective leaders emerged from the same local space in which they sought to organize. Though she valued the contributions and assistance of national groups, she did not want those groups to control the local movement. She believed that local people understood, more than anyone else, the challenges in their communities and could articulate how best to address them. "Don't [tell] me about somebody that ain't been in Mississippi two weeks," she argued, "and don't know nothing about the problems, 'cause they not leading us. And that's the truth."[30] Hamer went on to criticize white activists in the movement who took it upon themselves to anoint leaders of their choosing rather than allowing members of the community to have the final say on their representatives. "Time out for white people choosing the leader, hand picking the leader that [is] going to lead me 'cause we ain't going to follow."[31]

During the 1960s and '70s, Hamer made the case for empowering ordinary individuals to advance the fight for social justice. She emphasized the need to center everyday people in this struggle—to "let some of the grassroot people have a chance," as she explained it.[32] Hamer recognized the need for a diverse group of leaders at the grassroots level as a necessary step in the fight for Black rights and freedom. Alluding to the oppression of Black people in American society, Hamer observed in 1964, "I've gone to a lot of big cities, and I've got my first city to go to where this man wasn't standing with his feet on this black man's neck."[33] She later elaborated on this point with another analogy, arguing, "I've seen too many miseries and too many tricks. They say we should pull ourselves up by the bootstraps but how the hell we gonna do that when the man keeps stealing away the boots?"[34]

How then to keep the white man's feet off the Black man's neck and ensure that Black people had a chance to succeed? Hamer firmly believed it required a group effort. Progress called for ordinary people to come together, to pool their varied resources, to challenge racism and white supremacy—in every city, space, and context. "The only thing we can do, women and men, whether you [are] white or black, is to work together," Hamer explained.[35] She celebrated the power of each individual action and believed that singular acts of courage would accumulate over time to dismantle racist structures.

Hamer also advocated for effective leaders and criticized those who occupied leadership positions in society but failed to live up to the expectations of their roles. "We want people over us that's concerned about the people because we are human beings," she noted.[36] As she traveled across the country during the 1960s, she often addressed leaders who lacked courage. "We know we have a long fight," she noted, "because the leaders like the preachers and the teachers, they are failing to stand up today."[37]

"I used to have so much respect for teachers and preachers," she elaborated in the speech. "[But] how, how, how can you actually trust a man and have respect for him [when] he'll tell you to trust God, but he doesn't trust Him himself?"[38] Hamer's rhetorical question alluded to the inherent hypocrisy she saw in too many prominent members of the Black community—often individuals who were recognized as such solely for their profession, charisma, and education. Rather than stand in support with oppressed groups, they paid lip service to the movement, extending their support in words but not in deeds. "I don't want to hear you say, 'Honey, I'm behind you,'" Hamer explained. "Well, move, I don't want you back there. Because you could be two hundred miles behind. I want you to say, 'I'm with you.' And we'll go up this freedom road together."[39] For Hamer, the true test of any effective leader was their ability to stand firmly with members of the community in their moment of need—not in front of them or behind them but side by side. True leadership, in Hamer's view, required a group effort; it was not tied solely to one individual or organization in the movement.

For Hamer, the call to leadership extended to all Americans, regardless of social background and education. She therefore resisted the efforts of those who tried to diminish the contributions of leaders with limited formal education. "Don't worry about the qualifications," she told a packed audience in 1969, "because just like they learned it, you can too."[40] She addressed this issue again in 1971, while speaking at the NAACP Legal Defense Fund Institute in New York City: "But you see now, baby, whether you have a Ph.D., D.D., or no D, we're in this bag together. And whether you're from Morehouse or Nohouse, we're still in this bag together."[41] Hamer's remarks alluded to the class tensions in the movement, which often fueled deep divisions among activists. To some middle-class and elite Black Americans during the 1960s, Hamer would hardly qualify as a leader because of her limited formal education. The reality that her colleagues and peers sometimes shunned her on account of her education and social background disappointed Hamer. On several occasions, she addressed the disrespect she endured at the hands of other civil rights leaders whose conception of leadership did not include an impoverished and disabled Black woman with a sixth-grade education. In a 1969 interview with *New York Amsterdam News*, Hamer recalled being "insulted and embarrassed by [her] own people."[42] At the 1964 Democratic National Convention in Atlantic City, New Jersey, for example, Roy Wilkins, executive secretary of the NAACP, called Hamer an "ignorant woman"—expressing patriarchal condescension about her leadership capabilities and political knowledge.[43]

While these kinds of statements were meant to demean Hamer, she pushed beyond them and remained committed to using her voice to empower those around her. She resisted the idea that leadership should be reserved for those with formal education and resources. This posed a direct challenge to many civil rights activists—especially those of middle-class status and those who had prior experience in the realm of politics. Hamer therefore stood apart from many of her contemporaries, including those who questioned the leadership potential of young people. Similar to activists such as Ella Baker, Gloria Richardson, and Rosa Parks, Hamer embraced young people in the movement, emphasizing their vitality, vision, and ability to lead.[44] "I have high hopes in the young peoples of this nation, both black and white," she once noted.[45] No doubt her time with SNCC, which drew on a diverse group of young activists, strengthened Hamer's belief in the significance of empowering young leaders. Addressing Black students in one speech, Hamer encouraged them never to sit on the sidelines. "Stand up and be a man, a woman, wherever you are, because you're as much as anybody else," she insisted.[46] To that end, she devoted much of her time to supporting young activists, often working on college campuses to promote student political engagement. In June 1964, for example, Hamer helped to facilitate a weeklong voting rights training program for SNCC with several activists, including Julian Bond, at the Western College for Women in Oxford, Ohio. The training session, which offered instruction to the young activist students on how to facilitate voting registration in Mississippi, drew nearly three hundred participants.[47] For Hamer, these kinds of opportunities were vital to empowering young leaders in their efforts to help transform American society.

Hamer believed that focusing on one leader—or even a few—proved detrimental to social justice movements. "People will go to any limit just for personal power," she pointed out. "It doesn't really matter how the masses suffer, but just the few people, you know, controlling. . . . If there's going to be any survival for this country, there must be, we have to make democracy a reality for all people and not just a few," she added.[48] Hamer elaborated on this point in a 1971 speech, delivered in her hometown of Ruleville. She envisioned group-centered leadership as the only way to improve the conditions for Black people in the United States. "Community living and group decision making is local self-government," she explained. "It is this type of community self-government that has been lost over the decades and thus created decay in our poor rural areas in the South and our northern ghettos."[49] Hamer went on to argue that the lack of group-centered leadership was one of the factors that fueled social unrest in Black communities across the nation.[50] "This is what we have seen played back to us time and time again, first as peaceful demonstrations, and most recently in the form of violence and riots. If this nation is to survive we must return to the concept of local self-government with everyone participating to the maximum degree possible."[51]

"This is not to say, however, that we should not have a strong national or federal government," she added, "because these branches too must be responsive to the needs of all local and state governments through true representation of all men and women who have *total commitment* to a true *democratic process*."[52] Hamer's remarks reflected her deep commitment to advancing the core ideals of American democracy. Keeping the rights guaranteed by the US Constitution in mind, she advocated for the benefits of broad political participation—allowing all Americans to play an active role in shaping the laws and policies that dictate their everyday lives. These ideas guided her decision to help launch a movement that facilitated greater political participation among Black people in Mississippi.

"I'M FIGHTING FOR A PEOPLE'S MISSISSIPPI."

During the mid-twentieth century, Southern Democrats worked to block African Americans from casting ballots by utilizing an array of legal and extralegal tactics. By the early 1960s, an estimated 5 percent of Black residents in Mississippi were registered to vote—and the Democratic Party advocated an all-white slate of representatives for the state.[53] With SNCC and other organizations, Hamer resisted this state of affairs, pointing to the importance of fair representation on the national level. As early as 1963, she was involved in a series of efforts aimed at diversifying the Mississippi Democrats—allowing the concerns of Black residents in the state to be heard. In the fall of that year, she addressed the importance of Black political representation at the Freedom Vote rally in Greenwood, Mississippi.[54] In November 1963, civil rights activists in COFO had organized the Freedom Vote, a mock election to protest the denial of Black voting rights in the state. The Freedom Vote was a coordinated effort to reveal the extent of voter suppression and demonstrate that if given the opportunity, Black people in Mississippi would exercise their right to vote. The mock ballot included an interracial ticket with Dr. Aaron Henry, a Black pharmacist, running for governor and Edwin King, a white college chaplain, running for lieutenant governor. While the Freedom Vote was symbolic, it sent a clear message that Black people were determined to exercise their constitutional rights, countering a widespread view among white Southerners that Black people lacked interest in electoral politics.[55] In preparation for the vote, activists across the state held a series of Freedom Vote rallies to incite greater interest and support. The massive response to the Freedom Vote spoke volumes: between eighty thousand and ninety thousand Black residents in Mississippi participated.[56]

The 1963 Freedom Vote set the stage for the establishment of the Mississippi Freedom Democratic Party (MFDP) several months later. On April 26, 1964, Hamer joined forces with COFO activists Bob Moses, Annie Devine, Ella Baker, Victoria Gray, and others in an effort to challenge Mississippi's traditional Democratic Party, which had long excluded African Americans from participation.[57] She was the organization's central pillar, agitating to bring an end to discrimination in the Democratic Party.[58] The MFDP was open to all, regardless of race, thereby providing a counter to the regular Democratic Party that upheld a system of exclusion. "The long history of systematic and studied exclusion of Negro citizens from equal participation in the political processes of the state grows more flagrant and intensified daily," the MFDP explained.[59] In defiance of voter suppression tactics, the MFDP set out to give Black people in the state "an experience in political democracy."[60] Hamer and others had made attempts to work with the Mississippi Democratic Party to no avail; African Americans were continuously kept out of the Party's local, county, and state conventions. "When they wouldn't allow us to go into their regular Democratic meeting," she later recalled, "we organized what is now called the Mississippi Freedom Democratic Party."[61]

The MFDP embodied Hamer's political vision, which was based on the principles of American democracy. The state's all-white Democratic Party could not claim to represent the people of Mississippi when it excluded an estimated 500,000 Black residents. Anticipating those who would interpret her fight as an effort to advance an all-Black party, Hamer explained her vision for the MFDP during a speech: "I'm not fighting for a black Mississippi; I'm fighting for a people's Mississippi. I'm not fighting to seat an all-black government in the state of Mississippi, but I want you to know something, white people, it certainly ain't going to be an all-white one either."[62] As she emphasized on several occasions, the MFDP was an avenue to ensure that Black people would have a voice in electoral politics, thereby having an opportunity to shape local, state, and national politics.

In August 1964, only months after the MFDP's founding, Hamer and other members traveled to Atlantic City, New Jersey, to attend the Democratic National Convention. "When we went to Atlantic City," Hamer explained, "we didn't go there for publicity. We went there because we believed that America was what it said it was—the land of the free."[63] The delegation, which consisted of sixty-eight activists, arrived in Atlantic City to challenge the Mississippi Democratic Party and the validity of its all-white delegation to the convention. Hamer and the MFDP hoped the national party would compel the state party to give up seats to their delegation rather than suffer the embarrassment of exposing the lack of equal representation before a national audience. They also hoped to raise awareness of the broader struggles Black people in Mississippi faced as they attempted to exercise their constitutional right to vote, as well as the resistance civil rights activists encountered while organizing in the state.

Several weeks before the convention took place, members of the MFDP were shocked to learn of the brutal murders of James Earl Chaney, an African American activist from Meridian, Mississippi, and Michael Schwerner and Andrew Goodman, two Jewish activists from New York City. The three men, who were part of the Congress of Racial Equality (CORE), had been helping register Black residents to vote for the MFDP before they disappeared under suspicious circumstances. When their bodies were discovered on August 4, it reminded activists of their greatest fear and constant reality—those organizing for the rights and freedom of Black people could lose their lives, regardless of race.[64] While the murders sought to intimidate civil rights workers and quell the MFDP's work in the state, it achieved the opposite—it provided an impetus for the activists to demand immediate changes to the electoral process. The murders also served as a painful reminder to MFDP activists—and later the nation—that the fight for representation at the Democratic National Convention in Atlantic City was a matter of life and death for the delegation.

The experience in Atlantic City transformed Hamer. She encountered resistance from adversaries as well as from her presumptive allies. "That is the time when we found out what politics was like—not only in Mississippi, but in the United States," she recalled, "because I saw people threatening—I heard of people being threatened—because they dared to take a stand with the Mississippi Freedom Democratic Party."[65] Hamer persisted and delivered what would become the most well-known speech of her political career before the Credentials Committee at the convention. Her speech, televised to an audience of millions, addressed two central issues: voter suppression and state-sanctioned violence. While she was addressing the myriad of challenges Black people experienced in Mississippi, President Lyndon Johnson tried to block Hamer's speech, intentionally interrupting her testimony to give an impromptu press conference.

Notwithstanding the roadblocks she encountered in Atlantic City, Hamer managed to deliver an electrifying speech that captured the vision of the MFDP as a movement to empower African Americans in the state. The Democratic Party gave a weak rebuttal to Hamer's remarks, insisting that Black people had not been excluded without offering any compelling evidence to back their claim. They ultimately attempted to make the problem go away, recognizing that the presence of Hamer and her colleagues at the Democratic National Convention was an impediment to their usual proceedings. Leaders of the Democratic Party tried to convince the MFDP to accept two nonvoting seats at the convention. The offer was a far cry from what Hamer and her associates demanded. By extending an offer to join the convention floor without any voting privileges, the two-seat offer amounted to a symbolic gesture lacking any influence or actual representation.[66]

While Hamer vehemently resisted the two-seat offer, several civil rights leaders at the convention attempted to convince her otherwise. "I will never forget what they put us through," she recalled, and attributed her experiences at the convention to her "being a Mississippi housewife [and a farmer] and never exposed to politics."[67] From the vantage point of Rev. Martin Luther King Jr., NAACP leader Roy Wilkins, SCLC leader Andrew Young, and other male leaders, the seats offered by the Democratic Party represented a compromise that MFDP activists—and the national movement—could potentially harness in their favor. Activist Bayard Rustin, who served as an adviser for the MFDP at the convention, and MFDP chairman Aaron Henry agreed with this perspective, insisting that the compromise represented a step forward in the MFDP's attempts at recognition as a legitimate delegation for the state. Rustin also understood that a rejection of the compromise created a roadblock for future collaborations with the national Democratic Party. Collectively, the national civil rights leaders at the convention were especially invested in showing support for the Democratic Party—with their eyes on the presidential elections that would soon follow later that fall. They were hopeful that the election of Lyndon B. Johnson, with Hubert Humphrey as his running mate, would help advance the cause of civil rights in the long term. Accepting the compromise in the short term, they argued, would show support for the Democratic Party and help set the stage for securing civil rights legislation in the years to come.

Hamer was not oblivious to these concerns, but she was far less interested in making nice with the national Democratic Party than she was with securing rights and representation for the Black people of Mississippi. She later offered a scathing critique of Martin Luther King Jr. and other civil rights leaders for their stance, describing them as "tool[s] of the Johnson administration."[68] For Hamer, compromise with white public officials, whatever the motivation, left Black people empty-handed. "Fannie Lou Hamer . . . didn't seem to be interested in how we won the '64 election or how we kept our dignity," American politician Walter Mondale later observed, "she just wanted change [a]nd she wanted it now."[69] Hamer's urgency stemmed from her frustration with the slow pace of change in American politics. African Americans had waited long enough, Hamer reasoned, and the time for politicking and posturing was over. She pointed to a pattern of behavior among activists to compromise for the sake of progress—only to be further delayed in attaining their goals: "[T]hat's what [has] been accepted for the past hundred years. You always just take a little taste and you say yes sir, thank you. You just [accept] that, but when we rebelled then that made folks take a second look. We didn't take it. . . . To me it's very simple. If we was free almost a hundred years ago and if we are really free citizens what is we going to take a little something for?"[70] Hamer reasoned that it was high time for African Americans to take their fair share—*full* rights and actual representation, not a promise of future gains and symbolic gestures.

For these reasons, she rejected the two-seat compromise and saw its rejection as a moral and ethical stance. As she repeatedly reminded those who challenged her at the convention, the MFDP had traveled all the way to Atlantic City to demand representation and block the state party's plans to seat an all-white delegation—with the blessing of the national party. Two seats on the convention floor were a far cry from these demands. In Hamer's views, accepting such a compromise defied everything the MFDP stood for:

> They did have other leaders, that hadn't been in Mississippi, to tell us what we should expect and what we should accept and they wanted us to take a compromise—two votes at large. We refused to accept the compromise on the grounds of: if there's something supposed to be mine three hundred years ago, I just don't want anybody to hand me part of it today.[71]

Hamer's remarks alluded to her unwavering belief in the ideals of American democracy. As she consistently argued, the US Constitution and the Fifteenth Amendment granted Black people voting rights as citizens of the United States. The MFDP's demand for representation at the 1964 Democratic National Convention was a request to recognize a right already guaranteed to them. "All we want to do is be treated as human beings and . . . have a chance to elect our own officials," she later explained. "We want people in office that's going to represent us because so far we haven't had it."[72]

Hamer's strong resistance to the idea of a short-term compromise was also deeply rooted in her experiences as a Black Mississippian who had endured her share of hardships in the struggle for rights and freedom. She resisted the notion that the people of Mississippi should simply toe the line in agreement with national leaders—including those who knew little about the state and the unique challenges Black residents faced on a daily basis. Many of the civil rights leaders supporting the compromise, Hamer argued, lacked a full understanding of the local context informed by personal experiences and relationships, time spent in Mississippi, or knowledge of local affairs.

Although the national civil rights leaders at the Democratic National Convention framed their support of the two-seat compromise as part of "the big picture," the confluence of gender and class politics lay just beneath the surface. This attitude was on full display when Young insisted that Hamer adhere to the advice of national leaders with more experience in the realm of politics.[73] Others were especially offended by Hamer's direct style of communication and her refusal to display behavior they deemed appropriate. In a meeting with Senator Hubert Humphrey, the Democratic Party's presumptive nominee for vice president, Hamer directly pushed against the senator's recommendation that the MFDP accept what amounted to an unfair offer of two seats. With characteristic aplomb, Hamer posed a direct question to the senator to highlight the gravity of the situation: "Well, Mr. Humphrey do you mean to tell me that your position is more important to you than four hundred thousand black people's lives?" The question stung Humphrey who, according to Hamer, struggled to find the right words to respond.[74]

In the aftermath of the meeting with Humphrey, several of the national civil rights leaders worked to keep Hamer out of the negotiating discussions.[75] Their lack of confidence in Hamer's leadership abilities were revealed when King, Wilkins, and others arranged an impromptu meeting in King's suite with members of the Credentials Committee and two representatives of the MFDP, Joseph Rauh and Ed King. Hamer was not initially included.[76] When she and others became aware of the meeting, they quickly rushed over to join, forcing the meeting into the hallway when it was clear the suite was already full. The quick actions on Hamer's part emphasized her passion and her refusal to be sidelined by others—even prominent civil rights leaders. When one of Hamer's associates suggested that she "listen to the leaders" who were advocating the acceptance of the two-seat compromise, Hamer fervently resisted. "Who [is] the leader?" she asked. "I know you ain't been in Mississippi working with us. Who is he?" Reinforcing her point, she added, "I can't see a leader leading me nowhere if he's in N.Y. and I'm down here catching hell."[77]

Hamer's remarks shed light on the main forces underpinning her philosophy that local perspectives are valuable and even outweigh those of nationally visible leaders, who often know little about the local context. This was also made clear in Hamer's exchange with prominent Black politician and House of Representatives member Adam Clayton Powell Jr. who, after suggesting that she accept the compromise at the Democratic National Convention, asked Hamer if she knew who he was. Hamer confirmed her knowledge of the congressman but posed two rhetorical questions in response: "How many bales of cotton have you picked? How many beatings have you taken?"[78] For Hamer, lived experiences were just as valuable—perhaps even more so—than formal education, visibility, and political access. And even more, decisions could not be made solely at the whim of one person. In Hamer's vision, it required a collective effort. For this reason, Hamer refused to make decisions for all MFDP delegates—even when she was pressured to do so. "I said I'm not making a decision for the sixty-eight delegates," she later explained. "I won't do it."[79] Though she played an active role in deliberations, she maintained the view that the ultimate decision to reject the compromise needed to be backed by all the MFDP delegates.

These events underscored Hamer's unwavering commitment to group-centered leadership, which allowed for all voices to be involved in the decision-making process regardless of their gender, education, social background, or prior experience in politics.[80] SNCC leaders Ella Baker, James Forman, and Bob Moses understood this point. Not surprisingly, Hamer turned to them for advice on the matter. "I believe I'm right but I might be wrong," she said to them. "I respect you and I will respect your decision. Whatever you say, if you think I'm wrong, even though I felt like I was right, I would have done it." In their responses to Hamer, they reinforced the activist's position on the value of ordinary leaders in the movement—especially local leaders who understood the unique challenges facing their communities. "They told me," Hamer continued, "now look Mrs. Hamer, you're the people living in Mississippi and you people know what you've experienced in Mississippi, we don't have to tell you nothing [because] you make your own decision."[81]

Their remarks eased Hamer's concerns and reaffirmed her own convictions that a compromise was out of step with the goals of the MFDP. What Black people in Mississippi needed above all else was actual political representation—not a veneer of representation. With this in mind, Hamer, along with the help of Annie Devine and Victoria Gray, convinced the other MFDP delegates to reject the two-seat compromise.[82] Speaking before the convention's rules committee, Hamer passionately explained the limitations of such an offer: "We didn't come all this way for no two seats."[83] She elaborated further on this point in a subsequent interview: "We didn't come way up there from Mississippi, 68 delegates subject to being killed on our way back, and we didn't come all the way up there to compromise for no more than we'd gotten here. They only gave us two votes at large 'cause they knowed we wouldn't have had nothing. I said we just didn't come here for just that."[84] Hamer refused to capitulate for the sake of politics. Her allegiance to the Black people of Mississippi came first, and she was determined not to make concessions that could ultimately hurt those she cared most about in Ruleville and Sunflower County.

Although Hamer and the other MFDP delegates failed to secure the seats they had hoped to obtain when they arrived in Atlantic City, they left a lasting impression on all who were present. Walter Mondale, who later became vice president of the United States, recalled being deeply moved by Hamer's testimony: "She really blew it away." Her testimony was so powerful that Mondale later admitted he could hardly remember the other testimonies delivered at the convention: "As soon as Fannie Lou Hamer started, it was all forgotten."[85] African American baseball player Jackie Robinson reinforced these sentiments in a 1964 newspaper article. The "most moving of all-terrifying in its intensity and striking right at the heart of the awful situation," Robinson noted, "was the story told in ringing emotion-filled words by Mrs. Fannie Lou Hamer who told what happened to her after she led a group of 26 Negroes to register. . . . I don't believe there could have been many indifferent ears or dry eyes as the story of her outrage poured forth over the television screens," Robinson added.[86] His remarks mirrored those of countless others who were present at the convention—and even thousands who watched from the comfort of their homes. The MFDP's challenge to the Democratic Party raised national awareness of the fight for civil rights for Black people and laid bare American hypocrisy on matters of freedom and democracy. It was a testament to Hamer's leadership style and fundamental values.

In the aftermath of the 1964 Democratic National Convention, Hamer continued to play a vital role in mentoring and supporting young leaders in the movement and valuing their perspectives. In the summer of 1966, Hamer participated in the March Against Fear across Mississippi in support of James Meredith, the first African American to enroll at the University of Mississippi. Although Meredith's enrollment at the university marked a pivotal moment in the fight for civil rights, the violent response from local white residents underscored the massive hold of white supremacy.[87] Determined to "point out and challenge the all-pervasive overriding fear that dominates the day-to-day life of the Negro in the United States—and especially in Mississippi," Meredith planned a 220-mile one-man march, beginning on Sunday, June 5, 1966.[88] On the second day of the march, miles south of Hernando, Mississippi, a white man fired three rounds at Meredith.

As Meredith lay in a hospital bed recovering from his wounds, civil rights leaders, representing SCLC, the NAACP, the Urban League, CORE, and SNCC convened a meeting in Memphis, Tennessee, to plan a response. In an effort to ensure that the march would continue, several civil rights leaders, including Rev. Martin Luther King Jr., Roy Wilkins, and SNCC chairman Stokely Carmichael, agreed to gather at the location where Meredith had been attacked the following Sunday. As these activists finalized plans for the next leg of the march, they turned to Fannie Lou Hamer for help in coordinating local affairs.[89] She readily agreed to assist with plans, and on Sunday, June 12, she joined hundreds of activists determined to send a message that they would not be intimidated by white mob violence.[90]

While the March Against Fear provided a significant platform to challenge white supremacy, it also represented a moment of transition in the movement. As civil rights activists from various organizations came together that summer, their diverse perspectives and political approaches rose to the surface. Leaders in SCLC, the NAACP, and the Urban League emphasized the significance of civil disobedience in the effort to secure Black political rights—even in the face of white supremacist violence. They also hoped to use the march as an opportunity to encourage Black Mississippians to back the proposed 1966 Civil Rights Bill, which included provisions for ending discrimination in housing, education, and the workforce.[91]

Carmichael, Floyd McKissick of CORE, and other young activists in the movement, however, demanded a more radical response. They viewed the shooting of Meredith as the final straw and argued that nonviolence as a political approach was inefficient.[92] Instead they demanded greater political autonomy and advocated for Black self-defense, calling on the Deacons for Defense and Justice, a Louisiana-based Black paramilitary organization, to join the march.[93] Despite their many ideological differences, activists representing a variety of civil rights organizations moved ahead with plans to complete the March Against Fear. Hamer would play a vital role on the local level. She provided careful instructions about the specific route activists should take along the march and even led them in singing freedom songs.[94]

On June 16, Carmichael and two other organizers were arrested for trespassing as they attempted to set up camp at an elementary school in Greenwood, Mississippi. Following his release from prison later that evening, Carmichael reinforced his position on the matter of Black political autonomy, shouting the phrase "Black Power."[95] Carmichael's declaration electrified many SNCC activists and local residents who desired more concrete results. Black Power, however, caused consternation among many others, especially older activists in the movement who feared that a more radical approach would dismantle the movement. Hamer's response on the matter offered a glimpse into how she valued the contributions of young leaders in the movement, despite ideological differences. Although she fully supported nonviolent resistance, she also recognized the importance and utility of a more militant response to white supremacy. "I will agree with . . . Martin Luther King's 'nonviolent approach' in some cases," she once told a group of activists in Ruleville, Mississippi, "but in other cases, one has to take a more militant approach and I am not referring to turning the other cheek."[96] When a group of reporters suggested that Carmichael was stirring up trouble because of his more militant stance, Hamer carefully corrected them. "I think it's a very tragic thing that this country has driven people to this point in life," she argued. "The shame is not on the people, but on the country."[97] Her support for Carmichael, much like her actions at the 1964 Democratic National Convention, revealed her grounded approach to leadership. She respected Carmichael's leadership and believed it was important to allow him and other young activists to follow their own political instincts.

Hamer's commitment to supporting and empowering leaders was only matched by her passion and radical honesty, which served as a source of inspiration for many. As Bob Moses later recalled, "Mrs. Hamer . . . spoke from her heart. And she spoke about what was real to her from all of her experience. . . . And what came through, always, was her soul. . . . [W]hat you felt when she spoke and when she sang," Moses added, "was someone who was opening up her soul and really telling you what she felt and the pain that she had felt and the life that she had lived. And somehow she was able to convey that to people in a way in which [others] couldn't."[98] Hamer's uncanny ability to inspire others through her words, her unwavering commitment to providing a space for leaders of all backgrounds, and her desire to empower others to tap into their leadership potential served as a model—then as now.

CHAPTER FOUR

THE SPECIAL PLIGHT OF BLACK WOMEN

We have a job as black women, to support whatever is right, and to bring in justice where we've had so much injustice.

—FANNIE LOU HAMER[1]

In October 2020, rapper and songwriter Megan Thee Stallion penned a powerful op-ed in the *New York Times* titled "Why I Speak Up for Black Women."[2] The editorial appeared in the prominent newspaper weeks after news broke that Megan had been allegedly shot by a male acquaintance, Canadian rapper and singer Tory Lanez. In the days following the incident, Megan was subject to a barrage of public critiques and memes on social media. Some critics went as far as to blame Megan for the act of violence—pointing to her "scantily clad" outfits as somehow responsible for the act of violence.[3] Other observers deemed the incident "funny," focusing on the fact that Megan had suffered gunshot wounds to both feet.[4] Though the female rapper was initially silent on the matter, she decided to take a bold stance several weeks later, writing the op-ed to address the incident and the public's response. "The way people have publicly questioned and debated whether I played a role in my own violent assault," Megan wrote, "proves that my fears about discussing what happened were, unfortunately, warranted."

She went on to confront the problem of misogyny in society, which has allowed men to mistreat and disrespect women with little recourse: "[V]iolence against women is not always connected to being in a relationship. Instead, it happens because too many men treat all women as objects, which helps them to justify inflicting abuse against us when we choose to exercise our own free will." As Megan explained, this behavior pattern provides an additional hurdle for Black women, "who struggle against stereotypes and are seen as angry or threatening when we try to stand up for ourselves and our sisters." She drew connections between her own experiences and the experiences of countless other Black women in the United States who are "still constantly disrespected and disregarded in so many areas of life."[5]

As an artist, Megan used her massive platform to condemn violence against women, challenge patriarchy, and empower women across the nation. Her passionate editorial, and the courage needed to write it, served as a source of inspiration for many. While Megan used the space in the *New York Times* to call attention to the many challenges facing Black women during the twenty-first century—including high infant mortality rates and high rates of violence against Black transgender women—she also took the opportunity to encourage them. "[I]t's ridiculous that some people think the simple phrase 'Protect Black women' is controversial," Megan argued. "We deserve to be protected as human beings. And we are entitled to our anger about a laundry list of mistreatment and neglect that we suffer." Although she did not identify as a feminist in the article—or even mention the term—Megan articulated core Black feminist ideals, especially women's empowerment, an emphasis on the unique experiences of Black women, and the overlapping forms of oppression Black women face.[6]

Despite the challenges Black women face in a racist and patriarchal society, Megan emphasized that Black women were still leading the charge to transform American society. Her belief in the difference Black women could make in resisting patriarchy in all its forms is deeply rooted in history. She looked to Black women icons of the past—crediting Rosa Parks and "such legends as Shirley Chisholm, Loretta Lynch, U.S. Representative Maxine Waters and the first Black woman to be elected to the U.S. Senate, Carol Moseley Braun"—for hope and inspiration.[7] Megan's turn to the past is fitting as she tapped into a powerful message about the unique plight of Black women in American society that resonates throughout Black women's history. Like Fannie Lou Hamer fifty years earlier, Megan Thee Stallion sought to call attention to the interlocking systems of oppression that shape women's lives.

Although Hamer never self-identified as a feminist, she was deeply committed to the empowerment of women in society, especially in the realm of electoral politics and grassroots organizing, and she did not condone patriarchy or male chauvinism. Hamer also applied a race and gender analysis to her personal and political experiences—emphasizing the intersecting forces that shape Black women's lives in the United States. Despite her valuable contributions to Black feminist politics, Hamer resisted the label of *feminist*, much like many other Black women of the period. Her resistance stemmed from a history of distrust. More often than not, white feminists sidelined Black women in the women's liberation movement of the 1960s and '70s. The distrust, therefore, did not evolve out of thin air. Writer Toni Morrison argued as much in a 1971 editorial, aptly titled "What the Black Woman Thinks About Women's Lib." "What do black women feel about Women's Lib?" she asked. "Distrust. It is white, therefore suspect." Morrison's remarks capture the general disconnect between Black women and mainstream feminist movements of the twentieth century. Although many Black women were interested in the core principles of the women's liberation movement—especially the focus on expanding women's social, political, and economic rights—they rejected the movement's focus on dismantling patriarchy while ignoring racism.[8] Moreover, Black women found their contributions to the movement, and their specific concerns, largely overlooked. As Morrison explained, "In spite of the fact that liberating movements in the black world have been catalysts for white feminism, too many movements and organizations have made deliberate overtures to enroll blacks and have ended up by rolling them."[9] No doubt Hamer's refusal to embrace the term *feminist* or join the women's liberation movement reflects this history. Even more, it signaled Hamer's refusal to simply fall in line. She maintained her own views on women's rights—some of which aligned with the movement and many others that departed from it.

Ultimately, Hamer's ideas on women and gender, even the most controversial ones, significantly strengthened the mainstream feminist movement of the 1960s and '70s. Her life provided a model for how women could effectively lead in society and resist patriarchy in all its manifestations. But even more, Hamer joined other Black women in centering race and class in discussions of women's rights and progress. Long before the term *intersectionality* entered common parlance, Hamer articulated ideas that helped to advance this political vision. She understood her life in intersectional terms and resisted anyone, including white feminists, who recognized gender oppression but failed to grapple with the intersecting dimensions of race and class in particular. For these reasons, Hamer was especially critical of the women's liberation movement, pointing to the erasure of Black women's history and contributions.[10] She used her voice and influence in these spaces to remind activists of the unique place of Black women in American society. Her ideas and political activities ultimately "provide a genealogy for intersectional thought and black feminism," and exemplify how individuals who resist the label *feminist* can still effectively shape feminist politics.[11] Hamer's observations on gender and her own political activities helped to advance Black feminism in the United States, laying the groundwork for contemporary expressions of women's empowerment—much like the one articulated by Megan Thee Stallion.

"I'M TIRED OF BEING CALLED 'AUNTY.'"

Hamer's speeches and interviews capture the activist's ideas on women and gender. The theme of women's empowerment and respect ran through her earliest speeches. During the early 1960s, for example, Hamer publicly addressed the disrespect she and other Black women faced in a society that devalued the lives and contributions of Black people. She pointed to the common practice of white people referring to her as *girl* and *Aunty*—terms that failed to recognize Hamer's personhood.[12] "Because actually, I'm tired of being called 'Aunty,'" Hamer explained. "I wondered in life what [actual] time would they allow for me to be a woman? Because until I was thirty-six I was a girl: 'Girl this.' And now I'm forty-six and it's 'Aunty.' But I want you to know tonight: I don't have one white niece or nephew. And if you don't want to call me Mrs. Hamer, just call me plain 'Fannie' because I'm not your aunt."[13]

While reflecting on her experiences at the 1968 Democratic National Convention, Hamer pointed to the disrespect that Black women faced in public spaces. "Something disgusting to me," she explained, "[was] when one of the women that was with us at that convention, one of the black [women] . . . was not only flanked at that convention, but three security agent stamps was put on her bag. We was watched, some of us, like we was criminals."[14] Hamer's comments alluded to the ways white people criminalized Black women—a pattern of behavior that characterized the treatment of Black people in American society during the twentieth century. Hamer's disgust was rooted in the recognition that Black women, especially members of the working class, were subjected to mistreatment on account of stereotypes that framed Black women as criminals.[15] Even in the context of a political event, as Democrats gathered to select a new presidential nominee for the Democratic Party, Black women encountered suspicion and distrust from their white counterparts. Hamer's critiques extended beyond the criminalization of Black women. Many of her contemporaries at the earlier 1964 Democratic National Convention later recalled Hamer's frustration with the minimal female representation in the delegation—men held all the major positions. According to civil rights activist Jeanette King, Hamer "was quite angry about the male domination" and did not hesitate to speak her mind on the issue.[16] Her passionate advocacy on behalf of Black women was transformative for many who were present at the Convention. Wes Watkins, one of the delegates of the Mississippi Freedom Democratic Party, later credited Hamer for changing his views on women's rights and equality. "It made a feminist out of me," he admitted.[17]

Despite—and because of—their mistreatment in American society, Hamer argued that Black women occupied a unique place in society. Echoing a long line of Black women activists who came before her, including Black radicals Claudia Jones and Louise Thompson Patterson, Hamer maintained the belief that Black women were at the center of interlocking oppressions of race, gender, and class.[18] Because Black women occupied the most subordinate position within the national and global racial and gender hierarchies, they were uniquely positioned to advocate for rights and freedom. "We have a job as black women," Hamer insisted, "to support whatever is right, and to bring in justice where we've had so much injustice."[19] In this way, Hamer envisioned Black women as foundational to any movement for women's rights. Black women's liberation would therefore constitute the liberation of all women and all people. In the tradition of Black feminist thought, as reflected in the abolitionist movement of the nineteenth century, Hamer fused a desire to eradicate both racism and sexism in American society.[20] Her public presence and candid observations served as important reminders of the crucial role Black women played in advocating for women's rights alongside their demands for civil rights.

In 1972, journalist Franklynn Peterson drew these connections in a special feature on Hamer published in *Sepia* magazine: "Long before Women's Lib became a popular vogue, black women of courage like Harriet Tubman and Sojourner Truth made a reality of the women's liberation movement in their striving for freedom more than a century ago. In today's era, too, Women's Lib was far from news to black women when it hit the newspaper headlines and no one better symbolizes that soul sisters were far ahead of their time than Fannie Lou Hamer, who has sometimes been described as the mother of the black female political movement."[21] Peterson's remarks reinforced a point Hamer herself had long argued: Black women were forebears of the women's rights movement. Indeed, Hamer resisted the notion that Black women were somehow new to the women's rights movement or otherwise needed to be "awakened" by the women's liberation movement. She often referenced the decades of Black women's political work—such as that of abolitionist and women's rights activist Sojourner Truth—to underscore how vital Black women have always been in the fight for women's equality. Hamer's message emphasized this history as foundational to women's empowerment.

While Hamer passionately advocated for expanded rights and opportunities for women, she made it clear that her position was in no way meant to sideline Black men. On various occasions, she challenged what she viewed as white feminists' quest for liberation from men—a reaction to the era's focus on the need to free women from the confines and pressures associated with home and family as well as societal limitations placed upon women because of their gender.[22] Betty Friedan's 1963 book *The Feminine Mystique,* often credited as sparking the women's liberation movement, largely captured these sentiments—though it excluded Black women and glossed over working-class women.[23] The book vocalized the frustrations of middle-class and married white women, especially housewives, in American society. While the public call for women's liberation in the 1960s and '70s was far more expansive, there were certainly some married women who desired—and perhaps needed—liberation from their husbands. That was not the case for Hamer, and it was not the case for all women. "I'm not fighting to liberate myself from the black man in the South," she explained, "because, so help me, God, he's had as many and more severer problems than I've had. Because not only has he been stripped of the right to be a politician," she added, "but he has been stripped of the dignity and the heritage and all the things that any citizen of the country needs."[24] In another instance, she added, "I got a black husband, six feet three, 240 pounds, with a 14 shoe, that I don't want to be liberated from. But we are here to work side by side with this black man," she explained, "in trying to bring liberation to all people."[25]

Hamer's relationship with her husband, Pap, shed additional light on her ideas about gender roles. Their relationship did not subscribe to all the conventional expectations of what a woman or man should do in the home. The two maintained mutual respect for each other and shared the household responsibilities, including caring for their children. In describing her early entry into politics, Hamer often recalled Pap's supportive response when she shared her plans to attend the 1962 mass meeting in Ruleville: "In 1962, that Monday night after the fourth Sunday, I went to this mass meeting, after my husband told me, 'Well, I tell you what,' [he] said, 'I'll carry you out to that mass meeting tonight if you pick three hundred [pounds of cotton] today.'"[26] For Hamer, this was a source of pride—a story she recalled often to underscore the kind of relationship she had with her husband. Though Pap did not join Hamer at the mass meeting that evening, he extended his support for her interest in learning more about the movement by approving her plans on the condition that she would still meet the usual work expectations on the farm.

Hamer's remarks illuminate the dynamics of her relationship with Pap and the ways the two actively disrupted social norms. While the advent of the women's liberation movement did much to alter mainstream perspectives on gender roles and expectations, traditional Victorian ideals remained fixed in place in various sectors of society. By this measure, women were expected to attend to the matters of home and family while men participated in all aspects of public life. Years after the 1962 public meeting, while discussing her marriage with Pap, Hamer would describe the nature of their relationship:

> Pap is not like most men, too many refuse to let their wives travel all over the country. But, you see, we work together in Mississippi. We have absolute faith in one another. We understand each other and we like young people. When we have a free evening we'll go to the discotheques or night clubs where the young people go. We dance and learn their steps, listen to them talk, and enjoy ourselves.[27]

Hamer's remarks alluded to Pap's involvement in the movement. Although he did not play a prominent role, Pap supported Hamer's political activism. During the late 1960s and early 1970s, for example, Pap was involved in the running of Hamer's Freedom Farm, a community-based rural project to tackle poverty. At one point, Pap even assisted as farm manager and spearheaded several initiatives to support Hamer's work.[28] He also lent his support in the home as Hamer traveled extensively across the nation. That Hamer's husband would play such an active role in the affairs of the home as his wife led a vibrant political career is a testament to his disavowal of some conventional gender role ideals.[29] Hamer addressed this point during a 1976 interview: "We respect each other. We're not here separately, we're here together and I stand by him to see what we can do to set this country straight."[30] In this way, Hamer's relationship with Pap—especially their mutual love, trust, support, understanding, and willingness to compromise—captured the essence of women's empowerment.

While their day-to-day relationship certainly defied many conventional expectations, Hamer still held moderate views on gender roles—supporting women's empowerment in every possible way but not completely discarding traditional views about the roles men and women should play in the home and in society at large. Although she praised Pap for supporting her political career and extending a hand of support in their marriage, Hamer also insisted that Pap was fully in charge of the affairs of the home: "He, Mr. Hamer, is the boss of the house."[31] Echoing countless Black women activists of the twentieth century, Hamer also reinforced the idea that Black men's primary function was to serve as leaders and protectors, arguing that "in men, the strength of this nation lies. Stand up, black men, this nation needs you, mothers need you," she declared at a speech in 1971. "I call upon all men and women to stand up with pride and dignity," she added, "but especially black men."[32] In Hamer's vision, even the strongest women in society could not take the place of men, who Hamer framed as the ones who shouldered the responsibility to lead the nation forward:

> I am a woman, strong as any woman my age and size normally, but I am no man. I can think, but I am still a woman and I am a mother, as are most women. I can carry the message, but the burdens of the nation and the world must be shouldered by men. Decisions concerning life, comfort, and security must finally rest in the hands of men. Women can be strength for men, women can help with the decision making, but men will ultimately take the action.[33]

Hamer's remarks exemplify the ideological tensions that many Black women activists of various political persuasions grappled with during the twentieth century. This included Black nationalist women, who walked a fine line between leading and upholding the belief in the primacy of Black male leadership—in part because of how white patriarchy also sought to undermine Black men's dignity and place in society.[34]

While Hamer was deeply committed to empowering women and acknowledged the problem of gender discrimination, she reinforced the need for white liberal feminists to include race and class in their analysis. Gender discrimination undeniably shaped the experiences of women, but for women of color, it was by no means their only concern. Hamer, echoing other Black women activists, desired women's

advancement and equality but was equally concerned about addressing racism in society—a system of oppression that affected all Black
people, regardless of gender and class. Black women's dual concern—
the dismantling of racism and sexism—was not a new aspect of the
longer women's rights movements; it had been a consistent feature of
Black women's political activism, but many white liberal feminists
encountered it for the first time in the 1960s and '70s. As Congresswoman Shirley Chisholm later recalled, "A lot of women [in the wom-
en's liberation movement] . . . were stuck on the word 'sisters,' and
they thought we were all sisters. What we were saying is that sisters
had different agendas. It was a revelation to some of those [white]
women."[35] Chisholm's remarks highlighted one of Hamer's contributions to the women's liberation movement: she helped to broaden the
perspectives of white feminists who often viewed the world through
a narrow prism. Her public critiques of the movement served as a
means to help white feminists better understand the diversity of wom-
en's experiences, shaped by a range of social factors that extended
beyond gender.

Hamer was not short on advice for white liberal feminists, but they
were not the only ones on her mind. She also thought carefully about
the role of Black women in the movement, and she was ever mindful
of the way they were vilified in public discussions about the Black
community. She forcefully condemned the statements of sociologist
Daniel Patrick Moynihan, whose 1965 report *The Negro Family: The
Case for National Action*—dubbed the Moynihan Report—was an
indictment of Black women. By implicitly blaming "female-headed
households" for poverty in Black communities, Moynihan joined
countless other Americans who placed the blame on oppressed groups
for the challenges they faced—all the while overlooking systemic oppression. Hamer did not mince words when she told a news reporter
that "Moynihan who wrote about black matriarchal society, knows
as much about a black family as a horse knows about New Year's."[36]
She added, "We are women but we've always had to help, because we
know what they'd done to our men but we've always helped our husbands." Hamer reiterated, "There's nothing wrong with it."[37]

Hamer understood that Black women had a unique responsibility
to attend to the specific needs of their own families and communities.

She demonstrated this commitment through her efforts to end violence against women. During the 1960s and '70s, Hamer publicly denounced the violence that impoverished Black women in the South faced on a daily basis. She knew firsthand the pain and trauma associated with such violence. The 1963 Winona beating and sexual assault, as well as the forced sterilization she endured, were forever etched in Hamer's mind. These painful past incidents propelled Hamer to speak candidly about violence against Black women and girls.

Similar to other Black women activists of the period, including Rosa Parks, Hamer was deeply committed to defending and protecting Black women.[38] Hamer's response to the tragic case of Jo Etha Collier provides one example of her work to raise awareness of the issue and seek justice for victims' families. On May 25, 1971, three white men shot and killed Collier, an eighteen-year-old Black girl in Drew, Mississippi, as she traveled home after her graduation ceremony.[39] Although several news reports focused on the fact that the three men were under the influence of alcohol, Hamer and other local activists emphasized other likely motivations for the act of violence.[40] At the time of the shooting, Collier was an honors student and star athlete at Drew High School, a "formerly lily-white" school in the town.[41] Her graduation, only hours before the shooting, had been widely celebrated by her family and local residents.[42] Just as Collier was entering a local café, where she had plans to celebrate with loved ones, she was tragically gunned down by Wesley Parks, his brother, Wayne Parks, and their nephew, Allen Wilkerson. "She was black— that was the reason she was shot down," Hamer explained.[43] "I think they had watched this girl, because she was black and smart," Hamer later added. "This was too much, because they don't want to believe that black people have the capacity."[44]

In the aftermath of the shooting, Hamer took on a leading role in seeking justice for Collier's family. The tragic shooting coincided with Hamer's state senate campaign—a campaign in which she spoke openly about the need to address white supremacist violence.[45] Linking Collier's murder to that of countless others in Mississippi and across the nation—including the killings of Emmett Till, Medgar Evers, Malcolm X, and Martin Luther King Jr.—Hamer denounced racist violence as "sins" of the nation. "Miles of paper and film cannot record the many injustices this nation has been guilty of," she added.[46] As she worked to raise greater awareness of these injustices, Hamer was also deeply concerned with meeting the needs of Collier's family. Shortly after the shooting, she met with Collier's mother, Gussie Mae Love, in Ruleville. In the presence of reporters, the two women spoke at length in Hamer's home, addressing the shooting and the widespread problem of white supremacist violence in the state. In the days to follow, Hamer participated in several local demonstrations and traveled to Drew to meet with W. O. Williford, the city's mayor.[47]

At Collier's funeral, held on May 30, 1971, Hamer delivered a moving speech and announced plans to launch a fund to raise money for Collier's parents and siblings to help them move out of their dilapidated "tar-paper shack."[48] "So help me God," Hamer later told reporters, "I'll work my fingers to the bone to see that this family has a house."[49] While it's unclear if the family managed to purchase a new home, Hamer kept her word to offer financial support, and in September 1971 launched the Jo Etha Collier Building Fund after an extensive fundraising campaign.[50] Hamer remained in close contact after the shooting and was steadfast in her attempts to secure justice for the Love family.[51] In July of that year, Hamer brought Gussie Mae Love along with her to the founding meeting of the National Women's Political Caucus, held in Washington, DC.[52] Addressing members of the audience, Hamer appealed to mothers in attendance—"there's a lot of us [mothers] in this building today"—to draw attention to Love's presence in the room. She went on to share the painful story of Collier's death to emphasize the "racism and hate" that shaped Black women's lives in the United States.[53]

Months later, on October 19, 1971, Wesley Parks, the only shooter who had been indicted on murder charges, was convicted—but only on charges of manslaughter.[54] The reduced sentence was justified solely on legal grounds, but it was morally reprehensible. It underscored how much American society devalued Black lives—and in this instance, Black women and girls. "[I] want to know how come they can gun down an innocent, holy li'l chile from Drew, Mississippi, a black girl who is an image of the Lawd, they call that manslaughter," Hamer pointed out, "but when a white person gets killed, they call it murder!"[55] Hamer's criticism of the court decision highlighted the double standards of the criminal justice system, which served as a shield to protect white supremacists while leaving Black women—and all Black citizens—vulnerable. Similar to civil rights activist Gloria Richardson, Hamer deployed her anger toward the mistreatment of Black people to propel her efforts to fight for Black liberation.[56]

Although Hamer believed in empowering women through expanded political rights and opportunities, she never shied away from expressing views that ran counter to the platform of the women's liberation movement. This was especially true for reproductive rights. During the early twentieth century, women's rights activists in the United States viewed the fight for birth control as fundamental to women's liberation.[57] Though many women activists celebrated the approval of birth control by the Food and Drug Administration (FDA) on May 9, 1960, others passionately resisted the development. These debates would only intensify by the mid-1960s as a number of court cases concerning contraception began to set the stage for *Roe v. Wade*, the landmark 1973 Supreme Court case that would overturn restrictive abortion laws in the United States.[58] Though the topic of birth control sparked much disagreement among women, including suffragists and feminists, it remained at the forefront of discussions about women's autonomy in American society. By and large, the mainstream women's liberation movement actively supported birth control, emphasizing the important role it played in women's ability to control their lives and their futures. Some Black feminists of the period supported these campaigns, such as attorney Florynce "Flo" Kennedy, who played a central role in legalizing abortion and advocating reproductive rights during the 1960s.[59]

While Hamer certainly understood the motivations that compelled many women to endorse birth control, she resisted it on the grounds that it ran counter to her faith. "I respect my mother so much," she told the audience at a 1971 event at the University of Wisconsin–Madison, "that they didn't have them birth control pills because if they had them I probably wouldn't be standing here today."[60] Hamer's views on reproductive rights were no doubt shaped by her own personal experiences and family histories, especially her inability to bear children and her painful experience with a forced sterilization.[61] By one account, Hamer linked the issue of birth control to her own experiences while attending the 1969 White House Conference on Food, Nutrition and Health, convened at the request of President Richard Nixon. According to journalist Samuel Yette, a writer for the *Baltimore Afro-American*, Hamer grew agitated when she learned that several individuals at the conference were discussing birth control in one of the sessions.[62] She then forced her way into the session and took the opportunity to share her own painful experience of being sterilized years earlier. In doing so, Hamer sent the message that she viewed birth control use as an offense to those who longed for the opportunity to bear children, especially those who had experienced the violence of forced sterilizations.

Hamer also viewed abortion as an act of reproductive injustice.[63] According to prominent African American journalist Ethel L. Payne, Hamer also expressed "strong objections" at the 1969 gathering to a proposed policy that "would have put the Conference on Food, Nutrition and Health on record as favoring voluntary abortions for girls in disadvantaged groups."[64] In the presence of three thousand people, Hamer passionately denounced the plan, describing abortion as "murder" and "genocide." By the time Hamer concluded her remarks, the motion under consideration was quickly dismissed.[65]

At a 1971 event at Tugaloo College, Hamer reinforced her position on birth control and used the opportunity to express her lack of support for abortion rights. "The methods used to take human lives, such as abortion, the pill, the ring, et cetera, amounts to genocide," she argued. Without mincing words, she emphasized the impetus for her beliefs: "I believe that legal abortion is legal murder and the use of pills and rings to prevent God's will is a great sin."[66] Her statements reveal how deeply Hamer's political ideas were informed by her Christian beliefs—indeed, she directly tied her stance on contraception to her interpretation of scripture. Moreover, Hamer viewed birth control and abortion as social justice issues. She feared that both were simply white supremacist tools to regulate the lives of impoverished Black people and even prevent the growth of the Black population.[67] "I fight for the other kids too to give them a chance," she once argued while addressing her stance on birth control. "Because if you give them a chance," she added, "they might come up being Fannie Lou Hamers and something else."[68] Hamer's stance on reproductive rights defied what many others expected. However, she was certainly not alone. During the 1960s and '70s, a significant segment of Black activists passionately resisted birth control and abortion rights—often for the same reasons Hamer disavowed both. Members of the Black Panther Party and the Nation of Islam, for example, criticized contraception and decried abortion laws as efforts of the white ruling class to facilitate the genocide of the Black race.[69]

Despite being surrounded by many activists in the movement who championed reproductive rights, Hamer refused to budge on the issue during her lifetime. In this way, her personal life and experiences, as well as her religious views and family's history, guided her political action, offering one manifestation of the famous mantra of the women's movement: "The personal is political."[70] Notwithstanding Hamer's position on abortion rights and contraception, her bold stance against forced sterilizations—and her courageous decision to disclose her painful experiences to raise awareness—served as a source of inspiration for activists who supported reproductive justice. In 1977, for example, Barbara Smith, a founder of the pioneering Black lesbian feminist organization the Combahee River Collective, evoked Hamer's forced sterilization while leading a mass protest in support of abortion funding.[71]

"WHEN I LIBERATE MYSELF, I'M LIBERATING OTHER PEOPLE."

In 1971, Hamer delivered a powerful speech at the NAACP Legal Defense Fund Institute in New York City on the topic of women's liberation. As she had done many times before, Hamer began by centering Black women and their experiences. She took the opportunity to emphasize that Black women's lives are shaped by numerous hardships in American society, not solely gender oppression. "The special plight and the role of black women is not something that just happened three years ago. We've had a special plight for 350 years," she began, alluding to the history of chattel slavery in the United States. While her remarks were intended to offer insights into the experiences of the Black women too often erased from mainstream narratives,

Hamer did not resist the urge to take a jab at the women's liberation movement. By arguing that Black women's plight was not new, or "something that just happened three years ago," Hamer revealed her frustration with how public discussions on women's rights and liberation framed the movement as unprecedented. While the women's liberation movement certainly helped to raise greater awareness of gender inequality in American society, Hamer's remarks served as a bitter reminder that Black women needed no such consciousness-raising; their daily experiences—as well as the experiences of generations of Black women who preceded them—had already revealed to them the nature of gender oppression.[72] Along those lines, Hamer reminded audience members of her family history: "My grandmother had [a special plight]. My grandmother was a slave. She died in 1960. She was 136 years old. She died in [Mound] Bayou, Mississippi."[73]

Hamer went on to explain how she viewed liberation—a term that was central to the women's rights movement of the period. "I work for the liberation of all people," Hamer argued, "because when I liberate myself, I'm liberating other people."[74] White women were certainly included in this group. Hamer carefully explained the kind of liberation these women needed. It was a liberation from their own thinking and complicity:

> But you know, sometimes I really feel more sorrier for the white woman than I feel for ourselves because she been caught up in this thing, caught up feeling very special, and folks, I'm going to put it on the line, because my job is not to make people feel comfortable. You've been caught up in this thing because, you know, you worked my grandmother, and after that you worked my mother, and then finally you got hold of me. And you really thought, people—you might try and cool it now, but I been watching you, baby. You thought that you was more because you was a woman, and especially a white woman, you had this kind of angel feeling that you were untouchable. You know what? There's nothing under the sun that made you believe that you was just like me, that under this white pigment of skin is red blood, just like under this black skin of mine. So we was used as black women over and over and over.[75]

Hamer's remarks hit to the core of a fundamental problem with the women's liberation movement: how the majority of white women failed to acknowledge their own privilege and investment in white supremacy. American society conferred a special status for white women, tracing back to the era of slavery.[76] They were so "caught up in this thing," as Hamer argued, that too many white women in the movement lacked introspection and failed to acknowledge the way they had long contributed to the oppression of other women. She turned to her own personal experiences to reinforce the point. "You know I remember a time when I was working around white people's house," Hamer noted, "and one thing that would make me mad as hell, after I would be done slaved all day long, this white woman would get on the phone, calling some of her friends, and said, 'You know, I'm tired, because *we* have been working,' and I said, 'That's a damn lie.' You're not used to that kind of language, honey, but I'm gone tell you where it's *at*."[77]

In recounting this simple yet profound story, Hamer captured how interlocking systems of oppression—in this case, racism, sexism, and classism—shaped her life and the lives of other Black women. The domestic work of Black women in the intimate spaces of white people's homes often brought these issues to the surface.[78] Though Black women certainly shouldered the burden of sexism, it was by no means the only burden they carried. Hamer reminded white women that their race provided them freedom at the expense of Black women and other women of color: "So all of these things was happening because you had more. You had been put on a pedestal, and then not only put on a pedestal, but you had been put in something like [an] ivory castle." If the women's liberation movement removed the veil from many women's eyes, then Hamer argued white women should have to glimpse the struggles Black women had encountered for decades. "[W]hen you hit the ground," Hamer candidly explained, "you're gone have to fight like hell, like we've been fighting all this time."[79] It was a message of truth, difficult as it may have been for many white women to accept. But Hamer's message made it clear that for all of the real challenges white women endured on account of gender oppression, they had not experienced the depth of oppression and mistreatment Black women endured in American society. White women's position in society—as beneficiaries of whiteness and, often tacitly, white supremacy—afforded them more opportunities than Black women. Hamer therefore resisted any narrative that focused solely on gender oppression without a consideration of race oppression and class oppression.

This was a message she boldly conveyed to white liberal feminists at the first gathering of the National Women's Political Caucus (NWPC), an organization she helped to launch in July 1971. Established amid a surge of political movements that swept the nation, including the Black Power movement and the women's liberation movement, the NWPC set out to increase women's participation in "all areas of political and public life."[80] At the time of their founding, only one woman served in the US Senate and only twelve in the House of Representatives. The nation at the time had no woman serving as a governor and only a few served as mayors.[81] The NWPC set out to significantly transform the American political landscape. Although unsuccessful in her own bids for public office, Hamer was deeply committed to encouraging other Black women to take on public service and leadership positions.

No doubt Hamer also recognized the significant role these political collaborations could have on her future plans and continued prospects to hold public office. When she attended the 1971 gathering, Hamer was actively raising funds for her state senate campaign.[82] These motivations propelled Hamer to join forces with feminist icon Gloria Steinem, Congresswoman Bella Abzug, and others to help establish the NWPC as the largest women's political organization in the nation. Although the majority of the women involved in the Caucus were white, it drew several well-known women of color, including Congresswoman Shirley Chisholm, civil rights activist Myrlie Evers, Native American rights leader LaDonna Harris, New York City commissioner of human rights Eleanor Holmes Norton, Johnnie Tillmon of the National Welfare Rights Organization, and Dorothy Height, the president of the National Council of Negro Women.[83] Even among this illustrious group, Hamer stood out in her own unique way. She had already made a name for herself as a fierce advocate for voting rights. Hamer's passion for expanding women's political leadership, however, did not go unnoticed—many of Hamer's contemporaries viewed her as the "mother of the Black female political movement."[84]

Hamer lived up to this expectation at the NWPC's founding meeting at the Statler Hilton Hotel in Washington, DC, in July 1971. In the presence of more than three hundred women, including Jo Etha Collier's grieving mother, Hamer delivered a rousing speech that articulated the significance of an intersectional approach to women's political work. Referencing the earlier speeches of several white women at the Caucus meeting, Hamer tried to reorient audience members to the unique challenges facing Black Southerners. "Listening to different speakers," she explained, "I've thought about if they've had problems, then they should be black in Mississippi for a spell. . . . And when one of the speakers talked about how the white male rulers of the country would be coming to talk to women," she added, "you wouldn't believe the hell that I've gone through in the state of Mississippi."[85] Through these statements, Hamer's message was clear: one could not talk about oppression in the United States without factoring in race. The fight for women's rights would mean very little if it left Black people and other marginalized groups behind. For this reason, Hamer insisted, "I don't want [equal rights]. I've passed equal rights and I'm fighting for human rights, not only for the black man, for the red man, but for the white man and for all people of this country. Because America is sick and man is on the critical list."[86] Her statements underscored her expansive political vision—a vision that made it difficult for Hamer to ascribe to the brand of feminist politics many white women in the NWPC were advocating at the time. For Hamer and other Black women during this period, it was impossible to disentangle the fight for women's rights from civil and human rights. They were all interconnected.

Hamer turned to history as her guide, reminding the women in attendance that Black women had long been denied access to the vote—even as white women made significant advances. "As I stand here today my mind goes back to the problems that we have had in the past," Hamer explained. "And I think about the Constitution of the United States that says, 'With the people, for the people, and by the people.' And every time I hear it now," she continued, "I just double over laughing because it's not true; it hasn't been true."[87] For Hamer, women's rights and Black voting rights were equally integral parts of realizing the ideals of American democracy. "Now, we've got to make some changes in this country," she told the audience. "The changes we have to have in this country are going to be for the liberation of all people—because nobody's free until everybody's free."[88] Hamer's words presaged a vision of liberation and intersectional analysis that would also be advanced by feminists in groups like the Boston-based Combahee River Collective and the Third World Women's Alliance, a multiracial feminist organization founded by Black women in New York City in 1968.[89]

While Hamer was candid about the challenges ahead, she nevertheless offered assurances to those in attendance that they held the power in their hands to bring about the changes they desired. While the inclusive democracy guaranteed by the US Constitution was far from a reality, Hamer insisted, "We are going to make it true."[90] "Let's hook up these minorities and make one hell of a majority," she thundered.[91] Hamer's passionate delivery that afternoon—and the hope she inspired—could be felt by all. Even more, the power of her message resonated: the women's liberation movement could never hope to succeed without the presence and leadership of women of *all* backgrounds.

During the 1970s, the NWPC provided a space for Hamer to amplify her work around women's issues. Although she was critical of the women's liberation movement, Hamer found much value in working with white feminists and tried to use her influence to broaden their perspectives on race and class issues. The NWPC also provided a crucial avenue for Hamer to work alongside several Black women leaders who shared many of her political views. Such was the case with US Congresswoman Shirley Chisholm, with whom Hamer developed a close friendship. Born in 1924 in Brooklyn to Barbadian parents, Chisholm became the first Black woman in the House of Representatives.[92] She would later go on to run for president of the United States. In 1971, however, when she and Hamer began working together in the NWPC, Chisholm was finishing her first two-year term as a congresswoman, serving Brooklyn, New York. As a congresswoman,

Chisholm skillfully worked to advance feminist politics "within electoral and party politics."[93] Much like Hamer, she sought to address the challenges facing Black women, paying close attention to the intersecting dynamics of race, gender, and class. And much like Hamer, Chisholm adopted a direct approach and was uncompromising in her political aims. Not surprisingly, the two worked well together, and the NWPC provided an important space in which both women could agitate for expanded rights and opportunities for Black women.

At the NWPC convention, Chisholm and Hamer pushed other attendees to adopt an intersectional perspective. As Chisholm later explained, "Fannie and I attempted in a very assertive manner to tell the ladies that they had to pay attention to the concerns of women of color. Many of the ladies were quite surprised at what we had to say."[94] While the white women in the NWPC were seeking a "liberation of the spirit," Chisholm explained that she and Hamer were determined to help them broaden their perspective: "We felt it was important to be there and identified with the development of this organization so that our ideas would flow over the sisters."[95] Indeed, Chisholm and Hamer advocated for a women's organization that would not sideline the needs and concerns of Black America. According to Chisholm, Hamer caused great offense to some of the white women at the NWPC when she made it clear that Black women "would never join their organization unless they understood the particular depth of our concerns."[96] While some may have struggled to accept the tone of the message, Hamer's words reinforced a point she had long argued: no women's rights movement could ever succeed with a focus on gender oppression alone.

As Black women, Chisholm and Hamer did their best to convey to attendees that racism could not be ignored—it fundamentally shaped the lives of women of color and further compounded their experiences of sexism. Along these lines, the two women joined forces with other Black women at the inaugural meeting—including Myrlie Evers, Dorothy Height, and Beulah Sanders, vice president of the National Welfare Rights Organization—to advocate for the passage of an anti-racist resolution. The resolution maintained that the NWPC would not endorse or support racist candidates, regardless of their gender.[97] To their credit, the NWPC responded to these concerns; all members voted to pass the anti-racist resolution. It would come to represent the core of the organization's mission—to expand women's political opportunities without compromising their commitment to addressing the needs of women of color. By adopting this important resolution, the NWPC set out to prevent making the same mistakes that women's rights activists in the suffrage movement had made: supporting and accepting support from racist politicians in exchange for white women's advancement.[98]

The NWPC provided a significant vehicle for recruiting and training women of all backgrounds for public office. In November 1971, Hamer joined forces with US representative Bella Abzug, journalist Liz Carpenter, and labor activist Mildred Jeffrey to insist that women represent at least half of the delegates at the 1972 presidential nominating conventions. In a letter to Lawrence F. O'Brien, the Democratic chairman, Hamer and her collaborators argued that "failure to insure reasonable representation [of women] will undoubtedly result in serious credentials challenges by women's groups."[99] To boost women's political engagement, Hamer and other members in the NWPC also encouraged women across the nation to run for public office.[100] At one luncheon, cosponsored by the NWPC, Hamer reminded the women in attendance about the importance of electoral politics. "The air we breath[e] is politics," she remarked.[101]

With her own hopes of entering public office, Hamer skillfully capitalized on her involvement in the Caucus to boost her political prospects.[102] In 1971, she made the decision to run for office for the third and final time. Although her previous two runs were unsuccessful, she remained committed to the idea that she could have a meaningful impact on Mississippi through electoral politics. When she launched a campaign for state senate in 1971, running against the incumbent Robert Crook, Hamer immediately turned to others in the NWPC for assistance. They extended their full support. Betty Friedan traveled to Mississippi to deliver a speech in support of Hamer's run for office. "Electing women to offices in the state legislatures in 1971," Friedan explained to local reporters, "is the first step toward bringing women into the mainstream of the American political system."[103] NWPC member Liz Carpenter, a former White House aide, also traveled to Mississippi to support Hamer's run for office. During her visit, Carpenter gave several radio interviews, emphasizing the positive impact Hamer would have on the people of Mississippi and beyond.[104] Despite having broad support for her candidacy and national recognition, Hamer's campaign met the same fate as earlier attempts. She lost the election, 7,201 votes to 11,770 votes.

The personal disappointment did not thwart Hamer's passion for helping others. In 1972, despite battling poor health, Hamer traveled from Mississippi to Miami Beach, Florida, to support the nomination of Frances "Sissy" Farenthold for vice president of the United States.[105] "If she was good enough for Shirley Chisholm," Hamer declared, "then she is good enough for Fannie Lou Hamer."[106] Although Farenthold did not end up receiving the nomination, Hamer's actions and personal sacrifice exemplified her commitment to supporting women politicians. The core of her political work during the 1970s focused on empowering Black women leaders. In January 1972, for example, she attended a two-day symposium in Chicago titled "Black Women: The Ties That Divide and Bind—Program For Action." The symposium, sponsored by the Washington, DC, Black Women's Community Development Foundation, attracted two hundred women from Chicago and other cities across the nation.[107]

In a 1975 article for *Essence* magazine, journalist John H. Britton Jr. discussed the state of electoral politics in the United States, highlighting the role of Black women.[108] "Success in politics is possible for Black women," he argued, "but aspirants to public office should do little, if any romanticizing, about the qualifications necessary for victory in this anti-Black, anti-female environment."[109] After pointing out the numerous roadblocks Black women confronted in the political arena, Britton went on to assess the progress that had been made during the early 1970s. He noted that Black women were still significantly underrepresented in electoral politics—only 337 of the more than 520,000 elected offices in the nation were held by Black women. While Britton pointed to the need for greater representation, he also acknowledged that these figures, released in 1973, represented a 160 percent increase when compared to the number of Black women holding political office in 1969. This improvement, and the broader influence of Black women in American politics, he argued, could be attributed, in part, to the courageous efforts of Fannie Lou Hamer. "There is no male moral force in Mississippi," he explained, "that commands the respect of Fannie Lou Hamer."[110] Hamer's commitment to women's empowerment, her candid assessment of the women's liberation movement, and her ideas on gender—even the most controversial ones—as well as her tireless efforts to support others, buoyed Black women's political engagement in the 1970s.

CHAPTER FIVE

AN EXPANSIVE VISION
OF FREEDOM

I tell people I don't want no equal rights any more. I'm
fightin' for human rights.

—FANNIE LOU HAMER[1]

On July 12, 2016, Nigerian American activist Opal Tometi delivered a speech before the United Nations General Assembly. Only three years prior, Tometi had joined forces with queer activists Alicia Garza and Patrisse Cullors to launch Black Lives Matter (BLM), a global movement to end state-sanctioned violence. What began as a hashtag on social media following the acquittal of Trayvon Martin's murderer evolved into a protest movement that shook the nation to its core. After the 2014 police shooting of teenager Mike Brown Jr. in Ferguson, Missouri, BLM rose to national prominence, demanding justice for Brown's family and the thousands of unarmed Black people murdered by the police. From uprisings in cities across the nation to organized acts of resistance on college campuses, BLM transformed the American political landscape, shaping national discussions on race and policing. In the months leading up to the November 2016 presidential election in the United States, BLM forced several presidential candidates to confront the issue of state-sanctioned violence.

Although the movement began in the United States, it spread like wildfire across the globe. In only a matter of months, activists established BLM chapters in several major cities. In Toronto, for example, activists Janaya Khan and Yusra Ali cofounded a local BLM chapter in October 2014, following the police killing of Jermaine Carby in Brampton, Ontario.[2] Carby, a thirty-three-year-old Black man from Toronto, was shot and killed on September 24, 2014, during a routine traffic stop while traveling through the predominantly white suburbs of Brampton. In December 2014, activists in Japan gathered to launch an Afro-Asian solidarity march called Tokyo for Ferguson (#Tokyo4Ferguson) in the wake of the grand jury's acquittal of the police officer who gunned down Mike Brown Jr. in Ferguson, Missouri.[3] Displaying signs in both English and Japanese, these activists marched throughout the busy streets of Tokyo in solidarity with BLM activists in the United States. In the subsequent months, BLM marches and demonstrations began to sweep cities across Europe, including London, Paris, Amsterdam, and Berlin.[4] The wave of protests across the world further amplified BLM's concerted efforts to emphasize the global nature of state-sanctioned violence and anti-Black racism. In its early years (and in the years to follow), the founders of the movement also worked to foster transnational networks and solidarities between activists in the United States and those abroad. By 2016, the movement boasted an estimated twenty-six chapters across the world.[5]

Tometi's speech before the United Nations was part of this vital transnational work. Yet the occasion proved a historic moment in BLM's history—the first time one of its founders addressed the most powerful international body for human rights. Tometi's presence at the UN General Assembly therefore marked an important shift.[6] Reflecting on the historical significance of her appearance, Tometi pointed to the "urgent need to engage the international community about the most pressing human rights crises of our day. In the footsteps of many courageous civil and human rights defenders that came before," she continued, "I look to this meeting to be a forum for meaningful dialogue and action."[7]

This July 2016 event came on the heels of the high-profile police killings of two Black men: Alton Sterling on July 5 and Philando Castile on July 6.[8] The police shootings, both caught on video, sparked a wave of protests across the United States that summer. In hopes of addressing the problems of structural racism and discrimination, the

UN hosted a two-day debate that brought together world leaders and activists. Only six months prior, a group of UN researchers had called on US leaders to confront state-sanctioned violence and the "crisis of racial injustice."[9] They pointed out that "[i]mpunity for state violence has resulted in the current human rights crisis and must be addressed as a matter of urgency."[10] The two-day gathering in July 2016 was one significant step in the UN's efforts to address this crisis, and the decision to include Tometi as one of the featured presenters underscored BLM's central role in shaping national and global narratives on human rights. Reminiscent of a long line of Black activists who took their concerns before the UN, including activist and well-known singer Paul Robeson and lawyer William Patterson, Tometi presented a powerful message before the General Assembly—one heard and circulated to millions worldwide.[11]

She began her address with a moment of silence for Alton Sterling and Philando Castile, recognizing the gravity of the moment. She went on to emphasize three specific challenges in the campaign to advance human rights for all: global capitalism, white supremacy, and the suppression of democracy.[12] For Tometi, all three grew from the "root causes of inequality" and were shaped by a history of "colonialism, indigenous genocide, and the enslavement of people of African descent as the precursor."[13] Highlighting the devastating impact of racial capitalism, Tometi pointed to the ways marginalized groups are exploited across the globe: "The valuation of profit over people impedes human rights across much of the world. Capitalists' motivations consume natural resources, perpetuate violence against workers—especially women and girls—while contributing little to local economies." Citing national and international examples—from Detroit to Haiti to across the African continent—Tometi offered an incisive critique of how capitalist ventures have "strangled indigenous industries, privatized basic services, displaced over 65 million people, and decimated environments across Asia, Africa and the Americas."[14]

She went on to address the global problem of white supremacy, which created the circumstances for police killings in the United States and abroad. "These beliefs," she argued, "are deeply embedded into social and cultural fabrics throughout society and spread through media and entertainment, education, and other systems. A result of this is the cultivation of disdain against black people, and this anti-blackness has lethal consequences." The tragic police killings of Sterling and Castile underscored this fact as protests rocked the nation in July 2016. And as Tometi emphasized, Black people everywhere—in North America, Europe, Asia, and other parts of the world—are vulnerable to state-sanctioned violence. She therefore emphasized the need to view police killings in the United States as part of an ongoing human rights crisis. Tometi then reasoned that because state-sanctioned violence against Black people is a human rights issue, the response and solution required a global effort. "As communities face a myriad of challenges and hostility from the state, driven by neoliberal interests," Tometi argued, "they are advocating for their rights and asserting their human dignity."[15] Tometi went on to call on activists and world leaders to uphold an expansive political vision, modeled after BLM.[16] "We advocate with and are led by women, black immigrants, queer folks, people who are incarcerated, transgender, disabled, and people who practice different religions," she said. "We see this diversity and complexity as strength."[17]

By linking national concerns to global ones and calling for an expansive vision of rights and freedom, Tometi was, as she pointed out, walking "in the footsteps of many courageous civil and human rights defenders" who came before her. Fannie Lou Hamer was certainly one of these individuals. As an organizer during the 1960s and '70s, Hamer advocated an expansive vision of freedom—one that was fully inclusive of all marginalized groups in the United States and abroad. Hamer's visit to the African continent in 1964 had radically expanded her political vision—helping her see that the struggle for Black rights and freedom in the United States was, in the words of W. E. B. Du Bois, "but a local phase of a world problem."[18] As she traveled from place to place during the late 1960s and 1970s, Hamer often reminded activists to never fall into the trap of imagining that their local struggle was somehow disconnected from the struggles of other marginalized peoples. Embracing a defining feature of the Black intellectual tradition, Hamer resisted what she saw as any individual or collective effort to advance social progress for *some* rather than *all*.[19] "Now we've got to have some changes in this country. And not only changes for the Black man, and not only changes for the Black woman, but the changes we have to have in this country are going to be for the liberation of all people," Hamer argued in a 1971 speech before the National Women's Political Caucus. "I am not just fighting for myself and for the Black race," she explained. "But I am fighting for the Indians; I'm fighting for the Mexicans; I'm fighting for the Chinese; I'm fighting for anybody because as long as they are human beings, they need freedom."[20] Hamer summarized her position in five powerful words that she often repeated: "Nobody's free until everybody's free."[21] Those words are as timely and significant today as they were when she first expressed them.

"I FELT A CLOSENESS IN AFRICA."

Fannie Lou Hamer's travels abroad in 1964 helped her refine this message. As a field secretary for the Student Nonviolent Coordinating Committee (SNCC), she, along with eleven other activists, traveled to Guinea on a trip organized by entertainer and activist Harry Belafonte, an avid supporter of the organization.[22] It was the first and only time Hamer left the United States. During the 1960s, SNCC played a central role in advancing voter registration in the US South. In the summer of 1964, the group organized Freedom Summer, a volunteer campaign that drew over one thousand volunteers, mostly white college students from Northern cities.[23] The volunteers left their loved ones behind to spend the summer in Mississippi. Their goal was twofold: to register local Black residents to vote and to establish Freedom Schools—free grassroots schools designed to teach civic and political literacy. Within only ten days, local white supremacists murdered three volunteers and dozens more were beaten and arrested.

While the efforts of these activists were vital to challenging voter suppression in Mississippi and across the US South, the tragic incidents surrounding Freedom Summer, combined with the disappointment of the 1964 Democratic National Convention, weighed heavily on activists in SNCC.[24] Following Freedom Summer, Belafonte began to raise funds for a group of them to travel to the African continent. Belafonte believed the trip would invigorate the activists who had been working tirelessly to expand voting rights in the United States. "I had become quite sensitive to the fact that many of the people of SNCC were on burnout," he explained. "They had been on the front line for so long, doing so much, and many had been beaten and battered. What became clear to me was that they really needed a hiatus."[25] He recommended Guinea as the ideal place for SNCC activists to visit, pointing to the leadership and nation-building efforts of Guinea's first president Sékou Touré. In 1958, one year after Ghana gained its independence, Guinea declared its independence from France, signifying another triumph in the fight to end European colonialism in Africa.[26] Touré would lead the postcolonial nation forward, instituting a socialist government inspired by his own interest in Marxism.

Many Black Americans traveled to the African continent during this period, in most cases to join in celebration with African leaders and draw inspiration from their accomplishments. This was certainly true of Rev. Martin Luther King Jr. and Coretta Scott King, who joined a cadre of Black activists and artists—including labor organizer A. Philip Randolph, actress and vocalist Etta Moten Barnett, and political scientist Ralph J. Bunche—on a trip to Ghana in 1957. At the invitation of Kwame Nkrumah, Ghana's new prime minister, these African American activists participated in several ceremonial events in Accra.[27] While Ghana was certainly a popular destination for civil rights activists during the late 1950s and 1960s, others traveled to Guinea following its independence in 1958. In 1964, Malcolm X visited Guinea, where President Touré praised him for advancing the "struggle for dignity."[28] In 1969, Black Power activist Stokely Carmichael and his wife, South African singer Miriam Makeba, moved to Guinea, where they actively supported the Touré administration.[29] For many of these activists, Guinea not only represented a symbol of hope but also a pathway forward in the fight for civil and human rights.[30]

With Belafonte's help and support, SNCC arranged a three-week trip to Guinea in September 1964. While Belafonte led the initiative, Touré, according to activist John Lewis, had expressed interest in hosting "a group of young Americans who were involved in the civil rights movement."[31] The Guinean president hoped to provide an opportunity for young Guineans to meet with American civil rights leaders to exchange ideas and strengthen ties between both groups. SNCC activists were eager to take advantage of the opportunity and selected a group of twelve leaders, including John Lewis and Julian Bond, who would represent the organization on the trip. Hamer was one of four women included. SNCC activists Prathia Hall, Dona Richards, and Ruby Doris Smith Robinson joined Hamer on what would be a transformative trip for all involved.[32]

The group of activists left for Guinea on an Air Guinée flight on September 11, 1964. They flew from New York, stopping in Dakar, Senegal, en route to Guinea. From the outset, the experience was a life-altering one for Hamer. She was especially excited to travel outside the United States:

> You know, I had never been out of the state in my life, and after the convention in 1964 we needed rest. It was people like Harry Belafonte, and I don't know who else was involved, who supported [us] making it possible for eleven of us to go to Africa. Just to see Africa and try to—we had learned and heard so many things about Africa. I wasn't sure whether I would be frightened or what, because what little we had read about Africa was just wild. We didn't know really; we really didn't know that they were our people. Although we realized they were our ancestors, we didn't know how they act.[33]

Even before she arrived in Guinea, Hamer was deeply impressed with what she saw. She later pointed out how significant it was for her to see Black flight attendants and a Black pilot: "When I saw a man come out of the cockpit who was black, right away then this meant that it was going to be different from what I had been [used to], what had been taught to me. It was something different."[34] For Hamer, who had lived in Mississippi all her life—where Black people were still fighting to obtain some political and economic power—the image of a Black flight attendant and a Black pilot was especially meaningful and symbolic. It offered a glimpse into what she would witness when she arrived in Guinea—a newly independent nation governed by Black people.

When she finally completed the long journey to Guinea, Hamer marveled at the sight of President Sékou Touré and a delegation waiting at the airport. She and her colleagues were treated as honored guests and during their three-week stay had many opportunities to learn more about Guinea and its leadership under Touré. Throughout the visit, Hamer learned that Black people were not only in charge of transportation but also of every sector, including business and education.[35] Hamer and other SNCC activists frequently met with government officials in Guinea and had the opportunity to engage in a series of gatherings and conversations with President Touré. These meetings created a space for Hamer and her colleagues to discuss "civil and human rights occurrences in their respective countries, the similarities and differences between the problems in Africa and America, and how to help each other."[36]

The trip to Guinea, which lasted from September 11 to October 4, 1964, provided some much-needed respite from the rigors of Hamer's political work and extensive travels back home. Even more important, the experience forever crystallized in Hamer's mind the significance of Black political power and boosted her pride in her Blackness and African heritage:

> I saw some of the most intelligent people, you know, because I had never in my life seen where black people were running banks. I had never seen nobody behind a counter in a bank. I had never seen nobody black running the government in my life. So, it was quite a revelation to me. I was really learning something for the first time. Because then I could feel myself never, ever being ashamed of my ancestors and my background. I learned a lot. It taught me a lot while I was there. Because the welcome, and even the shame that we have here in this country, they don't have it there. In performing and all that kind of stuff, we have been made to feel ashamed of so many things that they're not.[37]

Hamer's words underscored how the 1964 trip to Guinea radically transformed her view of herself and left a lasting, positive effect on her psyche. "Being from the South we never was taught much about our African heritage," she later explained in her autobiography, *To Praise Our Bridges*. "The way everybody talked to us, everybody in Africa was savages and really stupid people."[38] Hamer's experience in Guinea completely upended such a view of Africa and African people. By connecting to her African roots and seeing other Black people lead with such dignity and grace, Hamer began to see herself in a new light. Living in the Jim Crow South during this period did very little to boost the morale of African Americans, who existed as second-class citizens and were "treated worse than dogs," as Hamer once told a group of reporters.[39] In Guinea, Black people could live in freedom, proudly displaying their cultural artifacts. She later emphasized how much the image of Black people leading and living freely served as a source of "inspiration." She took heart at the image of seeing Black people "just doing everything that I was used to seeing white people do."[40]

The experience of traveling to Guinea was also deeply personal for Hamer: "I felt a closeness in Africa."[41] Though she had no knowledge of her African ancestors, Hamer immediately felt a sense of familiarity with the people she encountered during her visit. "One thing I looked at so much was the African women. They were so graceful and so poised. I thought about my mother and my grandmother."[42] Hamer went on to decribe how the Guinean women resembled her relatives and even wore their hair and carried items on their heads in a smililar manner.[43] The sight brought her to tears, recognizing that she could have relatives in Guinea and would not even know it. "I probably got relatives right now in Africa, but we'll never know each other because we've been so separated that I'll never know them and they'll never know me," Hamer explained.[44] "I couldn't speak the French language and a lot of them couldn't speak English, but the comparison between my family and them was unbelieveable."[45]

While in Guinea, Hamer also had the opportunity to meet with several Guinean leaders who were very open and receptive to SNCC activists. For three hours on September 23, Hamer and her colleagues had the opportunity to meet with Alpha Diallo, the director general of the Ministry of Information and Tourism in Guinea and president of the African Association of Radio and Television Transmission.[46] Born in Conakry in 1935, Diallo had studied in France and returned to his native country where he would play an active role in Guinean politics. Throughout his political career, Diallo would hold several key positions in the Touré administration, including secretary of state for foreign affairs and head of Guinea's delegation to the United Nations.[47] During his meeting with Hamer and her colleagues, Diallo used the opportunity to discuss the challenges Guinea faced and how the nation's leaders hoped to address them. He pointed to some of the economic problems facing the country and how these challenges were directly tied to European colonialism. He highlighted some of their efforts to improve the economy and reminded the activists that Guinea was a socialist country—reaffirming the nation's commitment to ensure that everyone's needs would be equally met.[48] He also addressed how the United States could support the efforts of Guinean leaders. The director general emphasized the significance of the US extending "moral support to the Guinea cause."[49] He conveyed the message to SNCC activists that it was important to draw on the experiences of their trip to help inform Americans about the important developments taking place in Africa.[50]

During the meeting, Diallo spoke of his plans to travel to the United States, where he hoped to "observe the revolution in Negro affairs." He expressed confidence that the United States would grant full citizenship rights to African Americans, pointing to the significant historical developments taking place in the US and across the globe. He then proceeded to ask the activists to share their thoughts on the impending US presidential elections, scheduled to take place only two months later. Members of the SNCC delegation began to explain the challenges of electoral politics in the United States, pointing to the multiple ways Black people were barred from voting. Hamer took the opportunity to share with Diallo some of the challenges she encountered while trying to register to vote in Mississippi. Her statements helped to clarify some of Diallo's misconceptions about Black life under the system of Jim Crow.[51] Diallo was so moved by Hamer's presence and her candid account that he presented the activist with a gift—an African musical instrument—at the conclusion of the meeting.[52]

During their three-week stay, Hamer and the other members of the SNCC delegation had several other opportunities to meet with Guinean leaders who offered a glimpse into the inner workings of the newly independent African nation. In one instance, Hamer joined her colleagues in a meeting with representatives from the Ministry of Commerce, who offered a detailed discussion of the significance of cooperatives in Guinea.[53] Arguably the most important meeting

Hamer and her colleagues had in Guinea was with President Sékou Touré. Although they had several opportunities, some informal, to speak with Touré during their stay, their meeting with him on September 26, 1964, was especially meaningful.[54] The Guinean president began by emphasizing how the struggle for Black rights in the United States was deeply connected to the struggle for rights and freedom on the African continent. He went on to emphasize several key political points, which framed his own thinking and provided guidance for the activists in their own struggle for freedom in the United States.[55] "No solution of a problem can come about unless there is a consciousness that the problem exists," he began. "We must not underestimate the role of organization." He also cautioned SNCC activists to be mindful of who they identified as their leaders: "those who are selected to represent you [must be] carefully selected because the quality of their actions will affect society in one way or another." And finally, he advised the activists to always convey a public image of unity in the struggle, despite differences and even internal divisions. "Do not try to stress the contradictions in the black community. On the national plane, however, we must try to project unity," he concluded.[56]

Although Touré's words during this meeting and the many exchanges with the activists left a lasting impact on the entire SNCC delegation, they were especially transformative for Hamer. Belafonte, who had not only helped to fund the trip but also joined the delegation in Guinea, later recalled that Hamer was "the person who early on appeared to be the most affected by the trip."[57] Dona Richards, one of the four women in the SNCC delegation, reinforced this perspective in the aftermath of the trip. She later noted how Hamer had "come alive" in Guinea.[58] No doubt the experience was personally transformative, but even more so, the trip sparked a radical shift in Hamer's politics. She later described the entire experience as "just remarkable," reflecting on how much the trip opened her eyes and changed the way she would approach her political work in the years to follow.[59]

If Hamer's earlier painful experiences in Winona served to deepen her commitment to addressing state-sanctioned violence, then it was her 1964 trip abroad that helped to greatly expand her vision of Black liberation. The trip provided a significant opportunity for Hamer and her colleagues to forge transnational political alliances and propelled them to frame their struggle for liberation as part of a global struggle for freedom. The trip helped to internationalize SNCC, linking the activists to "a worldwide movement and community."[60] Hamer's exposure to Guinea and her dialogues and exchanges with President Touré and other African leaders during her visit also expanded her political perspective.[61] It helped her develop, more than ever before, a global racial consciousness and an increased desire to pursue transnational networks and solidarities.[62] When Hamer returned to the United States in October 1964, the trip's impact was evident—her speeches in the months and years to follow would center on the important links between the history and experiences of African Americans and other people of color abroad.

"MAKE DEMOCRACY A REALITY FOR ALL."

In the aftermath of the 1964 trip, SNCC activists forged an alliance with the Black nationalist leader Malcolm X, whom they had encountered while in West Africa. That year, Malcolm was on a six-month tour of West Africa and made a pilgrimage to Mecca. The tour provided the impetus for his decision to establish the Organization of Afro-American Unity (OAAU), which became a significant vehicle for Black internationalist organizing in the mid-1960s.[63] During his first public address on behalf of the new organization, Malcolm X—who by then had adopted the name El-Hajj Malik El-Shabazz following his trip to Mecca—explained that the new group would seek to organize "everyone in the Western Hemisphere of African descent into one united force" and, eventually, to "unite with our brothers on the motherland, on the continent of Africa."[64]

SNCC leaders would take hold of this internationalist vision in 1964, when they crossed paths with Malcolm X at an airport in Nairobi, Kenya.[65] At the time, two members of the SNCC delegation, John Lewis and Donald Harris, had decided to extend their stay in Guinea with plans to travel to various parts of Africa. Their unexpected encounter marked the beginning of a deeper relationship between SNCC and Malcolm X.[66] As the organization began to embrace a more militant and internationalist platform, they drew heavily on Malcolm's teachings. As James Forman, the former executive secretary of SNCC later explained, the organization's leaders began to shift further away from a focus solely on civil rights after engaging with Malcolm X's writings and speeches. Several years later, SNCC would declare itself a "human rights organization working for the liberation not only of Black people in the United States but of all oppressed peoples, especially those in Africa, Asia, and Latin America." That resolution, as Forman admitted, was one example of how Malcolm greatly influenced the organization.[67] In addition, SNCC members would collaborate with Malcolm X on various occasions and extended their support for his work during the mid-1960s. Malcolm offered the same support in return.[68]

On December 20, 1964, several weeks after returning to the United States from Guinea, Hamer shared the platform with Malcolm X at a political rally for the Mississippi Freedom Democratic Party (MFDP). The two respected each other and certainly welcomed the opportunity to collaborate that evening.[69] The event, held at the Williams Institutional CME Church in Harlem, brought together mostly African Americans in the city who came to support the MFDP's upcoming congressional challenge.[70] The structure of the iconic speech symbolized the political collaboration between Hamer and Malcolm. As Hamer delivered her speech in the Harlem church, Malcolm "worked extemporaneously to interpret and combine several core aspects of Hamer's address into his own."[71] This arrangement symbolized the connection between the two activists and their complementary approaches to leadership, relying on passion, deep conviction, and a determination to transform the lives of others. Not suprisingly, Hamer maintained deep admiration and respect for Malcolm X. In one instance, she described him as "one of the greatest men I had ever met in my life."[72] She praised his courage and his uncanny ability to articulate the concerns of Black people in Amerca: "He told exactly how every Negro in this country feels and didn't have the guts to say it."[73]

Hamer's description of Malcolm could easily have been applied to herself. Her boldness and candor did not go unnoticed. When she and Malcolm took the stage in Harlem in 1964, they electrified the room, laying bare the many problems of American society. Although Hamer addressed many of the same issues she had cited in her earlier speeches, her remarks that evening in Harlem signified her more expansive political vision—one that was certainly shaped by her travels abroad and her conversations with African leaders. After highlighting the many challenges Black people encountered in Mississippi, Hamer decried American foreign policy, pointing out the hypocrisy of US leaders who maintained a greater commitment to entering global conflicts rather than addressing domestic concerrns. "We have made an appeal for the president of the United States and the attorney general to please protect us in Mississippi," she began. "And I can't understand how it's out of their power to protect people in Mississippi. They can't do that, but when a white man is killed in the Congo, they send people there."[74]

Hamer's reference to the Congo in 1964 was also indicative of her awareness of the interrelated struggles between Black people in Mississippi and those in the Congo. Indeed, African American journalist William Pickens had made such an observation many years earlier, describing Mississippi as the "American Congo."[75] In Mississippi and in the Congo, Black people faced brutal labor conditions and unrelenting violence and terror. And in both contexts, white officials robbed the political rights and freedom from people of African descent.[76] In Mississippi, as in the Congo, a majority-Black labor force fueled local and national economies yet lacked access to landownership and legal protections. Congolese leader Patrice Lumumba directly confronted these issues, which would ultimately cost him his life. Born in 1925, Lumumba emerged as one of the leading African nationalists of the twentieth century. An uncompromising political leader, he advocated African unity, economic self-sufficiency, and true independence for Africa.[77]

In the wake of violent uprisings across the country, the Congo eventually gained its independence from Belgium on June 30, 1960. On January 17, 1961, Lumumba, the first democratically elected prime minister of the Congo, was assassinated in a coordinated transnational effort backed by the United States and Belgium in order to maintain imperial control in the region.[78] In the wake of independence, the Congo became embroiled in a series of political upheavals, both internal and external, against the backdrop of the Cold War.[79] Working to block the Soviet Union from gaining a foothold in the

African country, US leaders backed the presidential election of Cyrille Adoula, a lackluster candidate who had distanced himself from Lumumba.[80] President John F. Kennedy and members of his administration hoped Adoula's election might quell internal political tensions. The Congo Crisis, however, would continue for several years, and in August 1964, Stanleyville, the Congo's largest city, had fallen to rebels. On November 24, 1964, the United States sent troops to Stanleyville in an attempt to help Belgians regain control of the city and release the more than two thousand white foreigners who were being held hostage in the area.

These developments were foremost on Hamer's mind in December 1964, when she delivered her speech in Harlem. Her emphasis on the "white man in the Congo" alluded to the lengths to which white Americans were willing to go to help other white people held hostage in the Congo—yet they could not be bothered to address the challenges facing Black citizens on US soil. These realities deeply troubled Hamer, who categorically rejected the notion that Black people needed to be patient and keep waiting for their freedom. "For three hundred years, we've given them time," she reiterated. "And I have been tired so long, now I am sick and tired of being sick and tired."[81] Those powerful words would represent one of Hamer's most iconic and memorable phrases. Far beyond being a catchy expression, it would come to signify her dogged determination to expand the rights and freedom of Black people in the United States and in every part of the globe.

This expansive vision of freedom would form the core of Hamer's political message following her trip to Guinea. For Hamer, drawing the links between the experiences of Black people in the United States and those in Africa was not simply a matter of grappling with American foreign policy. The deep connection and relationship between African Americans and Africa guided her recognition. It was a connection and relationship that could not be disentangled. "I'll never forget one of the things that was told to me during the time that I was in Atlantic City," she recounted during a speech in Kentucky in the summer of 1968. "I got a letter and they had a lot of our pictures there and they had a red heart with something through the heart and they had a little reading under there that told me to go back to Africa."[82] Like so many African Americans before and after her, Hamer

felt the sting of that racist insult. Yet she took the opportunity to edu-
cate the mostly white audience members by addressing the letter publicly and reiterating that all Americans, with the exception of Native
Americans, were foreign to US soil. With her characteristic aplomb,
Hamer retorted:

> I don't know whether that man [who wrote the letter] is in that
> audience or not—but I tell him we'll make a deal: after they've sent
> all the Australians back to Australia, the Koreans back to Korea,
> the Chinese back to China, give the Indians their land back, and get
> on the Mayflower from whence they come, we will go home. See,
> it's time for America to wake up and know that we're not going to
> tolerate—we're not begging anymore.[83]

Hamer went on to remind audience members that they should not
be so quick to suggest that Black people "go back to Africa" when
Black people did not choose to leave Africa in the first place. "America created this problem," she explained. "[W]e were brought here
on the slave ships of Africa and not only was the dignity taken from
men—the black men—but also the women had to bear, not only their
kids, but they had to bear the kids for the white slave owners."[84] And
slavery was the root cause of many of the issues that plagued white
Americans. Without mincing words, Hamer boldly confronted those
who resisted integration: "I'm fed up and sick and tired of you saying
that you can't stand for integration when you started it, when they
started unloading the ships of the black people when we began to
come in from Africa. *You* started it because I have cousins as white
as any of you in here with blue eyes and gray hair—and a black man
didn't do it."[85]

In a speech delivered on May 27, 1970, at Loop College (now
Harold Washington College) in Chicago, Illinois, Hamer went on to
discuss American history, reflecting on how Europeans had snatched
people of African descent from their native lands and left them with
shards of memories and a constant feeling of displacement:

> I remember when I was walking the streets of Africa, in 1964. I went
> to a palace—and as we know most of our people came from the

West Coast of Africa—and walking the streets of Africa I saw a lot
of people that looked a whole lot like my grandmother. And I wept
like a baby because I said, "Now, right here—just like I'm living in
America. And the black people over here is my own people. I can't
even speak the language because you've taken it from me." They
didn't know me, and I didn't know them.[86]

In a subsequent speech, delivered in 1976, Hamer carefully drew
the connections between the experiences of Black people in the
United States and other marginalized groups. Without hesitation,
she offered a scathing critique of those who celebrated the bicenten-
nial anniversary of the founding of the United States and the passage of the Declaration of Independence. Addressing a predominantly
white audience, Hamer rhetorically asked: "How do you think black
people, Indian people, and any other oppressed folk feel celebrating
something that, years ago, that destroyed over twenty-five million of
my people that was being brought here on the slave ships of Africa?
Wiped out our heritage; raised families by our grandmothers; and
taking our name."[87]

The answer to the question was already implied: people of color
in the United States could not join in the celebrations. For people of
color, the founding of the United States represented the formal beginning of a centuries-long struggle for rights and freedom. Hamer
was not oblivious to the irony of the Declaration of Independence
upholding the rhetoric of "life, liberty, and the pursuit of happiness"
while Black Americans and other people of color on American soil
were being subjected to racial violence, hate, and terror. Reflecting on
the unique circumstances of Black people, who were brought against
their will to the New World, Hamer expressed deep anger and frustration. "I felt the anger of why this had to happen to us," she explained during one interview. "We were so stripped and robbed of
our background, we wind up with nothing. . . . And you know that
was a real crime."[88]

For Hamer, the rupture—cultural and otherwise—facilitated by
the transatlantic slave trade was further compounded by the nega-
tive and stereotypical depictions of African cultures that dominated
mass media. She addressed this issue in 1976. "When I watch . . .

television," she explained, "and this guy playing the role of Tarzan, and the navy—[I see] the kind of things that you have distorted and said about my people in Africa."[89] Hamer credited her 1964 trip to Africa as helping her recognize these distortions: "Going to Africa, meeting people, and having a chance year after year to meet my people from Africa, it's nothing for us to be ashamed of is being black." Reflecting her expansive vision of freedom, Hamer resisted a national framing of Black rights, arguing that "I am not fighting to be equal with [white Americans], but I'm fighting for human dignity."[90]

Hamer's emphasis on the need to advance human rights and dignity provided the basis for her views on American foreign policy. Much like her earlier observations about the Congo, Hamer was especially attentive to the ways US leaders forcibly inserted themselves into African affairs under the guise of protecting global democracy. In one of her last public speeches, delivered at the University of Wisconsin in 1976, Hamer denounced the United States government for "placing mercenaries and Central Intelligence Agents to kill my people in Angola."[91] Her comments alluded to the US involvement in the Angola Crisis from 1974 to 1975. On November 4, 1975, Cuban leader Fidel Castro had sent troops to Angola following South Africa's invasion of the country. It would later be revealed that US leaders were aware of the planned invasion of Angola and actually collaborated with South African troops in an effort to destabilize Angola—all the while disseminating a public image of noninvolvement. Hamer's charge that the Central Intelligence Agency (CIA) had plans to "kill my people in Angola" was consistent with the records that reveal how members of the CIA worked to hire and train private military contractors to fight members of the Angolan army.[92] This development, much like earlier events in the Congo, underscored how US leaders were far more interested in the business of empire-making—seeking to influence and dominate the affairs of other nations—than in addressing domestic issues related to race relations.[93]

Espousing an expansive vision of global liberation, Hamer boldly confronted American involvement in the Vietnam War—and she did so much earlier than Rev. Martin Luther King Jr. and many other civil rights activists did.[94] In 1965, while attending a demonstration in Lafayette Park in Washington, DC, Hamer spoke out against the Vietnam War shortly after she had sent a telegram to President Johnson asking him to "bring the people home from the Dominican Republic and Vietnam."[95] During this period, many Black leaders, including political strategist and pacifist Bayard Rustin, had yet to address US involvement in Vietnam, leaving Hamer as one of the lone voices in opposition to the war. While civil rights leaders like Rustin were initially silent on the Vietnam War, fearing that public denouncements would impede progressive coalition building, Hamer boldly confronted the issue.[96] "At that time, we felt very alone," she admitted, "because when we start saying, 'The war is wrong in Vietnam,' well, people looked at us like we were something out of space."[97] By 1968, many Black activists were boldly speaking out against Vietnam, following in Hamer's footsteps. Hamer remained consistent in her stance. While speaking at a rally in Berkeley in 1969, she condemned the actions of US leaders, pointing out their blatant hypocrisy: "I am sick of the racist war in Vietnam when we don't have justice in the United States. . . . And we are sick and tired of seeing people lynched, and raped, and shot down all across the country in the name of law and order and not even feeding the hungry across the country."[98]

Like many Black internationalists before and after her, Hamer refused to divorce developments taking place in the United States from global movements abroad. If Americans wanted peace and democracy in the world, Hamer emphasized, they needed to "start dealing with the problems in the United States, stop all of this urban renewal and model cities that's pushing people out of a place to stay and start dealing with facts of life."[99] From 1934 to 1962, the Federal Housing Administration (FHA) and the Veterans Administration (VA) administered more than $120 billion to fund urban renewal projects.[100] In an interview with Black communist Jack O'Dell, Hamer further addressed the underlying problems of urban renewal programs, which devastated Black communities during the 1950s and '60s. The FHA loans and other federal funds made available to cities to help them become economically viable lined the pockets of private developers—at the expense of poor Black people and other marginalized groups.[101] Less than 2 percent of the new real estate developed through these programs was made available to Black Americans and

Fannie Lou Hamer speaking at a hearing of the Senate Subcommittee on Employment, Manpower, and Poverty at the Heidelberg Hotel in Jackson, Mississippi.

Fannie Lou Hamer and others, participating in the March Against Fear.

Fannie Lou Hamer singing to a group of people during the March Against Fear.

Mrs. Hardy, Unita Blackwell, and Fannie Lou Hamer speaking at a hearing of the Senate Subcommittee on Employment, Manpower, and Poverty. Hamer appears on the right side of the photo.

Fannie Lou Hamer, Mississippi Freedom Democratic Party delegate, at the Democratic National Convention, Atlantic City, New Jersey, August 1964.

Fannie Lou Hamer participating in the March Against Fear through Mississippi, 1966, begun by James Meredith.

A head-and-shoulders portrait of civil rights leader Fannie Lou Hamer flanked by a man and woman, 1965.

Some of the keynote speakers, at the 1971 opening of the National Women's Political Caucus. Left to right: Betty Smith, former vice chairman of the GOP in Wisconsin; Dorothy Haener, international representative, Women's Department, United Automobile Workers Union; Fannie Lou Hamer, civil rights leader from Mississippi; and Gloria Steinem, member, Democratic National Policy Council. Mrs. Hamer announced that she would challenge Senator James O. Eastland, D-Miss., if he sought reelection the next year.

Fannie Lou Hamer of Mississippi addresses the delegates on the fight over Alabama credentials, during the second session of the 1968 Democratic National Convention.

other marginalized groups. Moreover, these federally funded projects led to the destruction of 20 percent of city housing units that were occupied by Black people.[102] More than 60 percent of those displaced by these urban renewal programs were Black Americans, Latinx people, and other racial minorities.[103]

Hamer decried these programs, which she aptly described as "Negro removal" programs.[104] "They want to tear the homes down and put a parking lot there," Hamer explained. "[But] where are those people going? Where will they go?"[105] She emphasized how these renewal programs were simply new manifestations of white supremacy and reminded US leaders that their actions were on display for the world to see: "The world is looking at America and it is really beginning to show up for what it is really like. 'Go Tell It on the Mountain.' We can no longer ignore this, that America is not 'the land of the free and the home of the brave.'"[106]

For Hamer, the "facts of life" to which she alluded were unmistakable: "We got to change some curriculum and in making the change, we can have more peace, and real democracy when we bring the boys home and some of the billions of dollars that's being spent in Vietnam can go into rural areas like Mississippi."[107] Addressing those who insisted that the war in Vietnam was necessary to prevent the global spread and influence of communism, Hamer pointed out the holes in such logic by emphasizing how developments taking place at home shaped Americans' perspectives of global issues. Although she did not embrace communism, she resisted US leaders who tried to use it as a cover for their own moral failings:

> We want a change throughout the country, and the only way we can have a change is to bring those men home from Vietnam. People have been greatly punished—they have been criticized—because we are in a racist war that don't give a man a chance, that carry him to Vietnam. And I don't believe, you know, the first escape boat this country got to get away on is communism. Now, I know as much about communism as a horse know about New Year, but nobody and that mean nobody, have to tell me that it's not something wrong with the system. And no communist have to tell me that I'm without food and clothing and a decent place to live in this country.[108]

In effect, Hamer underscored how the efforts to draw a stark contrast between American democracy and communism were fundamentally undermined by how the United States mistreated its Black citizens. "The whole world is watching us today," she reiterated during a 1969 MFDP rally in Lexington, Mississippi.[109]

As the decade came to a close, Fannie Lou Hamer joined a chorus of voices in the United States who were agitating for human rights and calling attention to the devaluation of Black lives at home and abroad. When the Massachusetts-based Pan-African Liberation Committee (PALC) called for a boycott of the Gulf Oil Corporation in 1973 because of its business—and tacit support of colonialism—in Portuguese territories in Africa, Hamer extended her full support.[110] Organized by Randall Robinson, then a Harvard law student who went on to establish TransAfrica, PALC led a nationwide effort to call attention to the Gulf Oil Corporation's role in financing Portuguese colonial rule in Angola, Mozambique, Guinea-Bissau, and the Cape Verde islands.[111] "As Europe's poorest country," PALC leaders pointed out, "Portugal is incapable of financing its wars against African people alone."[112] By demanding a boycott of all Gulf Oil Corporation products, PALC extended their support for African liberation movements of the period and turned to some of the nation's leading Black activists and intellectuals for their endorsement. Hamer lent her support to the 1973 boycott and endorsed PALC's statement, alongside more than fifty leaders, including Afro-Trinidadian theorist C. L. R. James, Congressman John Conyers of Michigan, African American journalist Ethel L. Payne, and poet Don L. Lee (Haki R. Madhubuti).

Later reflecting on US involvement in Vietnam and on the African continent, Hamer expressed hope that US leaders would cease imposing their will on others while they left issues unaddressed at home. The fight for democracy, she pointed out, was disingenuous if the United States was only interested in democracy for some and not *all*. "We'll be able to stand and fight together for the things that we rightfully deserve," she passionately argued, "not in Vietnam, not in Biafra, but right here in the United States to make democracy a reality for all of the people of the world regardless of race or color."[113]

At the core of her political vision was a belief that the freedom of one marginalized group was deeply connected to the liberation of other marginalized groups. The mantra "Nobody's free until everybody's free" captures the essence of Hamer's expansive political vision. For Hamer, the quest for freedom was incomplete if it failed to take into account all oppressed peoples, regardless of race, age, ability, religion, gender, class, or sexuality. And this perspective was still limited in scope if it only considered those living within the confines of the borders of the United States. Her vision of liberation was also deeply internationalist. In her political philosophy, the fight for the rights and liberation of marginalized people in the United States connected to the freedom struggles of other people of color around the world. By linking local and national concerns with global ones, Hamer set a precedent for future generations of Black activists.

CHAPTER SIX

TRY TO DO SOMETHING

You can pray until you faint, but if you don't get up and try to do something, God is not going to put it in your lap.

—FANNIE LOU HAMER[1]

In 2017, Rev. Dr. William J. Barber II and Rev. Dr. Liz Theoharis launched a joint campaign to confront poverty in the United States. Framing the task of dismantling poverty as both a moral imperative and human rights issue, Barber and Theoharis have worked to build a powerful and dynamic movement that now boasts tens of thousands of active participants. Named the Poor People's Campaign: A National Call for Moral Revival, their movement and vision drew inspiration from Rev. Martin Luther King Jr.'s efforts. In 1967, the year before his assassination, King had announced plans for the original Poor People's Campaign at a staff retreat for his organization, the Southern Christian Leadership Conference (SCLC). He intended for a group of two thousand people to descend on Washington, DC, to demand a redistribution of economic power. King's vision of a multiracial coalition working to improve the socioeconomic conditions for all Americans, regardless of race, was not carried out until after his tragic death.[2] Under the leadership of Ralph Abernathy, SCLC decided to move forward with the campaign in April 1968.

The first procession, led by Coretta Scott King, attracted hundreds of protesters who gathered in Washington, DC, on Mother's Day in May 1968.[3]

Barber and Theoharis have picked up the mantle, working to build a "broad, fusion movement that could unite poor and impacted communities across the country."[4] On Mother's Day in 2018—fifty years after Coretta Scott King led a procession in Washington, DC—the new Poor People's Campaign came to fruition, attracting over five thousand Americans of diverse backgrounds. For six weeks, from May to June 2018, activists and leaders gathered in Washington, DC, and in state capitals to lead teach-ins, mass meetings, and other local events to demand better living conditions for those living in poverty in the United States.[5] Their task is not an easy one. Poverty persists as a major problem in the United States despite its status as the wealthiest nation in the world. A 2018 survey reveals that 95.3 million Americans are currently low income and one in seven are living in poverty.[6] This figure is hardly any different from statistics for the previous year, which revealed that 95 million Americans were impoverished or classified as low income.[7] Today, an estimated 43.5 percent of the US population is either living in poverty or considered low income.[8] "Income inequality and wealth disparity have increased under Republicans and Democrats over the past four decades," Barber and Theoharis argue, "but now there is increased policy disdain for the poor."[9]

At the heart of tackling poverty, they point out, is a radical shift in our perceptions of the poor. The Poor People's Campaign therefore aims to dispel two myths that continue to shape the ideas of Americans, which, in turn, create a significant impact on public policy. First, campaign organizers have worked to remind all Americans that poverty is not the fault of the poor. In a nation that still touts the idea that one can simply succeed through sheer will and determination, the Poor People's Campaign has laid bare how the systemic problems in the US shape individual experiences and outcomes, resulting in limited access to wealth. Second, campaign leaders have worked to dispel the myth that "there is not enough for all of us to survive and thrive."[10] To the contrary, they emphasize how the redistribution of wealth as well as several other steps, including changes in federal spending and an increased minimum wage, can effectively improve the lives of impov-erished Americans—and, by extension, all Americans.[11]

Rev. Barber reiterated this message during a 2019 speech at the University of California, Berkeley, in which he called on Americans of all races and socioeconomic backgrounds to fight for economic justice.[12] He reminded attendees that the US Constitution empowered all Americans to "alter any political system" that becomes "danger-ous and detrimental to the principles of life, liberty, and the pursuit of happiness for everyone." Within this framework, Barber asked his audience to work toward advancing social justice and the "general welfare" of all. "Any pretense about liberty, [that] does not establish justice, that does not provide for the common defense, that divides people rather than pulls them together, [. . .] it undermines the pro-moting of the general welfare is contrary to what is put on paper," he passionately argued.[13] Reflecting on the courageous activists of the past who embraced such a vision, he evoked Fannie Lou Hamer, who worked tirelessly to improve the lives of Black people and other marginalized groups during her lifetime. It was a fitting gesture that symbolically linked the two activists and leaders—intellectually and spiritually—across the annals of time.

More than fifty years before Rev. Barber collaborated with Rev. Theoharis to launch a nationwide movement to address systemic poverty, Fannie Lou Hamer grappled with the same concern in her community of Ruleville, Mississippi. For Hamer, the struggle to end poverty in Mississippi—much like other social ills—required a con-certed effort on the part of each individual American. She believed that each of us has the responsibility to work toward building the just and equal society we envision. Like Barber and Theoharis, Hamer viewed the struggle for economic justice as a moral imperative, rooted in her Christian faith and upbringing. She forcefully articulated this message at a mass meeting in Indianola, Mississippi, in September 1964 in the presence of hundreds of Black residents at a Baptist church. "You can pray until you faint," she explained, "but if you don't get up and try to do something, God is not going to put it in your lap."[14] She elaborated further in a later interview: "90% of the people of Missis-sippi have always gone to church, always believing that things would finally happen. But we found that things just don't change like that.

You have to make them change."[15] In Hamer's perspective, faith was no substitute for individual action—the will to make a change, rather than relying solely on others to make one's life better. Her unwavering belief in the significance of individual action provided impetus for her own efforts to launch Freedom Farm, a community-based rural and economic development project, as a strategy for tackling poverty in Mississippi during the late 1960s and 1970s.

"I HAVE A PRINCIPLE, I HAVE A CHARGE."

Living in Mississippi shaped Fannie Lou Hamer's views on poverty.[16] The granddaughter of enslaved Black people, Hamer grew up in a life of sharecropping, working diligently on a white family's plantation with no prospect for landownership herself. Like countless other Black people in the Jim Crow South, Hamer worked under the weight of the oppressive and exploitative sharecropping system with no end in sight. Later in life, Hamer would speak about her difficult childhood, which was often marred by hunger. Hamer told stories of how her mother struggled to feed the twenty Townsend children, mentioning how Lou Ella would make "flour gravy" by mixing "flour with a little grease."[17] Hamer's parents struggled to meet the family's basic needs with scant financial resources. As the activist recalled years later, "For most of that time, we never had shoes," and they had to endure the difficulties of sharecropping with their feet wrapped in rags.[18] Hamer's account mirrored that of many other African Americans living in Mississippi during the early twentieth century. A study of Indianola by anthropologist Hortense Powdermaker captured the devastating effects of sharecropping in the South during the 1930s. Of the thousands of Black people who worked as sharecroppers, Powdermaker found that only 25 to 30 percent received a fair settlement for crops at the end of the year.[19] Half of the Black families in the Mississippi Delta during this period could not afford to maintain a nutritious diet.[20]

Franklin D. Roosevelt's New Deal exacerbated the difficult economic conditions associated with Black farming in Mississippi in the 1930s. While the programs sought to improve the socioeconomic circumstances for all Americans, they ultimately left behind the most vulnerable groups, including African Americans.[21] The 1933 Agricultural Adjustment Act (AAA) intended to increase failing crop prices by paying landowners to reduce their crop production. As written, the AAA required landowners to share the payment with their tenants and sharecroppers. But few landowners were willing to share these payments and, as a result, held on to these funds while displacing thousands of land tenants, sharecroppers, and small landowners— many of whom were African American.[22] Increased mechanization in the 1940s further accelerated the rapid decline in land tenancy and sharecropping.[23] These developments devastated Black Southerners who relied heavily on sharecropping and farming as both a way of life and a means of survival. These realities, combined with increasing racial violence and terror, fueled the second wave of the Great Migration, in which an estimated 4.5 million Black Southerners relocated to Northern and Western cities from 1945 to 1970.[24]

By 1960, 75 percent of all families in the Mississippi Delta lived below the poverty line of $3,000.[25] In Quitman County, Mississippi, the median annual income of a Black family was an estimated $819 while residents in Washington County fared only slightly better with an average annual income of $1,600.[26] In Sunflower County, where Hamer resided, the population in 1960 was estimated at 46,000 people—67 percent of them African American.[27] More than half of the Black residents in Sunflower County worked in the fields of agriculture and 70 percent of African American men were employed as "farmers, farm managers, laborers, and foremen."[28] With increased mechanization, residents in Sunflower County struggled to make ends meet as they sought other ways to support their families. The lack of access to quality education—only 10 percent of the Black population in Sunflower County had more than six years of education— further exacerbated dire socioeconomic conditions. Black residents in Mississippi during the 1960s suffered from extreme unemployment, homelessness, hunger, and malnutrition in a state that not only failed to offer any kind of aid but also actively worked to block African Americans from receiving support.[29]

Hamer's life experience underscored the impossibility of breaking free from poverty in a system designed to prevent African Americans from accessing financial resources and educational opportunities. In a 1963 speech at a Freedom Vote rally in Greenwood, Mississippi, Hamer reflected on how poverty shaped her life well beyond the years of her childhood. "I've 'kept the faith,'" she told the audience. "You know, it had been a long time—people, I have worked, I have worked as hard as anybody. I have been picking cotton and would be so hungry . . . wondering what I was going to cook that night."[30] Her words illuminated the cruelty of the sharecropping system, which robbed African Americans of benefiting from their time and labor, leaving them with very little in return. For Hamer, her life of sharecropping effectively came to a halt when she became actively involved in the civil rights movement. When she was forced to leave W. D. Marlow's plantation—as retaliation for her bold decision to register to vote—Hamer walked away and never returned.

Yet she never turned her back on her people—those who toiled day after day in the Mississippi Delta and beyond. As a woman of faith, Hamer viewed the effort to serve others as part of her life's mission, ordained by God. She often quoted the biblical verse Luke 4:18 as a reaffirmation of her life's work to help those in need: "The Spirit of the Lord is upon me because he has anointed me to preach the gospel to the poor. He has sent me to heal the brokenhearted, to preach deliverance to the captive, and recover the sight to the blind, to set at liberty to them who are bruised, to preach the acceptable year of the Lord." Even as the circumstances of her life changed and she gained national prominence for her work as an activist, Hamer remained deeply connected to her community. She empathized with those who struggled to make ends meet because she had experienced their pain and consistently struggled with poverty throughout her life—all while working to improve conditions for others. In one instance, she reflected on the fact that her socioeconomic conditions had changed very little since she joined the civil rights movement:

In 1962, 1963, 1964 and '65, when it was some of us traveling from place to place without money, without food, and at all times we didn't have really decent clothes. I remember at one time when we was traveling from place to place a co-worker of mine, we would have sometime just enough money to get a sour-pickled wiener, and a pop to go from place to place, we drank that and we would eat that wiener together and we would go on to one place to the other, and my blood pressure went up to 230![31]

Hamer's passionate yet lighthearted delivery of this story could hardly shield audience members from the pain she had endured. Here she was diligently working and advocating for others while she could not always meet her basic needs. She shrugged it off, focusing less on herself and instead centering the needs of others. And she remained ever positive, pointing out to listeners that as bad as circumstances might have been during this period, it was no different from the norm: "Now some of the time since then I got hungry, but I got consolation because I had got hungry before I got in it. Wasn't going to be no more hungry now than I was then."[32]

A selfless leader, Hamer worried less about her own circumstances than she did about the lives of those who surrounded her—Black and white. "I'm not fighting for a black Mississippi," she once remarked. "I'm fighting for a people's Mississippi."[33] Few things angered Hamer as much as witnessing those with wealth make policy decisions that alienated the poor. In Hamer's view, those who had the means had the responsibility to help others. And those who were empowered as leaders in society bore the responsibility to lift others up, not tear them down. As she traveled from place to place, she took notice of the conditions of Black people in local communities and carefully observed how some local leaders, including many preachers, showed little interest in improving the socioeconomic circumstances for all. At a speech before members of the National Council of Negro Women (NCNW), the largest Black women's organization in the United States during the 1960s, Hamer directly confronted the problem of indifference and class divisions in Black communities:

> You see in the Delta area of Mississippi, I watched Friday night— was two weeks ago—I watched our principal, our professional men, and these chicken-eating ministers stand up and vote against the poor Negro people and the poor white in Sunflower County. You see if you are professional and if you are a nonprofessional, if you are not giving service to your fellow man, well, you can be as

fancy-dressed as you want to be, but just don't go to church because it's no good. Because we are our brother's keeper.[34]

Hamer's scathing critique of local preachers was grounded in her religious beliefs. She reiterated her embrace of Luke 4:18 and called on people of faith to never lose sight of their God-given purpose to help those in need. For Hamer, this was the only way to live a life of dignity: "[T]oday we have professional people in the state of Mississippi—teachers and preachers—[who] don't have the dignity—they have these degrees but they don't have the dignity and respect for their fellow man to stand up for a cause."[35]

Hamer saw this as the only way to lead a life of faith: "If we are not concerned about each other, going to the field working for three lousy dollars a day, coming out so tired we can hardly cook what little we have, then stop saying something about I'm a Christian."[36] She called out religious leaders who used biblical verses as a cover to avoid doing anything to assist people in need. Alluding to the biblical promise of a "land of milk and honey," Hamer expressed disgust with those who seemed so preoccupied with heaven that they paid no attention to the challenges facing people on Earth. "I'm sick and tired of seeing these cats telling me that I should expect milk and honey," she told white audience members in Kentucky.[37] "I can't drink sweet milk, and I don't eat honey. . . . That ain't going to work no more, honey," she continued. "You know, and I'm tired of being fed, 'He said, "Thy will be done on earth as it is in heaven."' Now, I know some of the stuff that's going on down here. God don't want this stuff in heaven. That means, we're going to have to push these men and these women and put them in office."[38]

Hamer did not reserve her criticism for only religious leaders. She did not tolerate anyone with means who abandoned those in need, especially politicians and policy makers. And she was not afraid to name names. In several speeches, she called out Jamie L. Whitten, the US congressman whose district included Sunflower County, for his complete disregard of Black and poor people.[39] A member of the Democratic Party, Whitten served as the chairman of the House Appropriations Subcommittee on Agriculture, a powerful group that provided more than $20 million in farm subsidies for white residents who owned large plantations in the region. Yet Whitten actively blocked data collection about poverty in the region in an effort to keep federal funding out of the hands of Black residents and extended only $4 million in aid to those living in poverty in Sunflower County.[40] His actions, rooted in white supremacy, served to keep African Americans in a state of need while white plantation owners, who were already in a better economic position, received additional aid to boost their wealth. Hamer would decide to run against Whitten in 1964 in an effort to remove him from office. As she pointed out, politicians like Whitten had "been in Washington thirteen years and he is not representing the people of Mississippi because not only do they discriminate against the poor Negroes, they discriminated . . . against the poor whites."[41] While she was unsuccessful in her bid to unseat Whitten, Hamer used her voice and her growing influence in the region to raise greater attention to the myriad ways white politicians worked to undermine Black economic progress in the South.

During the mid-1960s, Hamer took on Senator James Eastland, another white politician who served the interests of white planters at the expense of Black residents in Mississippi. Born in Doddsville, Mississippi, in 1904, Eastland became a wealthy landowner in Sunflower County and a well-known senator who proudly advocated racial segregation. From the beginning of his Senate term in 1941 until his resignation in 1978, Eastland wielded significant influence in the region. In the aftermath of the 1954 *Brown v. Board of Education* Supreme Court decision, Eastland's prominence rapidly grew on the national scene as he unabashedly stood in the way of Black political progress.[42] Two years later, he became the chair of the Judiciary Committee, a position he leveraged to resist civil rights legislation and advance white supremacist policies. Though she lacked the resources and prestige that Eastland enjoyed, Hamer did not hesitate to openly condemn the senator's practices and demand that all Americans take notice of how Eastland significantly contributed to African Americans' devastating economic and social conditions in Mississippi. During several public speeches, Hamer went so far as to evoke Eastland's name when offering background on her life's story:

I'm from the ruralest of the ruralest, poorest of the poorest U.S.A.—
the home of Senator James O. Eastland, Sunflower County, where
we have thirty-eight thousand blacks, seventeen thousand whites,
fourteen thousand potential voters (black), eight thousand white,
150 percent of the white are registered, and we don't have quite 50
percent of the blacks registered. And the reason I say "150 percent
of the white are registered" is because they's still voting that's dead
and they's still voting that's not born in Mississippi.[43]

By calling attention to Eastland in this way, she reinforced a message to white America that Sunflower County was one of the poorest
in Mississippi because of man-made forces. Hamer also emphasized
the intentionality of white supremacists to do everything within their
power to keep Black people in a subordinate position and always in financial need. Like Congressman Whitten, Senator Eastland exploited
federal funding—taking funds from the government to line the pock-
ets of white planters at the expense of the most vulnerable residents
in the region.[44]

These actions were not only devastating for Black people in Mississippi, but they also placed their children—and by extension, the future
of the South—at great risk. In her 1967 speech before members of the
NCNW, Hamer highlighted the specific needs of Black children in the
Mississippi Delta. She likely framed her speech along these lines in recognition of the Council's decades-long work with racial uplift in Black
communities. Founded by Mary McLeod Bethune in 1935, the NCNW
helped to "unite black women's sororities, professional organizations,
and auxiliaries" during the twentieth century.[45] The NCNW provided
a wealth of grants and scholarships for Black women and actively supported the War on Poverty programs in the Mississippi Delta as well
as development projects in Africa during the 1960s.[46]

Speaking before members of the NCNW, Hamer took the opportunity to highlight the Black children in Sunflower County living in
poverty. "We have in Sunflower County fourteen hundred children
that we were able to get out of the ghettos, out of the country, and
most of these children had never seen a commode in their lives. Some
of these children had never had their faces washed in a face bowl—but

you see, I care." She went on to call out "the professional Negro"—no doubt alluding to some who sat in the audience listening—who were more committed to joining the "power structure" rather than supporting efforts to end poverty in Black communities.[47] While she was disappointed by the actions of some members of the Black middle class and elite, Hamer reassured the audience that she would not falter in her efforts. "I am going to stand. You see, I have a principle and not only do I have a principle, I have a charge."[48] In Hamer's view, it was her responsibility to uplift others and to draw from her own painful experiences to empower others and improve their condition. Working to better the lives of Black children was especially important to Hamer because, as she once explained it, "I don't want my children to come through what I had to come through. I want to make Mississippi a better place for *all* the kids, not only the wealthy white kids."[49] This mission was central to Hamer's commitment to advancing a democratic vision of the United States. As Hamer reminded audiences across the country, it was impossible to "make democracy work" when only some Americans had access to rights and resources.[50]

Hamer reiterated this message in the summer of 1968, when she traveled to Kentucky to deliver a talk to a predominately white audience.[51] One of the subjects of her criticism was President Lyndon B. Johnson's Great Society programs, the largest reform agenda in the United States since FDR's New Deal.[52] Against the backdrop of the civil rights movement, Johnson announced the introduction of the Great Society programs during his State of the Union address in 1964. Through the Great Society programs, Johnson hoped to address virtually every societal problem, including disease, pollution, and poverty. The programs, which were all part of Johnson's War on Poverty, included several new initiatives but also built on earlier reform programs, including some that were introduced during the Progressive Era (1890–1920) and, most notably, the New Deal. Three core programs—Medicare, Medicaid, and the Economic Opportunity Act—were based on the earlier New Deal programs. Yet the Great Society programs attempted to address the issue of race, and their approach to social reform entailed advancing several civil rights initiatives, including the 1964 Civil Rights Act and the 1965 Voting Rights Act.[53] Hamer recognized the value and utility of these programs, but she was not especially impressed by them as they fell short of their promises. Much like the New Deal programs, those of the Great Society failed to reach those who needed help the most: Black Americans.

Hamer considered these programs a missed opportunity and emphasized the need for Americans to do a lot more if they hoped to dismantle white supremacy.[54] In areas like the Mississippi Delta, the Great Society programs might as well have been an attempt to place a Band-Aid on a gushing wound; they failed to address the underlying problem of structural racism, which excluded African Americans and other people of color from a wealth of resources and opportunities. In a 1968 speech in Kentucky, Hamer pointed to the weaknesses of the program—captured in its dubious name: "If this society of yours is a 'Great Society,' God knows I'd hate to live in a bad one."[55] Hamer boldly uttered those exact words to Johnson in a telegram. Though she was once hopeful that Johnson's initiatives might in fact improve conditions for Black people, Hamer came to view the War on Poverty as simply a "war against poor people."[56] She especially decried the discriminatory practices occurring at the local level, which excluded impoverished Black people from participating in programs designed to help eliminate poverty.

This was evident when it came to the matter of food stamps—an initiative that grew out of the New Deal. As part of the Great Society programs, Johnson introduced the Food Stamp Act of 1964, which was meant to prevent hunger and improve the social conditions of impoverished Americans. The program, however, required people to purchase food stamps. According to the act, Americans were expected to "purchase their food stamps, paying an amount commensurate with their normal expenditures for food."[57] Such an arrangement failed to consider the many Americans, especially rural Black people working as sharecroppers, who simply could not afford to purchase food stamps—no matter what the cost. In a 1971 speech at the University of Wisconsin, Madison, Hamer emphasized how the Food Stamp Act failed to meet the needs of rural Black people. She opened up about her own personal experiences to underscore the gravity of the situation:

> We know what has happened in the past with food stamps, welfare, and all of this kind of stuff. And it is not only in the South—it's up

South and down South—where our people have suffered from malnutrition. One of my daughters stayed in the hospital six weeks, suffering from malnutrition. And I remember other things with other
people where kids literally starved almost to death. And then I start
traveling throughout this country to try to do something about the
problem. So, I would come to Madison, Wisconsin, New York City,
California, and all over the county trying to raise funds to purchase
food stamps. But the real crime, I think it's a crime, that if a man
and woman is hungry, that they have to pay for the food stamps
when thousands of people in the state of Mississippi have made less
than five hundred dollars in 1970.[58]

The growing competition for resources further compounded the
problems Hamer described as federal funds were diverted to meet the
needs of the Vietnam War and to address race riots in urban areas.[59]
All of these circumstances meant that the Great Society programs,
while meaningful, had little positive impact on the lives of Black
Southerners living in poverty. Hamer called on Americans to do more
to alleviate poverty by devising strategies that would specifically meet
the needs of those in dire circumstances. "It's time for us to wake up,
and if we [are] going to make democracy a reality, we have to work
to eliminate some of the problems with not only blacks but the poor
whites as well."[60]

When speaking to white audiences, Hamer did not shy away from
discussing religion and repeatedly reminded them of her spiritual calling to help the poor:

But you're not better than the black man because the fourth chapter
of St. Luke and the eighteenth verse, where Christ was dealing with
poor people . . . said, "The spirit of the Lord is upon me because he
has anointed me to preach the gospel to the poor." And that didn't
just mean black, that meant people. And to show you we're no different, the seventeenth chapter of Acts and the twenty-sixth verse
says, "has made of one blood all nations." So whether you're white,
black, or polka dot, we made from the same blood brother, and we
are on our way.[61]

The Bible clearly shaped Hamer's worldview and ideas about poverty.[62] Helping the poor, according to Hamer, was a divine responsibility and therefore a moral imperative. It also required taking actionable steps. Hamer believed that God was on her side, but she also understood that faith alone could not bring an end to racial injustice in this country. And faith alone could not end poverty. Although her resources were minimal, she was determined to match faith with action and envisioned ways she could help members of her community. Recognizing the limitations of the Great Society programs, Hamer wanted policies and initiatives that would empower impoverished Black people: "To have a great country, not only will we have to have political power, but we will have to have economic power as well."[63]

Hamer's painful personal experience with malnutrition further bolstered her desire to eliminate poverty in the Mississippi Delta. While speaking to a journalist for *Sepia* magazine in 1972, Hamer elaborated on the challenges her family faced while dealing with hunger and poverty. "My own daughter is sixteen-years-old," she explained. "She was in the hospital a few years ago. They fed her glucose because she was suffering from malnutrition."[64] While Hamer was forthcoming about her daughter Vergie's experience, she was silent about her daughter Dorothy, who died in 1967 because of chronic malnutrition.[65] Her refusal to publicly discuss Dorothy's death no doubt signaled the depth of Hamer's pain. What she could not articulate in words, she expressed through her deeds. Freedom Farm provided an avenue for Hamer to extend a helping hand to others—and in so doing, spare them from some of the pain she had endured.

"FOOD IS USED AS A POLITICAL WEAPON."

In 1969, Fannie Lou Hamer set out to tackle the issue of poverty by launching the Freedom Farm Cooperative (FFC), a community-based rural and economic development project.[66] With a donation of $10,000 from Measure for Measure, a charitable organization based in Wisconsin, Hamer was able to purchase forty acres of land in her hometown of Ruleville, Mississippi, with plans to develop the land to provide resources for local residents in need.[67] That year, the NCNW, under the leadership of activist Dorothy Height, donated fifty pigs to Freedom Farm, thereby establishing a "pig bank" that was meant to be self-replenishing.[68] Freedom Farm also worked to ensure its members would have adequate and stable housing. The FFC grew to over 640 acres and provided a crucial means for local farmers to have some sense of financial and even political autonomy.

Freedom Farm also grew out of Hamer's desire to address the weaknesses of the Great Society programs that had failed to financially uplift Black Southerners. "I had been going around a lot of areas and [seeing] folks just not having enough to get food stamps," she explained in a 1972 interview. "We just thought if we had land to grow stuff on, then it would be a help to us." In her autobiography, *To Praise Our Bridges,* Hamer elaborated further, offering a scathing critique of federal poverty programs that exploited the poor: "We are 91 percent of the poor here in Sunflower County and we are going to control 91 percent of all the poverty money that comes through here. They have stolen from us for too long. That's why these crackers got involved in the poverty program—just another way to steal from black folks."[69] In setting up the FFC, Hamer was especially careful about how donations would be spent to keep the Farm running. She explained her rationale during an interview: "Because I've seen government-funded programs with cooperatives and after you get through making the proposal with a stack of paper this high and after you finish paying all the administration from twenty-five thousand dollars to twelve thousand dollars it would be exactly two dollars to go to the program. The only person that's paid at this point is the secretary."[70]

As someone who had worked for many years as a sharecropper, Hamer knew firsthand the difficulties that emerged from a lack of landownership. She also understood the economic power associated with having one's own land and resources. "Living on the farm, on some plantation, they still don't give you a place to grow stuff. So we founded Freedom Farms in 1969. . . . In February, we got some money, just donations, to put an option on forty acres of land."[71] As thousands of Black people from Mississippi abandoned the region because of a loss of job opportunities, Hamer's Freedom Farm provided a much-needed alternative. It offered a significant opportunity for local residents to "stay in the South, live off the land, and create a healthy community" in the Mississippi Delta.[72] The decision was a practical one—and a matter of survival. As Hamer once remarked, "Down where we are, food is used as a political weapon. But if you have a pig in your backyard, if you have some vegetables in your garden, you can feed yourself and your family, and nobody can push you around. If we have something like some pigs and some gardens and a few things like that, even if we have no jobs, we can eat and we can look after our families."[73] The conditions of life in Mississippi were so dire that the very idea of having one's own land—"with some pigs and some gardens"—was a powerful act of resistance. Hamer saw the way white political leaders in the South attempted to use poverty and the threat of hunger to block African Americans from seeking political rights. "Where a couple of years ago white people were shooting at Negroes trying to register, now they say, 'go ahead and register—then you'll starve.'"[74] In this way, Hamer linked Black economic rights with political rights, recognizing that the two could not be divorced from each other in the Jim Crow South.

Hamer's Freedom Farm Cooperative therefore created employment opportunities for local residents; the members of the cooperative were local farmers who had lost their jobs and were displaced as a result of mechanization in the state.[75] Those who joined were expected to pay a modest membership fee of one dollar per month. Those who were unable to pay the fee were not excluded from the Farm.[76] The cooperative focused on three primary concerns to help improve the socioeconomic conditions of local residents. First, Freedom Farm provided housing for those who needed a place to stay. During the early 1970s, it developed the Delta Housing Development Corporation, which provided housing for more than seventy families.[77] It also provided resources and support for small-business owners with agricultural knowledge. And finally, Freedom Farm attended to the nutritional needs of the poor in the Mississippi Delta. "I don't be ashamed when someone comes here," she explained, "and I can go in the kitchen and fry some ham, and open some soup, and have some vegetables, because we put it up. It's not only essential that you have food, but it's healthy food."[78]

Hamer managed to fund and expand these programs with the help of several supporters, including activist and celebrity Harry Belafonte, leaders of the NCNW, and student organizations at Harvard

University.[79] Through numerous local and national fundraising efforts, Hamer brought widespread attention to Freedom Farm. By September 1969, she was able to raise an estimated $19,000 and extended a national call for an additional $24,000 to buy 780 acres of land.[80] She took great pride in her ability to create a practical solution to a persistent problem in her community: "This is the first kind of program that has ever been sponsored in this country in letting local people do their thing theirselves," she once explained.[81]

By creating a space for these families, Hamer sought to empower local Black residents. The board of directors of Freedom Farm were local Black residents, and Hamer's right-hand man, Joseph "Joe" Harris, was a young Black businessman from Sunflower County and former member of SNCC who served as the FFC's business manager.[82] Born in 1945, Harris had obtained a degree from Tougaloo College in 1965. Hamer allowed Black people to lead and also encouraged Black farmers' entrepreneurial aspirations.[83] As she explained, "You give a man food he can eat for a few days, but if you give us the tools we can produce for ourselves."[84] Her actions were rooted in the idea of Black self-sufficiency—an underlying current in Black political thought for decades. "You see what it is. They [whites] not going to do nothing for you and don't want you to do nothing for yourself," she explained in a 1970 interview.[85] "We have to build our own power," she pointed out in her earlier autobiography.[86] Although Hamer never embraced Black nationalism, her unwavering commitment to the ideals of Black self-sufficiency and autonomy mirrored the ideas and activities of Black nationalists in the United States and in other parts of the globe. For example, decades before Hamer launched Freedom Farm, James Stewart, a leader in the Universal Negro Improvement Association (UNIA) established Liberty Farm in Oregonia, Ohio, during the 1940s.[87]

Few details have survived about the farm in Ohio, but Stewart went on to establish a new Liberty Farm thousands of miles away in West Africa during the late 1940s. Born in Morehead, Mississippi, in 1903, Stewart relocated to Liberia in 1949 as part of a wave of Black Americans exploring opportunities outside of the repressive Jim Crow South.[88] His efforts were also a response to Marcus Garvey's earlier call for building commercial farms in Liberia—a necessary step in the fight to increase Black economic power on a global scale. With the assistance of Liberian president William V. S. Tubman, Stewart purchased two hundred acres of land in the remote area of Gbandela, where he launched Liberty Farm. Along with several members of his family as well as some UNIA members and local indigenous people, Stewart planted several cash crops and built modern buildings and an elementary school.[89] While Stewart's Liberty Farm was not identical to Hamer's Freedom Farm, both projects underscored the significance of economic self-sufficiency in Black political life and culture. And like Stewart's Liberty Farm, Hamer's Freedom Farm created opportunities for Black people to earn a living off the land and launch their own entrepreneurial ventures.

The vast majority of families involved in Hamer's Freedom Farm were African American. However, Hamer extended help to anyone in need, regardless of their race. As she explained, "All of the qualifications that you have to have to become a part of the co-op is you have to be poor."[90] In a 1970 interview with Black novelist Paule Marshall for *Vogue* magazine, Hamer reinforced this point, arguing that "hunger has no colour line. And I'd walk a mile for any man who is hungry, Black or white."[91] In Hamer's view, the act of bringing Black and white Mississippians together at Freedom Farm was not only necessary to challenge poverty in the region; it was also a step toward building interracial political collaborations. Echoing Rev. Martin Luther King Jr., who envisioned the Poor People's Campaign as a way to bring Black and white people together to seek economic justice, Hamer saw Freedom Farm as a vehicle for African Americans to build "a coalition with the poor whites" in Mississippi.[92] As she emphatically explained during a 1970 interview, "That's where the political power will come from."[93]

The families that worked on Freedom Farm collaborated with one another and followed a strict set of rules to ensure its viability and continued growth. This was especially true for the use of the pig bank. As Hamer explained in 1970, "Every person who receives a pig has to sign a pig agreement—not to sell him or trade him off, but to keep that pig, and from each litter, give back two to the bank."[94] Freedom Farm's participants also planted and harvested a variety of crops, including sweet potatoes, kale, tomatoes, and string beans.[95] Their community garden yielded crops that served more than 1,600 families in the Mississippi Delta, as well as other parts of the country. An estimated 10 percent of the crops grown at Freedom Farm went to local residents who could not work in the fields. During the early 1970s, Hamer's Freedom Farm shipped the surplus to Black families from Mississippi who had relocated to Northern cities.[96]

In addition to providing food and housing, Hamer's Freedom Farm offered a wealth of educational resources and opportunities for families with young children. The circumstances of life had ripped Hamer away from formal schooling at a young age, but she deeply valued education. With some of the donations they had received, the FFC distributed several scholarships to local Black students to help them attend college.[97] During the late 1960s, Hamer revealed her commitment to education by playing an instrumental role in bringing the Head Start program to Sunflower County. Funded by the federal government, Head Start gave impoverished Black children access to early childhood education.[98] The goal of the program was to "stimulate the educational, emotional, physical, and social growth of pre-school children."[99] It also created more job opportunities for local residents, including Hamer's husband, Pap, who worked as a bus driver for Head Start.[100] Hamer was at first very resistant to the program, reflecting her overall ambivalence about the Great Society programs. However, Hamer's love for children and desire to help lift others out of poverty provided the impetus for her to back the program.[101] With funding from the NCNW, Freedom Farm launched the Fannie Lou Hamer Daycare Center in the early 1970s to provide childcare help for low-income mothers seeking employment.[102]

Just as Freedom Farm expanded its reach and impact, the antipoverty program experienced a series of setbacks that ultimately led to its closure by 1976. After surviving several tornadoes that hit Sunflower County in 1971, the members of Freedom Farm had to reallocate some of the funds for disaster relief. While they managed to plant and harvest new crops following the tornadoes, the workers continued to encounter a string of challenges. By 1972, Freedom Farm struggled to obtain new donors. A series of droughts and floods led to a significant loss of crops, making it impossible for Hamer to compensate Freedom Farm employees. In a final blow, in 1974, Joe Harris, the thirty-year-old business manager of Freedom Farm, died suddenly, and Hamer became ill shortly thereafter. In 1976, Hamer sold the land in an effort to pay back taxes owed to the state and county.[103] The experience was a devastating blow to Hamer, who had invested significant time, energy, and resources to build Freedom Farm.

The closure of Freedom Farm, however, could not detract from the powerful lesson Hamer taught others through her anti-poverty efforts. Hamer's own discussion of her activism around poverty captures the depth of her resolve and the power of her determination to make a difference. In October 1970, writer June Jordan traveled to the Mississippi Delta to survey the conditions of Black life.[104] Among her many stops during her stay in the region, Jordan paid a visit to Hamer to meet the activist who had "electrified the 1964 National Democratic Convention and the whole nation."[105] On a tour of Freedom Farm, Hamer expressed sheer excitement at what she had managed to accomplish. Pointing to the rows of turnips, collards, and mustard greens, Hamer emphasized the significance of Black people in Mississippi having their own land and resources: "You see, this mean[s] you got your milk, and you got your vegetables, your meat— and then you got your living. And that's the only way you survive in Mississippi . . . if you control your own life."[106] For Hamer, whose personal experiences had taught her the importance of having control of one's life, Freedom Farm represented the infinite possibilities of Black economic and political power.

Despite its end in the late 1970s, Freedom Farm left a lasting legacy and a valuable lesson that encapsulated the words Hamer uttered years earlier: "You can pray until you faint, but if you don't get up and try to do something, God is not going to put it in your lap."[107] With the FFC, Hamer had indeed done something—and it was transformative. She had matched her deep religious faith with concrete action, utilizing what little she had to initiate radical changes. Her individual act sparked a vibrant anti-poverty movement throughout the Mississippi Delta and beyond. This bold act inspired many Americans during the 1960s and 1970s—and it remains a source of inspiration today.[108]

UNTIL ALL OF US
ARE FREE

On March 14, 1977, several months shy of her sixtieth birthday, Fannie Lou Hamer passed away at the Delta Health Center in Mound Bayou, Mississippi. She had entered the hospital weeks earlier after learning that her breast cancer had recurred. In the final years of her life, as she worked to keep Freedom Farm afloat, Hamer's health had deteriorated. In January 1972, while protesting an act of violence against a young Black girl in Ruleville, Hamer suddenly collapsed in the picket line. She was immediately taken to the Delta Health Center. Since joining the civil rights movement in 1962, Hamer had worked tirelessly to assist others—traveling across the country, raising money and launching several initiatives in Sunflower County such as Freedom Farm, and raising her children—all the while spending little time attending to her own health needs.[1]

After Hamer's collapse that afternoon in 1972, doctors listened to her describe a list of ailments that included blurry vision, fatigue, and aches and pains—all associated with untreated type 2 diabetes and hypertension, which had contributed to Hamer's heart disease. The struggle to keep Freedom Farm afloat, which relied primarily on the funds she earned through speaking tours, weighed heavily on Hamer's emotional health during her stay at the Health Center. In the ensuing weeks, Hamer took some time to rest and received follow-up treatment at Meharry Medical Center in Nashville, Tennessee. She even paused her speaking tour for six months, finally intent on attending to self-care and recovery. She seemed to be on the mend.[2]

By April 1972, however, she began to take on more commitments. That month, she opened up her home to Dr. Neil R. McMillen, a professor at the University of Southern Mississippi, for what was supposed to be a series of oral interviews about her life and political work. Yet she struggled to make it through the planned interviews, still battling fatigue.[3] Despite these ongoing concerns, she made the sacrifice to attend several events that year, including the 1972 Democratic National Convention in Miami Beach, Florida. When McMillen returned to Hamer's home nearly a year later to continue conducting the interview they had started, Hamer admitted that she was still not in good health. "Is it serious?" McMillen asked. "Yes, I think so," she replied. "I'm thankful that I made it this far," she said, characteristically adding, "I don't know how many more steps I'll have to make, but I'll keep going."[4]

Hamer's statements captured her resolve to keep fighting for civil and human rights—even at the expense of her own health. And her words foreshadowed what was to come as she resumed her speaking tour and continued working at Freedom Farm. In January 1974, she was readmitted to the hospital for "nervous exhaustion." In the months to follow, she would make several hospital visits, and in the spring of 1976, Hamer underwent a mastectomy.[5] When her friend Eleanor Holmes Norton learned that Hamer could not afford the prosthesis she desired, Norton purchased one.[6] This small gesture lifted Hamer's spirits during an otherwise challenging period.

Hamer's growing list of health concerns led to more financial difficulties. With each hospital visit and new medications, Hamer and her husband, Pap, sank deeper and deeper into debt. During this period, Pap, who was well into his sixties, took on a new job to bring in more income.[7] The couple relied on the kindness of strangers—several activists and friends donated funds to aid with Hamer's medical expenses. "I have been unable to get around to work during the past 26 months and for that reason the chest is at rock bottom," she admitted to Rev. Marion Elaine Myles in letter dated August 23, 1976.[8] Though she maintained her resolve to keep fighting, Hamer had indeed hit rock bottom. She battled depression in these last few months, expressing much frustration and immense disappointment that many of the individuals she had supported were nowhere to be found. June Johnson, one of the activists who had been jailed and beaten with Hamer years earlier in Winona, later recalled finding Hamer agitated during a visit. Hamer had asked a neighbor to come by to comb her hair, and hours later, they had not arrived.[9] What appeared to be a small matter was a deeply painful experience for Hamer—she had spent her life putting others before herself and, in this particular moment, the love and sacrifices she had extended were not being reciprocated.

Although she lamented the ways too many people looked the other way, Johnson's arrival that afternoon was one expression of love that Hamer needed—and appreciated—in these last few weeks of her life. Thankfully, it was not the only one. In those last few months, Hamer witnessed an outpouring of love in the community and beyond for her life's work and contributions. Most notably, local activists came together to celebrate Fannie Lou Hamer Day in fall 1976, honoring her with a Paul Robeson Award for humanitarian service. During the celebration, attendees pooled their resources to aid Hamer with medical expenses, raising more than $2,000 that evening.[10]

In February 1977, while battling illness and bouts of depression, Hamer agreed to do a phone interview with African American journalist Annette J. Samuels for the *New York Amsterdam News*. It was a follow-up interview to one that had taken place a year earlier. Although she was going through a dark period, Hamer likely agreed to do the interview in hopes of securing some financial support for her mounting medical bills. Perhaps she also welcomed the opportunity to reflect on all that she had accomplished in her life, sensing that the end was near. The interview, one of the last Hamer gave before her passing, highlighted her remarkable political career as well as the many challenges she had endured in her lifetime. As she had done countless times before, Hamer shared with Samuels the experience of attending the 1962 mass meeting in Sunflower County, Mississippi, where she met SNCC activists for the first time. "I had never heard that I had the right to vote," she reiterated. "I was curious. So I went to the meeting."[11] She then went on to recount the first time she attempted to register to vote, traveling with eighteen activists from Ruleville to Indianola: "That was the beginning of my getting involved in the civil rights movement."[12]

Although the interview focused primarily on Hamer's political career, it also highlighted various aspects of Hamer's personal life. She and Samuels discussed Hamer's relationship with Pap, noting that the two had been married for thirty-one years. When asked about how her political work affected her marriage, Hamer emphasized a point she had made many times before: "He, Mr. Hamer, is the boss of the house. We respect each other." Emphasizing the spirit of unity that guided their relationship, both at home and in public, Hamer added, "I stand by him to see what we can do to set this country straight."[13] Though she spoke positively about her relationship with Pap, Hamer admitted that her health challenges and the financial problems were taking a toll on the family. Following the death of her daughter Dorothy in 1967, Hamer took in Dorothy's young daughters, Lenora and Jacqueline, both of whom she formally adopted in 1969. With very limited financial resources in 1977, Hamer explained to Samuels that Lenora, age ten, and Jacqueline, age nine, were helping Pap in the cotton fields to ensure the family would have food to eat. "We still have hanging over our heads a $2,000 doctor bill from when I [got] sick two years ago," Hamer added.[14]

The financial challenges in the Hamer home only intensified in the weeks to follow. One month after the interview with Samuels, Hamer was readmitted, for the last time, to the Delta Health Center for treatment related to breast cancer, as well as her ongoing heart disease and diabetes. In a brief interview with Samuels, Pap expressed deep concern about how the recent hospitalization would further impact their finances. "It's never too good," he told Samuels. "And now with Fannie in the hospital again, we're going to have even more bills coming in."[15] Concerns about bills, however, would wane in comparison to the devastating news that would soon follow. After several days of crying in agony as she lay in a hospital bed and singing the hymns that had brought comfort many times before, Hamer passed away from heart failure on March 14, 1977. The news of her death spread rapidly throughout Mississippi, across the nation, and around the globe.

Six days later, thousands of people gathered in Ruleville, Mississippi, to honor Fannie Lou Hamer, known affectionately as "Mrs.

Hamer."[16] The funeral drew a remarkable group of prominent figures from the civil rights–Black Power era, with activists and leaders present to pay their respects to Hamer. These included Hamer's mentor Ella Baker; former chairman of SNCC Stokely Carmichael (Kwame Ture); the national director of the Urban League, Vernon Jordan; former SNCC chairman and future US congressman John Lewis; Dorothy Height, president of the National Council of Negro Women (NCNW); and former SNCC chairman H. Rap Brown (Jamil Abdullah Al-Amin).[17] President Jimmy Carter authorized a military plane to take Andrew Young, then US ambassador to the United Nations, Congressman Charles Diggs, and several others to Hamer's funeral.[18] Young delivered a moving eulogy, praising Hamer's life of courage and sacrifice and emphasizing her remarkable influence on the lives of all Americans. "No one in America has not been influenced or inspired by Mrs. Hamer," he said. Young, who had played an instrumental role in getting Hamer out of the Winona jailhouse in 1963, credited her political work—Hamer's "sweat and blood"—for sowing the seeds of change in America.[19] "None of us would have been where we are now, had she not been there then," he later remarked.[20] Carmichael, with whom Hamer had organized during the 1960s, affirmed Young's assessment at the funeral, pointing out that so many people were present "not because she is Mrs. Hamer, but because she is us—she is the best of us."[21]

This message reverberated all across the nation. Two months after Hamer's death, Marcia Gillespie, editor in chief of *Essence* magazine, penned a moving essay on Hamer's life and legacy. She told the story of how she had traveled to Ruleville, Mississippi, to meet Hamer, one of her heroines, six years earlier. "I walked into the bare little airport," Gillespie explained, "and was immediately embraced— ample bosom, big arms, a smile with a touch of gold, a moon face that showed the tracks of pain and sorrow and eyes that spoke of a soul at peace. I was home."[22] As she had always done, Hamer made her visitor feel at home, welcoming Gillespie and allowing the journalist to spend a few days with the family. It was a recurring scene in the Hamer household—people walked in and out to break bread with Hamer, listening intently to her words of wisdom and basking in her love and hospitality. For Gillespie, the encounter with Hamer in 1971 was transformative:

> I met a woman who defied any little platform or pedestal I might have wished to place her on. I met a woman whose commitment to making this a decent world was total. A woman who lived a life of faith, who reminded me of the power of prayer and hope, who would not belittle herself by hating, who long discovered that her capacity for loving was boundless, who gave it freely and easily without fear of rejection or depletion. I met a woman beautiful because she loved, a fighter because of love and indomitable in her love. She made me want to do better, be bigger and I basked in her warmth.[23]

Gillespie's remarks captured the beauty and essence of Hamer's life and legacy. Hamer's courage and passion were contagious; she had the remarkable ability to leave a positive impact on anyone who crossed her path. As this book attests, Hamer has been a transformative figure in my own life. In the Christian ideal, she lived her life in sacrifice of others—always seeking ways to improve their circumstances. A passionate advocate for social justice, Hamer devoted her life to securing civil and human rights. And when she spoke, she spoke with a clear sense of purpose and radical honesty that had the ability to pierce through one's soul. Long after Hamer's death, her powerful words—political visions, freedom dreams, and hopes for the nation—live on.

"WE'VE GOT TO DO THE WORK."

On Saturday, August 19, 2020, Kamala Harris confidently walked across the stage at the Democratic National Convention at the Wisconsin Center in Milwaukee, Wisconsin. The Convention, shared remotely to curb the spread of COVID-19, drew only a portion of its usual in-person attendance. Yet that evening, millions of Americans tuned in to hear then-Senator Harris of California accept the nomination for vice president of the United States. Harris, the daughter of

Indian and Jamaican immigrants, made history that night, following in the footsteps of Black journalist Charlotta Bass, also from the state of California.[24] In 1952, Bass became the first Black woman to run for vice president in the United States, running alongside Progressive Party presidential candidate Vincent Hallinan, an attorney from San Francisco.[25] Although the campaign was unsuccessful—Hallinan and Bass only garnered 14,000 votes—it set the stage for Kamala Harris's run sixty-eight years later.[26]

When Harris took to the stage at the 2020 Democratic National Convention, the historic importance of the moment was undeniable. In only a matter of months, she would become the first Black woman and first person of Indian descent to be elected vice president on a winning party ticket. On the evening of August 19, however, she stood before a live and televised audience to formally accept the nomination and express her gratitude to those who made it possible. "Greetings America. It is truly an honor to be speaking with you," Harris began. "That I am here tonight is a testament to the dedication of generations before me. Women and men who believed so fiercely in the promise of equality, liberty, and justice for all." Reflecting on the hundredth anniversary of the passage of the Nineteenth Amendment, Harris acknowledged the courageous women who had "organized, testified, rallied, marched, and fought—not just for their vote, but for a seat at the table."[27] These women, she noted, provided a source of inspiration for us all "to pick up the torch, and fight on. Women like Mary Church Terrell and Mary McLeod Bethune. Fannie Lou Hamer and Diane Nash. Constance Baker Motley and Shirley Chisholm. We're not often taught their stories," she added. "But as Americans, we all stand on their shoulders."[28]

By evoking Fannie Lou Hamer that evening, Kamala Harris reinforced the activist-intellectual's enormous significance in shaping United States history. Alongside a cadre of other courageous Black American women, Hamer, the Mississippi sharecropper turned activist, occupied a meaningful place in Harris's personal and political narrative. Far beyond offering a source of inspiration, Hamer's ideas helped to frame Harris's political vision that evening. After highlighting her family's history and the values and lessons she learned from her relatives along the way, Harris turned her attention to the state of

affairs in the United States. She emphasized some of the most pressing national concerns, including the failures of the Trump administration, high unemployment, and the coronavirus pandemic. Though
she acknowledged how the virus devastated the lives of millions of
Americans, Harris underscored how structural racism fueled health
disparities in the United States. "While this virus touches us all, let's
be honest; it is not an equal opportunity offender," Harris remarked.
"Black, Latino and Indigenous people are suffering and dying disproportionately. This is not a coincidence," she further explained. "It is
the effect of structural racism." Pointing to disparities and inequities in
all sectors of American society—including health care, education and
technology, housing and employment, and policing and criminal justice—Harris called on Americans to take an active role in dismantling
structural racism. "And let's be clear," she noted, "there is no vaccine
for racism. We've got to do the work." Evoking Hamer for the second
time that evening, Harris insisted that because of our linked fate, all
Americans must join the fight to create a more inclusive democracy:
"We've got to do the work to fulfill that promise of equal justice under
law. Because none of us are free . . . until all of us are free."[29]

Vice President Kamala Harris's reference to Hamer's political vision at the 2020 Democratic National Convention is a testament to
the enduring power of her ideas even generations later. Hamer had
reiterated this message on numerous occasions, before diverse audiences throughout the US South and other parts of the nation, during
the 1960s and '70s. It signified the basis of Hamer's political philosophy—the belief that we must all work together, as Americans, for
the betterment of society. Those words—"none of us are free until all
of us are free"—captured the essence of Hamer's political work and
vision. She loved Black people and vigorously fought to improve their
socioeconomic status in American society, yet she did not limit her
work and focus to Black people alone. A courageous freedom fighter,
Hamer fought for the rights and liberation of all marginalized people.
She used her powerful voice to propel others to do better—and to
be better.

In Hamer's vision, which still resonates today, liberation cannot occur in fragments—it can only take place in a holistic fashion.
The political gains of one group mean little if other groups remain

disenfranchised. And likewise, if one group suffers, other groups cannot experience real joy. The mantra "None of us are free until all of us are free" also reinforces the idea that the fight for justice must be a global one and intersectional in nature, attending to the overlapping systems of oppression that shape the lives and experiences of each individual. Hamer's political vision was grounded in the spirit of unity, solidarity, and, most of all, *action*. By emphasizing how our fates are linked, Hamer called upon everyone in the United States to play an active role in building an inclusive democracy—one that would live up to the constitutional ideals on which the nation was founded. The work of democracy remains unfinished, and the roadblocks are many, but Hamer's vision of America and her enduring message to all Americans offer a way forward.

ACKNOWLEDGMENTS

I am grateful to God for helping me write this book. The process has been challenging, but He surrounded me with so many kind individuals during the journey. Although I cannot possibly name every individual who helped me over the past few years, I extend my deepest thanks to everyone who contributed to this project in some way—no matter how small. I appreciate every kind word and gesture. They all went a very long way in making this project come to fruition.

I dedicate this book to my husband, Jay, and our son, "Little Jay." They have been such a blessing to me and a constant source of love and support. My son is too young to read this book, but I hope he will pick it up in the future and be transformed by Fannie Lou Hamer's words—as I have been.

I am grateful for the other members of my family, especially my mom, whose personal sacrifices made it possible for me to pursue the path of becoming a professional historian and writer. I am also thankful for my community of friends and mentors near and far, who enthusiastically supported the project and showed up for me over the last few months to ensure that I would finish this book. I am immensely grateful to my wonderful agent, Lucy Cleland, for her guidance, wisdom, and support.

I could not have finished writing without the help of some amazing research assistants. I especially owe a debt of gratitude to Richard Mares, Tiana Wilson, and Cordelia Brazile. Several scholar-friends read parts of the manuscript and offered invaluable feedback along the way. Special thanks to Eddie Bonilla, Maegan Parker Brooks, E. Tsekani Browne, Ashley D. Farmer, Joseph R. Fitzgerald, Stephen G. Hall, LaShawn D. Harris, Davis W. Houck, Chana Kai Lee,

Lisa Levenstein, Russell Rickford, David Romaine, Phillip Luke Sinitiere, and Jeanne Theoharis.

One of the most rewarding aspects of writing this book has been the opportunity to connect with Fannie Lou Hamer's wonderful family. I am especially grateful to Jacqueline Hamer Flakes and Monica Land for their enthusiasm and support.

Working with Beacon Press has been an absolute pleasure. Gayatri Patnaik has been a wonderful editor, offering incisive editorial guidance at every step of the process. I am honored that we had the opportunity to work together on this project. Her enthusiasm for the project from idea to completion means so much to me. Thanks also to Helene Atwan for her faith in the project.

I could not have finished this book without the support of the Carr Center for Human Rights Policy at the Harvard Kennedy School. A yearlong fellowship at the Carr Center provided valuable resources and the dynamic intellectual community I needed to make it to the finish line. I would especially like to thank Sushma Raman and Mathias Risse for their kindness and remarkable leadership and vision.

Finishing this book in the midst of a global pandemic and widespread political uprisings was a dizzying experience. In the aftermath of the police killings of George Floyd, Breonna Taylor, Tony McDade, and many others, I wrestled with a mix of emotions, including disillusionment, rage, and immense sadness. In so many ways, Fannie Lou Hamer's timeless words carried me through. I found hope and inspiration in her story and the fortitude to keep pushing for social change. After reading this book, I hope that will be the same for you.

Thank you, all—*from the bottom of my heart.*

NOTES

INTRODUCTION: A LONG FIGHT AHEAD

1. Fannie Lou Hamer, "'The Only Thing We Can Do Is Work Together,' Speech Delivered at a Chapter Meeting of the National Council of Negro Women in Mississippi, 1967," in *The Speeches of Fannie Lou Hamer: To Tell It Like It Is*, ed. Maegan Parker Brooks and Davis W. Houck (Jackson: University Press of Mississippi, 2011), 73.

2. SNCC Legacy Project, "Our Mrs. Hamer," Civil Rights Movement, Archive, Remembrances of Mrs. Hamer on Her 100th Birthday, October 2017, https://www.crmvet.org/mem/hamer.htm.

3. Annette Samuels, "Fannie Lou Hamer," *New York Amsterdam News*, February 12, 1977.

4. John Egerton, *A Mind to Stay Here: Profiles from the South* (London: MacMillan, 1970), 98.

5. Samuels, "Fannie Lou Hamer."

6. Jerry DeMuth, "Fannie Lou Hamer: Tired of Being Sick and Tired," *The Nation*, June 1, 1964, https://www.thenation.com/article/archive/fannie-lou-hamer-tired-being-sick-and-tired.

7. Lynne Olson, *Freedom's Daughters: The Unsung Heroines of the Civil Rights Movement from 1830 to 1970* (New York: Simon & Schuster, 2001), 255.

8. Olson, *Freedom's Daughters*, 255.

9. Fannie Lou Hamer, "'I'm Sick and Tired of Being Sick and Tired,' Speech Delivered with Malcolm X at the Williams Institutional CME Church, Harlem, New York, December 20, 1964," in *The Speeches of Fannie Lou Hamer*, 62.

10. Keisha N. Blain, "'God Is Not Going to Put It in Your Lap.' What Made Fannie Lou Hamer's Message on Civil Rights So Radical—And So Enduring," *Time*, October 4, 2019, https://time.com/5692775/fannie-lou-hamer.

11. Heather Booth, "As Remembered by Heather Booth," Civil Rights Movement, Archive, Remembrances of Mrs. Hamer on Her 100th Birthday, 2017, https://www.crmvet.org/mem/hamer.htm.

12. Keisha N. Blain, "Fannie Lou Hamer's Dauntless Fight for Black Americans' Right to Vote," *Smithsonian Magazine*, August 20, 2020,

https://www.smithsonianmag.com/history/fannie-lou-hamers-dauntless -fight-for-black-americans-right-vote-180975610.

13. Fannie Lou Hamer, "'Is It Too Late?,' Speech Delivered at Tougaloo College, Tougaloo, Mississippi, Summer, 1971," in *The Speeches of Fannie Lou Hamer*, 133.

14. "Ruleville, Mississippi (MS) Poverty Rate Data: Information about Poor and Low-Income Residents," see City Data, Poverty Rate Data (2019), City-Data.com, http://www.city-data.com/poverty/poverty -Ruleville-Mississippi.html, accessed December 18, 2020.

15. John A. Tures and Seth Golden, "No African American Has Won Statewide Office in Mississippi in 129 Years—Here's Why," *The Conversation*, June 17, 2019, https://theconversation.com/no-african -american-has-won-statewide-office-in-mississippi-in-129-years-heres -why-118319.

16. Hamer, "'The Only Thing We Can Do Is Work Together,'" 73.

17. Fannie Lou Hamer, "'Until I Am Free, You Are Not Free Either,' Speech Delivered at the University of Wisconsin, Madison, Wisconsin, January 1971," in *The Speeches of Fannie Lou Hamer*, 121.

18. Key works on Hamer include Chana Kai Lee, *For Freedom's Sake: The Life of Fannie Lou Hamer* (Urbana: University of Illinois Press, 2000); Earnest N. Bracey, *Fannie Lou Hamer: The Life of a Civil Rights Icon* (Jefferson, NC: McFarland, 2011); Maegan Parker Brooks, *A Voice That Could Stir an Army: Fannie Lou Hamer and the Rhetoric of the Black Freedom Movement* (Jackson: University Press of Mississippi, 2014); Kay Wright Mills, *This Little Light of Mine: The Life of Fannie Lou Hamer*, 2nd ed. (1993; reprint, Lexington: University Press of Kentucky, 2007); Monica M. White, *Freedom Farmers: Agricultural Resistance and the Black Freedom Movement* (Chapel Hill: University of North Carolina Press, 2018); Maegan Parker Brooks, *Fannie Lou Hamer: America's Freedom Fighting Woman* (Lanham, MD: Rowman and Littlefield, 2020); Karen D. Crozier, *Fannie Lou Hamer's Revolutionary Practical Theology: Racial and Environmental Justice Concerns* (Boston: Brill, 2020); Kate Clifford Larson, *Walk with Me: A Biography of Fannie Lou Hamer* (New York: Oxford University Press, 2021).

CHAPTER ONE: LET YOUR LIGHT SHINE

1. Fannie Lou Hamer, "'I Don't Mind My Light Shining,' Speech Delivered at a Freedom Vote Rally in Greenwood, Mississippi, Fall 1963," in *The Speeches of Fannie Lou Hamer*, 6.

2. Clayborne Carson, *In Struggle: SNCC and the Black Awakening of the 1960s* (Cambridge, MA: Harvard University Press, 1981); Faith S. Holsaert, Martha Prescod Norman Noonan, Judy Richardson, Betty Garman Robinson, Jean Smith Young, and Dorothy M. Zellner, eds., *Hands on the Freedom Plow: Personal Accounts by Women in SNCC* (Urbana: University of Illinois Press, 2012); Charles M. Payne, *I've Got*

the Light of Freedom: The Organizing Tradition and the Mississippi Freedom Struggle, 2nd ed. (Berkeley: University of California Press, 2007); and Barbara Ransby, *Ella Baker and the Black Freedom Movement: A Radical Democratic Vision* (Chapel Hill: University of North Carolina Press, 2003).

3. Crozier, *Fannie Lou Hamer's Revolutionary Practical Theology*, 22.
4. Fannie Lou Hamer, interview by Neil McMillen, Center for Oral History and Cultural Heritage, University of Southern Mississippi, April 14, 1972, and January 25, 1973, transcript, 4.
5. Hamer, interview by McMillen, 4.
6. Hamer, "'I Don't Mind My Light Shining,'" 5.
7. Hamer, "'I Don't Mind My Light Shining,'" 6.
8. Fannie Lou Hamer, "It's in Your Hands," in *Black Women in White America: A Documentary History*, ed. Gerda Lerner (1972; reprint, New York: Vintage Books, 1992), 609. It is significant to note that there is some discrepancy in the county of Hamer's birth. Though she often indicated she was born in Montgomery County, she was actually born in Tomnolen, Mississippi, which is located in Webster County.
9. Brooks, *Fannie Lou Hamer*, 12; Lee, *For Freedom's Sake*, 1.
10. Fannie Lou Hamer, "Autobiography of Fannie Lou Hamer," July 1976, 1–6, Box 1, Folder 1, Biographical Information, Fannie Lou Hamer Collection, Department of Archives and Special Collections, J. D. Williams Library, University of Mississippi.
11. Brooks, *Fannie Lou Hamer*, 12.
12. Eugene Dattel, *Cotton and Race in the Making of America: The Human Costs of Economic Power* (Lanham, MD: Ivan R. Dee, 2009); Sven Beckert, *Empire of Cotton: A Global History* (New York: Penguin Books, 2014); Edward E. Baptist, *The Half Has Never Been Told: Slavery and the Making of American Capitalism* (New York: Basic Books, 2014).
13. Hamer, interview by McMillen, 3.
14. DeMuth, "Fannie Lou Hamer: Tired of Being Sick and Tired."
15. James D. Anderson, *The Education of Blacks in the South, 1860–1935* (Chapel Hill: University of North Carolina Press, 1988).
16. Leon Litwack, *Been in the Storm So Long: The Aftermath of Slavery* (New York: Knopf, 1979).
17. Brooks, *Fannie Lou Hamer*, 21.
18. Lee, *For Freedom's Sake*, 5.
19. Hamer, interview by McMillen, 3.
20. Brooks, *Fannie Lou Hamer*, 20; Mills, *This Little Light of Mine*, 13.
21. Hamer, interview by McMillen, 3.
22. Jack O'Dell, "Life in Mississippi: An Interview with Fannie Lou Hamer," *Freedomways* 5, no. 2 (Spring 1965): 231–32.
23. Harriet A. Washington, *Medical Apartheid: The Dark History of Medical Experimentation on Black Americans from Colonial Times to the Present* (New York: Doubleday, 2008), 47–50.

24. Rae-Ellen W. Kavey and Allison B. Kavey, *Viral Pandemics: From Smallpox to Ebola and COVID-19* (New York: Routledge, 2020).

25. Although Hamer generally referred to her bout with polio as the source of her limp, it is also likely that the limp was the result of a childhood accident in which her brother dropped her in the bathtub. See Brooks, *Fannie Lou Hamer*, 27; Mills, *This Little Light of Mine*, 10.

26. Lee, *For Freedom's Sake*, 2.

27. Hamer, "Appendix: Interview with Vergie Hamer Faulkner by Maegan Parker Brooks, July 14 and July 17, 2009," in *The Speeches of Fannie Lou Hamer*, 202.

28. Brooks, *Fannie Lou Hamer*, 24–25.

29. Egerton, *A Mind to Stay Here*, 96.

30. Egerton, *A Mind to Stay Here*, 96.

31. Charles Marsh, *God's Long Summer: Stories of Faith and Civil Rights* (Princeton: Princeton University Press, 1997), 10–48.

32. Crozier, *Fannie Lou Hamer's Revolutionary Practical Theology*, 4.

33. Crozier, *Fannie Lou Hamer's Revolutionary Practical Theology*, 5.

34. Brooks, *Fannie Lou Hamer*, 14; Lee, *For Freedom's Sake*, 7.

35. Laura Ratliff, interview by Chana Kai Lee, December 21, 1985, Ruleville, Mississippi, in Lee, *For Freedom's Sake*, 7.

36. Cathy Aldridge, "What Makes Fannie Lou Hamer Run?," *New York Amsterdam News*, September 13, 1969; Fannie Lou Hamer, "On Being a Sharecropper," *Songs My Mother Taught Me*, recorded 1963, Smithsonian Folkways Recordings, 2015, CD and MP3.

37. Aldridge, "What Makes Fannie Lou Hamer Run?"

38. Hamer, "'Until I Am Free, You Are Not Free Either,'" 123.

39. Hamer, "Autobiography of Fannie Lou Hamer," 1–6.

40. Fannie Lou Hamer, *To Praise Our Bridges: An Autobiography* (Jackson, Mississippi: KIPCO, 1967), 6.

41. Hamer, *To Praise Our Bridges*, 6.

42. Hamer, *To Praise Our Bridges*, 6.

43. Hamer, *To Praise Our Bridges*, 6.

44. Brooks, *Fannie Lou Hamer*, 25.

45. Brooks, *Fannie Lou Hamer*, 25.

46. Hamer, *To Praise Our Bridges*, 9.

47. Hamer, *To Praise Our Bridges*, 9.

48. June Jordan, *Fannie Lou Hamer* (New York: Thomas Y. Crowell, 1972). Jordan based the book on interviews she conducted with Hamer during the early 1970s.

49. Brooks, *Fannie Lou Hamer*, 17; Lee, *For Freedom's Sake*, 11.

50. Brooks, *Fannie Lou Hamer*, 17.

51. Hamer, *To Praise Our Bridges*, 11.

52. Lee, *For Freedom's Sake*, 17.

53. Brooks, *Fannie Lou Hamer*, 26.

54. Author unknown, "Biography: Mrs. Fannie Lou Hamer," Box 3, Folder 4, "Biographical Information," Fannie Lou Hamer Papers, Amistad Research Center at Tulane University, New Orleans.

55. Fannie Lou Hamer's grandniece Monica Land was the first to discover this information in local records. Brooks, *Fannie Lou Hamer*, 26. Census records appear to support Land's findings. US Census Bureau, "Sixteenth Census of the United States, 1940, Sunflower County, Mississippi," Enumeration District: 67–52, Census Place: Sunflower, Mississippi; Roll: m-t0627–02067; Page: 10A; "Enumeration District: 67–52," Ancestry.com; National Archives in St. Louis, Missouri, "WWII Draft Registration Cards for Mississippi, October 16, 1940–March 31, 1947," St. Louis, Records of the Selective Service System, 147, Box 200, Ancestry.com.

56. Brooks, *Fannie Lou Hamer*, 26.

57. Evelyn Brooks-Higginbotham, *Righteous Discontent: The Women's Movement in the Black Baptist Church, 1880–1920* (Cambridge, MA: Harvard University Press, 1993); Victoria Wolcott, *Remaking Respectability: African American Women in Interwar Detroit* (Chapel Hill: University of North Carolina, 2001); and Cheryl Hicks, *Talk with You Like a Woman: African American Women, Justice, and Reform in New York, 1890–1935* (Chapel Hill: University of North Carolina Press, 2010).

58. Brooks, *Fannie Lou Hamer*, 26.

59. Brooks, *Fannie Lou Hamer*, 26.

60. Brooks, *Fannie Lou Hamer*, 26; Lee, *For Freedom's Sake*, 18.

61. Paule Marshall, "Fannie Lou Hamer: Hunger Has No Color Line," *Vogue*, June 1, 1970, 192.

62. Lee, *For Freedom's Sake*, 20.

63. Hamer, *To Praise Our Bridges*, 11. It is significant to note that Hamer delivered her autobiography orally in a series of recordings made by Julius Lester and Maria Verela. For more context on the process of producing the autobiography, see the SNCC Digital Gateway: https://snccdigital.org/our-voices/learning-from-experience/part-5.

64. Brooks, *Fannie Lou Hamer*, 29.

65. Hamer, "Autobiography of Fannie Lou Hamer," 1–6.

66. Fannie Lou Hamer, "'America Is a Sick Place, and Man Is on the Critical List,' Speech Delivered at Loop College, Chicago, Illinois, May 27, 1970," in *The Speeches of Fannie Lou Hamer*, 105.

67. Hamer, "'America Is a Sick Place, and Man Is on the Critical List,'" 106.

68. Tera W. Hunter, *To 'Joy My Freedom: Southern Black Women's Lives and Labors After the Civil War* (Cambridge, MA: Harvard University Press, 1997), 4–5.

69. Ransby, *Ella Baker and the Black Freedom Movement*.

70. Carson, *In Struggle*.

71. Brooks, *Fannie Lou Hamer*, 33.

72. Brooks, *Fannie Lou Hamer*, 36.

73. Hamer, interview by McMillen, 4.

74. Thomas E. Patterson, *The Vanishing Voter: Public Involvement in an Age of Uncertainty* (New York: Alfred Knopf, 2002), 5.

75. Fannie Lou Hamer, "'We're On Our Way,' Speech Delivered at a Mass Meeting in Indianola, Mississippi, September 1964," in *The Speeches of Fannie Lou Hamer*, 50.

76. Hamer, "'America Is a Sick Place, and Man Is on the Critical List,'" 107.

77. Megan Landaucr and Jonathan Wolman, "Fannie Lou Hamer . . . Forcing a New Political Reality," *Daily Cardinal*, October 8, 1971, Box 3, Folder 13, "News Clippings," Fannie Lou Hamer Papers, Amistad Research Center.

78. SNCC Legacy Project, "Our Mrs. Hamer."

79. Bracey, *Fannie Lou Hamer*, 159.

80. Martha S. Jones, *Vanguard: How Black Women Broke Barriers, Won the Vote, and Insisted on Equality for All* (New York: Basic Books, 2020).

81. Fannie Lou Hamer, "Federal Trial Testimony, Oxford, Mississippi, December 2, 1963," in *The Speeches of Fannie Lou Hamer*, 9.

82. Christopher J. Lebron, *The Making of Black Lives Matter: A Brief History of an Idea* (Cambridge: Oxford University Press, 2017), 27–28.

83. Ida B. Wells-Barnett, "How Enfranchisement Stops Lynchings," *Original Rights Magazine* 1, no. 4 (June 1910): 42–53.

84. Lebron, *The Making of Black Lives Matter*, 28.

85. Hamer, "'We're On Our Way,'" 55.

86. Fannie Lou Hamer, "'Nobody's Free Until Everybody's Free,' Speech Delivered at the Founding of the National Women's Political Caucus, Washington, D.C., July 10, 1971," in *The Speeches of Fannie Lou Hamer*, 136.

87. Hamer, "'I'm Sick and Tired of Being Sick and Tired,'" 62.

88. Hamer, "'I'm Sick and Tired of Being Sick and Tired,'" 63.

89. *The Life of Fannie Lou Hamer: Never Turn Back*, dir. Bill Buckley (1983; Rediscovery Productions, 2011).

90. Hamer, "'Nobody's Free Until Everybody's Free,'" 136.

91. Fannie Lou Hamer, "'What Have We to Hail?,' Speech Delivered in Kentucky, Summer 1968," in *The Speeches of Fannie Lou Hamer*, 82.

92. Hamer, "'What Have We to Hail?,'" 82.

93. Michael J. Pfeifer, ed., *Global Lynching and Collective Violence: Volume 2: The Americas and Europe* (Urbana: University of Illinois Press, 2017).

94. Neil R. McMillen, *Dark Journey: Black Mississippians in the Age of Jim Crow* (Urbana: University of Illinois Press, 1989), 229–30.

95. The specific location of Till's murder is unknown. However, it is likely that it took place in Sunflower County. Devery Anderson, *Emmett Till: The Murder that Shocked the World and Propelled the Civil Rights Movement* (Jackson: University Press of Mississippi, 2015), 94; and Timothy B. Tyson, *The Blood of Emmett Till* (New York: Simon & Schuster, 2017), 64, 123–24.

96. Tyson, *The Blood of Emmett Till*, 5–7.

97. Tyson, *The Blood of Emmett Till*, 51–55.

98. Anderson, Emmett Till, 276–77; Chris Myers Asch, *The Senator and the Sharecropper: The Freedom Struggles of James O. Eastland and Fannie Lou Hamer* (New York: New Press, 2008), 167; "What Happened to the Key Figures in the Emmett Till Case?," *Clarion Ledger*, September 13, 2018, https://www.clarionledger.com/story/news/2018/09/13/what-happened-key-figures-emmett-till-case/1275626002.

99. Fannie Lou Hamer, "Testimony Before the Subcommittee on Elections of the Committee on House Administration, House of Representatives, Washington, D.C., September 13, 1965," in *The Speeches of Fannie Lou Hamer*, 68.

100. Hamer, "'Nobody's Free Until Everybody's Free,'" 136.

101. *The Life of Fannie Lou Hamer: Never Turn Back*, dir. Bill Buckley.

102. Hamer, "'We're On Our Way,'" 52.

103. Hamer, "'We're On Our Way,'" 52.

CHAPTER TWO: TELL IT LIKE IT IS

1. Hamer, "'I'm Sick and Tired of Being Sick and Tired,'" 62.

2. Ryan Grim, "The Transcript of Sandra Bland's Arrest Is as Revealing as the Video," *Huffington Post*, July 22, 2015, https://www.huffpost.com/entry/sandra-bland-arrest-transcript_n_55b03a88e4b0a9b94853b1f1.

3. Abby Ohlheiser and Abby Phillip, "'I Will Light You Up!' Texas Officer Threatened Sandra Bland with Taser During Traffic Stop," *Washington Post*, July 22, 2015, https://www.washingtonpost.com/news/morning-mix/wp/2015/07/21/much-too-early-to-call-jail-cell-hanging-death-of-sandra-bland-suicide-da-says. In addition to the officer's dashcam video, the encounter was recorded on Bland's cell phone. However, it would take several years for the Waller County police to release the cell phone recording of Bland's arrest. At the time of the incident, the public was only made aware of the recording on the officer's dashcam.

4. Cristina Maza, "Did Bland Commit Suicide? 'Too Many Questions,' Texas Officials Say," *Christian Science Monitor*, July 21, 2015, https://www.csmonitor.com/USA/USA-Update/2015/0721/Did-Sandra-Bland-commit-suicide-Too-many-questions-Texas-officials-say. Also, see the documentary *Say Her Name: The Life and Death of Sandra Bland*, dir. Kate Davis and David Heilbroner (HBO Documentary Films, 2018).

5. Amina Khan, "Getting Killed by Police Is a Leading Cause of Death for Young Black Men in America," *Los Angeles Times*, August 15, 2019, https://www.latimes.com/science/story/2019–08–15/police-shootings-are-a-leading-cause-of-death-for-black-men.

6. Andrea J. Ritchie, *Invisible No More: Police Violence Against Black Women and Women of Color* (Boston: Beacon Press, 2017). The #SayHerName movement, launched in 2015, sheds light on Black women's vulnerability to state-sanctioned violence.

7. Mari Haywood, "Philadelphia LGBT Community Asks What—Or Who—Killed Transgender Woman Nizah Morris 10 Years Ago,"

GLAAD, April 23, 2013, https://www.glaad.org/blog/philadelphia-lgbt -community-asks-what-or-who-killed-transgender-woman-nizah -morris-10-years-ago.

8. Matthew Speiser, "An 18-Year-Old Woman Was Found Dead in Her Jail Cell Last Week," *Business Insider,* July 22, 2015, https://www .businessinsider.com/kindra-chapman-died-in-police-custody-2015–7.

9. Aja Romano, "A Transgender Woman Was Shot in Baltimore and No One Is Talking About It," Daily Dot, March 1, 2020, https://www .dailydot.com/irl/transgender-sex-worker-mya-hall-death-nsa.

10. Kimberlé Crenshaw, Andrea Ritchie, et al., *Say Her Name Report: Resisting Police Brutality Against Black Women* (African American Policy Forum, Center for Intersectionality and Social Policy Studies, July 2015), https://aapf.org/sayhernamereport.

11. Aaron E. Carroll, "Doctors and Racial Bias: Still a Long Way to Go," *New York Times,* February 25, 2019, https://www.nytimes.com/2019 /02/25/upshot/doctors-and-racial-bias-still-a-long-way-to-go.html.

12. Kidada Williams, *They Left Great Marks on Me: African American Testimonies of Racial Violence from Emancipation to World War I* (New York: New York University Press, 2012), 6.

13. On Hamer's early life, see Lee, *For Freedom's Sake,* 1–22.

14. Hamer's recollection of this event is filled with some inaccuracies. Although she notes that Pullum was lynched in 1925, he was actually lynched two years prior—on December 14, 1923. Hamer biographer Maegan Parker Brooks also points out that Hamer was most likely not a witness to this lynching but would have become aware of this story later in life. The story of Pullum's lynching circulated widely in the region. See Brooks, *Fannie Lou Hamer,* 18–19.

15. Hamer incorrectly recalled Joe's last name as "Pulliam" in oral histories.

16. O'Dell, "Life in Mississippi: An Interview with Fannie Lou Hamer," 233. On O'Dell, see Jack O'Dell and Nikhil Pal Singh, *Climbing Jacob's Ladder: The Black Freedom Movement Writings of Jack O'Dell* (Berkeley: University of California Press, 2012).

17. O'Dell, "Life in Mississippi: An Interview with Fannie Lou Hamer," 233.

18. Litwack, *Been in the Storm So Long.*

19. McMillen, *Dark Journey,* 229. Of this number, twenty-three of the victims were white men and one was a white woman.

20. McMillen, *Dark Journey,* 229.

21. Ida B. Wells-Barnett, *The Red Record: Tabulated Statistics and Alleged Causes of Lynching in the United States* (Chicago: Donohue & Henneberry Printers, 1895).

22. Paula Giddings, *Ida: A Sword Among Lions; Ida B. Wells and the Campaign Against Lynching* (New York: Amistad, 2008); Mia Bay, *To Tell the Truth Freely: The Life of Ida B. Wells* (New York: Hill and Wang, 2010); and Michelle Duster, *Ida B. the Queen: The Extraordinary Life and Legacy of Ida B. Wells* (Miami: Atria/One Signal, 2021).

23. Ida B. Wells, *Crusade for Justice: The Autobiography of Ida B. Wells,* ed. Alfreda Duster, 2nd ed. (Chicago: University of Chicago Press,

2020), 267; and Kristina DuRocher, *Ida B. Wells: Social Activist and Reformer* (New York: Routledge, 2016), 279.

24. Brooks, *A Voice That Could Stir an Army*, 19.
25. O'Dell, "Life in Mississippi: An Interview with Fannie Lou Hamer," 233.
26. O'Dell, "Life in Mississippi: An Interview with Fannie Lou Hamer," 234.
27. DeMuth, "Fannie Lou Hamer: Tired of Being Sick and Tired."
28. DeMuth, "Fannie Lou Hamer: Tired of Being Sick and Tired."
29. Brooks, *A Voice That Could Stir an Army*, 36–37.
30. Payne, *I've Got the Light of Freedom*.
31. Brooks, *A Voice That Could Stir an Army*, 37.
32. Hamer, interview by McMillen, 6.
33. Fannie Lou Hamer, "'We're on Our Way,' Speech Delivered at a Mass Meeting in Indianola, Mississippi, September 1964," in *The Speeches of Fannie Lou Hamer*, 47.
34. Brooks, *A Voice That Could Stir an Army*, 38.
35. Hamer, "'America Is a Sick Place, and Man Is on the Critical List,'" 108.
36. Hamer, "'America Is a Sick Place, and Man Is on the Critical List,'" 108.
37. Hamer, "'America Is a Sick Place, and Man Is on the Critical List,'" 108.
38. Hamer, "'I'm Sick and Tired of Being Sick and Tired,'" 59.
39. Hamer, "'I'm Sick and Tired of Being Sick and Tired,'" 59.
40. Hamer, interview by McMillen, 5.
41. Fannic Lou Hamer, "'To Tell It Like It Is,' Speech Delivered at the Holmes County, Mississippi, Freedom Democratic Party Municipal Elections Rally in Lexington, Mississippi, May 8, 1969," in *The Speeches of Fannie Lou Hamer*, 90–91.
42. Bridgett A. King, *Voting Rights in America: Primary Documents in Context* (Santa Barbara, California: ABC-CLIO, 2019), 137.
43. "Fannie Lou Was 'Tired' of Racial Discrimination," *Baltimore Afro-American*, March 26, 1977.
44. Fannie Lou Hamer, "Testimony Before a Select Panel on Mississippi and Civil Rights, Washington, D.C., June 8, 1964," in *The Speeches of Fannie Lou Hamer*, 37.
45. Hamer, *To Praise Our Bridges*, 12.
46. Egerton, *A Mind to Stay Here*, 98.
47. Lee, *For Freedom's Sake*, 49–52.
48. Bracey, *Fannie Lou Hamer*, 85.
49. Bracey, *Fannie Lou Hamer*, 85.
50. Phyl Garland, "Builders of a New South: Negro Heroines of Dixie Play Major Role in Challenging Racist Traditions," *Ebony*, August 1966, 30.
51. O'Dell, "Life in Mississippi: An Interview with Fannie Lou Hamer," 234.
52. Danielle McGuire, *At the Dark End of the Street: Black Women, Rape, and Resistance—A New History of the Civil Rights Movement from Rosa Parks to the Rise of Black Power* (New York: Alfred A. Knopf, 2010); Williams, *They Left Great Marks on Me*.
53. Lee, *For Freedom's Sake*, 58–59. For an in-depth examination of Hamer's public accounts of the Winona beating, see Davis W. Houck,

"Fannie Lou Hamer on Winona: Memory, Trauma, and Recovery," in Richard J. Jensen, ed., *Social Controversy and Public Address in the 1960s and Early 1970s: A Rhetorical History of the United States,* Vol. IX (East Lansing: Michigan State University, 2017), 1–38.

54. Houck, "Fannie Lou Hamer on Winona: Memory, Trauma, and Recovery," 27.

55. Hamer, "'America Is a Sick Place, and Man Is on the Critical List,'" 113.

56. Hamer, "'America Is a Sick Place, and Man Is on the Critical List,'" 113.

57. McGuire, *At the Dark End of the Street.*

58. Fannie Lou Hamer, interview by Robert Wright, August 9, 1968, Oral History Collection, Civil Rights Documentation Project, Moorland–Spingarn Research Center, Howard University, Washington, DC, quoted in Lee, *For Freedom's Sake,* 40.

59. Hamer, "'America Is a Sick Place, and Man Is on the Critical List,'" 111.

60. Bracey, *Fannie Lou Hamer,* 88.

61. Bracey, *Fannie Lou Hamer,* 41.

62. Lee, *For Freedom's Sake,* 81.

63. Washington, *Medical Apartheid,* 189.

64. Brooks, *Fannie Lou Hamer,* 30.

65. Brooks, *Fannie Lou Hamer,* 30.

66. William Bradford Huie, "The Shocking Story of Approved Killing in Mississippi," *Look,* January 24, 1956. For an examination of this confession, its impact, and an investigation into the facts of Till's lynching, see Anderson, Emmett Till; Dave Tell, "Confession and Race: Civil Rights, Segregation, and the Murder of Emmett Till," in *Confessional Crises and Cultural Politics in Twentieth-Century America* (University Park: Penn State University Press, 2015), 63–90.

67. Bracey, *Fannie Lou Hamer,* 42; Brooks, *Fannie Lou Hamer,* 27.

68. Thomas W. Volscho, "Sterilization Racism and Pan-Ethnic Disparities of the Past Decade: The Continued Encroachment on Reproductive Rights," *Wicazo Sa Review* 25 (Spring 2010): 17–31.

69. Dorothy Roberts, *Killing the Black Body: Race, Reproduction, and the Meaning of Liberty* (New York: Vintage, 1998), 72–73.

70. Roberts, *Killing the Black Body,* 8; Kim Severson, "Thousands Sterilized, A State Weighs Restitution," *New York Times,* December 9, 2011, https://www.nytimes.com/2011/12/10/us/redress-weighed-for-forced-sterilizations-in-north-carolina.html.

71. Roberts, *Killing the Black Body;* Jennifer Nelson, *Women of Color and the Reproductive Rights Movement* (New York: New York University Press, 2003); McGuire, *At the Dark End of the Street.* On medical activism in the Black community, see Alondra Nelson, *Body and Soul: The Black Panther Party and the Fight Against Medical Discrimination* (Minneapolis: University of Minnesota Press, 2011).

72. Washington, *Medical Apartheid,* 205.

73. Kelly Fulkerson Dikuua, "[Un]informed Consent: Eugenics, Forced Sterilization and Medical Violence in the Jim Crow United States and Apartheid Southern Africa" (PhD diss., Ohio State University, 2019).

74. Rebecca M. Kluchin, *Fit to Be Tied: Sterilization and Reproductive Rights in America, 1950–1980* (New Brunswick, NJ: Rutgers University Press, 2011), 177.

75. John Dittmer, *Local People: The Struggle for Civil Rights in Mississippi* (Urbana: University of Illinois Press, 1995), 118–19.

76. Hamer, "Testimony Before a Select Panel on Mississippi and Civil Rights," 41.

77. Hamer, "Testimony Before a Select Panel on Mississippi and Civil Rights," 41.

78. Anne Overbeck, *At the Heart of It All?: Discourses on the Reproductive Rights of African American Women in the 20th Century* (Berlin: De Gruyter Oldenbourg, 2019), 157.

79. Brooks-Higginbotham, *Righteous Discontent.*

80. Overbeck, *At the Heart of It All?*, 157.

81. Overbeck, *At the Heart of It All?*, 157.

82. Overbeck, *At the Heart of It All?*, 157.

83. Laura Woliver, *The Political Geographies of Pregnancy* (Chicago: University of Illinois, 2002), 86.

84. McGuire, *At the Dark End of the Street*, 192.

85. Lebron, *The Making of Black Lives Matter*, 1–34.

86. "Fannie Lou 'Tells It Like It Is,'" *Harvard Crimson*, November 23, 1968.

CHAPTER THREE: WE WANT LEADERS

1. Hamer, "'We're On Our Way,'" 54.

 2. Keisha N. Blain, "A Short History of Black Women and Police Violence," The Conversation, June 12, 2020, https://theconversation.com/a-short-history-of-black-women-and-police-violence-139937.

 3. Errin Haines, "Family Seeks Answers in Fatal Police Shooting of Louisville Woman in Her Apartment," *Washington Post*, May 11, 2020, https://www.washingtonpost.com/nation/2020/05/11/family-seeks-answers-fatal-police-shooting-louisville-woman-her-apartment.

 4. Taryn Finley, "#BirthdayForBreonna Initiative Marks What Would've Been Breonna Taylor's 27th Birthday," *Huffington Post*, June 5, 2020, https://www.huffpost.com/entry/breonna-taylor-birthday-remembrance_n_5ed953cfc5b67abc999475ff.

 5. Alisha Haridasaani Gupta, "Birthday for Breonna: A Campaign to Mourn and Honor," *New York Times*, June 6, 2020, https://www.nytimes.com/2020/06/06/us/birthday-breonna-taylor-black-lives-matter.html.

 6. Mary Retta, "Cate Young on Breonna Taylor's Birthday Memorial and the Fight For Justice for Black Women," *Teen Vouge*, June 5, 2020, https://www.teenvogue.com/story/cate-young-breonna-taylors-birthday-memorial.

 7. Finley, "#BirthdayForBreonna Initiative Marks What Would've Been Breonna Taylor's 27th Birthday."

 8. Gupta, "Birthday for Breonna: A Campaign to Mourn and Honor."

 9. Gupta, "Birthday for Breonna: A Campaign to Mourn and Honor."

10. Gupta, "Birthday for Breonna: A Campaign to Mourn and Honor"; Bianca Austin, "Justice for Breonna Taylor (official) (#BREEWAYY)," GoFundMe, August 4, 2020, https://www.gofundme.com/f/9v4q2 -justice-for-breonna-taylor.

11. Bianca Austin, "Justice for Breonna Taylor (official) (#BREEWAYY)."

12. Jason Slotkin, "Louisville's Police Department Fires an Officer Involved in Breonna Taylor's Death," NPR, June 19, 2020, https://www.npr.org /sections/live-updates-protests-for-racial-justice/2020/06/19/880864286/ louisvilles-police-department-fires-an-officer-involved-in-breonna-taylor -s-deat. In January 2021, the department terminated the two other officers involved in the shooting. See Dylan Lovan, "2 Detectives Involved in Breonna Taylor's Death Are Fired," Associated Press, January 6, 2021, https://apnews.com/article/breonna-taylor-cops-fired-910c87438 ebc09e74eac8a4f4678fb63; Marisa Iati, "Louisville Police Move to Fire Two More Officers Involved in Raid That Killed Breonna Taylor," *Washington Post*, December 29, 2020, https://www.washingtonpost .com/nation/2020/12/29/breonna-taylor-officers-fire.

13. Hamer, "'We're On Our Way,'" 55.

14. As a participant in the Highlander Folk School, an interracial leadership training school in Monteagle, Tennessee, Hamer was part of a network of dynamic Black women leaders in the civil rights movement, including Diane Nash, Septima Clark, and Rosa Parks. On Highlander, see David P. Levine, "The Birth of the Citizenship Schools: Entwining the Struggles for Literacy and Freedom," *History of Education Quarterly* 44, no. 3 (Autumn 2004): 388–414.

15. Hamer, interview by McMillen, 30.

16. Ransby, *Ella Baker and the Black Freedom Struggle*.

17. Payne, *I've Got the Light of Freedom*.

18. Wesley Hogan, *Many Minds, One Heart: SNCC's Dream for a New America* (Chapel Hill: University of North Carolina Press, 2007); and Howard Zinn, *SNCC: The New Abolitionists* (Boston: Beacon Press, 1964; Chicago: Haymarket Press, 2017).

19. Ransby, *Ella Baker and the Black Freedom Movement*, 245.

20. Ella Baker, "Bigger than a Hamburger," *Southern Patriot* 18 (June 1960).

21. Ransby, *Ella Baker and the Black Freedom Movement*, 6, 239.

22. Ransby, *Ella Baker and the Black Freedom Movement*, 300.

23. Jacqueline A. Rouse, "Examination of Black Female Grass Roots Leaders in Mississippi During the 1960s: Annie Devine, Fannie Lou Hamer and Annie Rankin," *Negro History Bulletin* 63, no. 1/4 (January–December 2000): 23–30; Belinda Robnett, *How Long? How Long? African American Women in the Struggle for Civil Rights* (New York: Oxford University Press, 1997).

24. Fannie Lou Hamer, interview by Anne and Howard Romaine, Anne Romaine Interviews, 1966–1967, November 1966, Ruleville, Mississippi, transcript, 2, Archives Main Stacks, SC 1069, Folder 1, WIHVR2050-A, Freedom Summer Digital Collection, Wisconsin Historical Society,

Madison, https://content.wisconsinhistory.org/digital/collection/p15932coll2/id/13726.

25. Hamer, interview by Anne and Howard Romaine, 2.

26. SNCC Legacy Project, "Our Mrs. Hamer."

27. Hamer, interview by Anne and Howard Romaine, 1–2.

28. Ransby, *Ella Baker and the Black Freedom Movement*, 304; Dittmer, *Local People*, 108.

29. Hogan, *Many Minds, One Heart*, 196.

30. Hamer, interview by Anne and Howard Romaine, 9.

31. Hamer, interview by Anne and Howard Romaine, 9.

32. Fannie Lou Hamer, "Testimony Before the Democratic Reform Committee, Jackson, Mississippi, May 22, 1969," in *The Speeches of Fannie Lou Hamer*, 97.

33. Hamer, "'I'm Sick and Tired of Being Sick and Tired,'" 62.

34. "Fannie Hamer Mourned," *Los Angeles Sentinel*, March 24, 1977.

35. Fannie Lou Hamer, "'The Only Thing We Can Do Is to Work Together,' Speech Delivered at a Chapter Meeting of the National Council of Negro Women in Mississippi, 1967," in *The Speeches of Fannie Lou Hamer*, 73.

36. Hamer, "'We're On Our Way,'" 54.

37. Hamer, "'We're On Our Way,'" 49.

38. Hamer, "'We're On Our Way,'" 55.

39. Hamer, "'We're On Our Way,'" 56.

40. Hamer, "'To Tell It Like It Is,'" 93.

41. Hamer, "It's in Your Hands," 613.

42. Aldridge, "What Makes Fannie Lou Hamer Run?"

43. Aldridge, "What Makes Fannie Lou Hamer Run?" Hamer discusses the incident with Wilkins in her 1966 interview with Anne and Howard Romaine. See Hamer, interview by Anne and Howard Romaine, 5.

44. On Parks, see Jeanne Theoharis, *The Rebellious Life of Mrs. Rosa Parks* (Boston: Beacon Press, 2013), 234; on Richardson, see Joseph Fitzgerald, *The Struggle Is Eternal: Gloria Richardson and Black Liberation* (Lexington: University of Kentucky Press, 2019); on Baker, see Ransby, *Ella Baker and the Black Freedom Movement*.

45. Fannie Lou Hamer, "'If the Name of the Game Is Survive, Survive,' Speech Delivered in Ruleville, Mississippi, September 27, 1971," in *The Speeches of Fannie Lou Hamer*, 143.

46. Hamer, "'What Have We to Hail?,'" 83.

47. Howard Allen, "Prep for 'Long Hot Summer': 300 College Students Train for 'Operation Mississippi,'" *Call and Post* (Cleveland), June 27, 1964.

48. Hamer, "'We Haven't Arrived Yet,' Presentation and Responses to Questions at the University of Wisconsin, Madison, Wisconsin, January 29, 1976," in *The Speeches of Fannie Lou Hamer*, 184.

49. Hamer, "If the Name of the Game Is Survive, Survive,'" 142.

50. Keisha N. Blain, *Set the World on Fire: Black Nationalist Women and the Global Struggle for Freedom* (Philadelphia: University of Pennsylvania Press, 2018), 3.

51. Hamer, "'If the Name of the Game Is Survive, Survive,'" 143.
52. Hamer, "'If the Name of the Game Is Survive, Survive,'" 143. Emphasis in the original.
53. Hamer, interview by Anne and Howard Romaine, 2.
54. Brooks and Houck, eds., *The Speeches of Fannie Lou Hamer*, 3.
55. William H. Lawson, *No Small Thing: The 1963 Mississippi Freedom Vote* (Jackson: University Press of Mississippi, 2018).
56. Vicki Crawford, "African American Women in the Mississippi Freedom Democratic Party," in *Sisters in the Struggle: African American Women in the Civil Rights–Black Power Movement*, eds. Bettye Collier-Thomas and V. P. Franklin (New York: New York University Press, 2001), 123.
57. Mills, *This Little Light of Mine*, 105; Crawford, "African American Women in the Mississippi Freedom Democratic Party," 121–38.
58. Mills, *This Little Light of Mine*, 105.
59. "The Mississippi Freedom Democratic Party; Considerations Underlying the Development of the Mississippi Freedom Democratic Party," Baker—Ella Baker Papers, 1959–1965, Archives Main Stacks, SC 628, WIHVB490-A, Freedom Summer Digital Collection, Wisconsin Historical Society, Madison, https://content.wisconsinhistory.org/digital/collection/p15932coll2/id/18091.
60. "The Mississippi Freedom Democratic Party; Considerations Underlying the Development of the Mississippi Freedom Democratic Party," Ella Baker Papers, 1959–1965, 2.
61. Hamer, "'What Have We to Hail?,'" 77.
62. Hamer, "'To Tell It Like It Is,'" 89.
63. Hamer, interview by Anne and Howard Romaine, 5.
64. Lisa Anderson Todd, *For a Voice and the Vote: My Journey with the Mississippi Freedom Democratic Party* (Lexington: University Press of Kentucky, 2014), 241.
65. Hamer, "'What Have We to Hail?,'" 77.
66. Mills, *This Little Light of Mine*, 121–22, 127–30. It is significant to note that they wanted the two seats to be occupied by Aaron Henry, an African American activist, and Rev. Ed King, a white minister, to show an "integrated" compromise.
67. Hamer, interview by McMillen, 15.
68. "CORE Says: 'Fight Fire with Fire . . . ': New Era In: Non-Violent Tactics . . .," *Norfolk Journal and Guide*, July 9, 1966.
69. Morgan Ginther, "The Mississippi Delegation Debate at the 1964 Democratic National Convention: An Interview with Former Vice President Walter Mondale," *Southern Cultures* 20, no. 4 (Winter 2014): 108.
70. Hamer, interview by Anne and Howard Romaine, 23.
71. Hamer, "'What Have We to Hail?,'" 78.
72. Hamer, interview by Anne and Howard Romaine, 8.
73. Lee, *For Freedom's Sake*, 87–90; Mills, *This Little Light of Mine*, 128–129.

74. Hamer, interview by Anne and Howard Romaine, 10.

75. Mills, *This Little Light of Mine*, 125.

76. Lee, *For Freedom's Sake*, 91–92.

77. Fannie Lou Hamer, interview by Robert Wright, August 9, 1968, Oral History Collection, Civil Rights Documentation Project, Moorland–Spingarn Research Center, Howard University, Washington, DC, quoted in Lee, *For Freedom's Sake*, 98.

78. Brooks, *Fannie Lou Hamer*, 84.

79. Hamer, interview by Anne and Howard Romaine, 11.

80. Lee, *For Freedom's Sake*, 92.

81. Hamer, interview by Anne and Howard Romaine, 7–8.

82. Mills, *This Little Light of Mine*, 129–30.

83. Mills, *This Little Light of Mine*, 32.

84. Hamer, interview by Anne and Howard Romaine, 12.

85. Ginther, "The Mississippi Delegation Debate at the 1964 Democratic National Convention," 111.

86. Jackie Robinson, "Tribute to Mississippi Negroes," Jackie Robinson Says, *Tri-State Defender*, September 12, 1964.

87. Aram Goudsouzian, *Down to the Crossroads: Civil Rights, Black Power, and the Meredith March Against Fear* (New York: Farrar, Straus and Giroux, 2015); James Meredith, *Three Years in Mississippi* (Jackson: University Press of Mississippi, 2019).

88. "Mississippi Story: The Word Is Fear Pressures in the Movement Laws and Rights," *New York Times*, June 12, 1966, https://www.nytimes.com/1966/06/12/archives/mississippi-story-the-word-is-fear-pressures-in-the-movement-laws.html.

89. Brooks, *Fannie Lou Hamer*, 113.

90. Mills, *This Little Light of Mine*, 177.

91. The 1966 Civil Rights Bill was ultimately defeated in the US Senate.

92. Goudsouzian, *Down to the Crossroads*, 24.

93. Akinyele Umoja, *We Will Shoot Back: Armed Resistance in the Mississippi Freedom Movement* (New York: New York University Press, 2014); and Charles E. Cobb Jr., *This Nonviolent Stuff'll Get You Killed: How Guns Made the Civil Rights Movement Possible* (Oxford: Oxford University Press, 2014).

94. Brooks, *Fannie Lou Hamer*, 115.

95. Peniel E. Joseph, *Stokely: A Life* (New York: Basic Civitas, 2014), 99, 114–15.

96. Hamer, "'If the Name of the Game Is Survive, Survive,'" 142.

97. Carlotta Washington, "Freedom Fighter Still Seeking Human Right," *Call and Post*, February 28, 1970.

98. Robert Moses, interview by Blackside, Inc., *Eyes on the Prize: America's Civil Rights Years (1954–1965)*, May 19, 1986, Henry Hampton Collection, Film and Media Archive, Washington University Libraries, St. Louis, http://repository.wustl.edu/concern/file_sets/j3860870r.

CHAPTER FOUR: THE SPECIAL PLIGHT OF BLACK WOMEN

1. Hamer, "It's in Your Hands," 613.
2. Megan Thee Stallion, "Why I Speak Up for Black Women," *New York Times,* October 13, 2020, https://www.nytimes.com/2020/10/13/opinion/megan-thee-stallion-black-women.html.
3. Bethonie Butler, "Megan Thee Stallion Was Mocked After Being Shot. As She Reclaims the Narrative, Black Women Recognize Her Pain," *Washington Post,* July 31, 2020, https://www.washingtonpost.com /arts-entertainment/2020/07/31/megan-thee-stallion.
4. Julia Craven, "Violence Against Black Women Is Not a Meme," Slate, July 30, 2020, https://slate.com/news-and-politics/2020/07/memes-of -megan-thee-stallion-shooting.html.
5. Stallion, "Why I Speak Up for Black Women."
6. Beverly Guy-Sheftall, ed., *Words of Fire: An Anthology of African-American Feminist Thought* (New York: New Press, 1995); Patricia Hill-Collins, *Black Feminist Thought: Knowledge, Consciousness, and the Politics of Empowerment* (New York: Routledge, 2000); Stephen Ward, "Third World Women's Alliance: Black Feminist Radicalism and Black Power Politics," in *The Black Power Movement: Rethinking the Civil Rights–Black Power Era,* ed. Peniel E. Joseph (New York: Routledge, 2006), 119–44.
7. Stallion, "Why I Speak Up for Black Women."
8. Ashley D. Farmer, *Remaking Black Power: How Black Women Transformed an Era* (Chapel Hill: University of North Carolina Press, 2017), 71.
9. Toni Morrison, "What the Black Woman Thinks About Women's Lib," *New York Times,* August 22, 1971.
10. Mills, *This Little Light of Mine,* 273.
11. Erik S. McDuffie, *Sojourning for Freedom: Black Women, American Communism, and the Making of Black Left Feminism* (Durham, NC: Duke University Press, 2011), 24.
12. Hamer, "'We're On Our Way,'" 55.
13. Hamer, "'We're On Our Way,'" 55.
14. Hamer, "Testimony Before the Democratic Reform Committee, Jackson, Mississippi, May 22, 1969," 96.
15. Kali Nicole Gross, *Colored Amazons: Crime, Violence, and Black Women in the City of Brotherly Love, 1880–1910* (Durham, NC: Duke University Press, 2006).
16. Mills, *This Little Light of Mine,* 232–33.
17. Wes Watkins, interview by Kay Wright Mills, Washington, DC, December 26, 1989, quoted in *This Little Light of Mine,* 233.
18. For information on Claudia Jones and Louise Thompson Patterson, see McDuffie, *Sojourning for Freedom.*
19. Hamer, "It's in Your Hands," 613.
20. Martha S. Jones, *The Vanguard: How Black Women Broke Barriers, Won the Vote, and Insisted on Equality for All* (New York: Basic Books, 2020).

21. Franklynn Peterson, "Fannie Lou Hamer: Mother of 'Black Women's Lib,'" *Sepia* 21 (December 1972): 16.

22. Bonnie J. Morris and D-M Withers, *The Feminist Revolution: The Struggle for Women's Liberation* (London: Virago, 2018); Rosalyn Baxandall and Linda Gordon, eds., *Dear Sisters: Dispatches from the Women's Liberation Movement* (New York: Basic Books, 2000); Kathleen C. Berkeley, *The Women's Liberation Movement in America* (Westport, CT: Greenwood Press, 1999); and Guy-Sheftall, *Words of Fire*.

23. Betty Friedan, *The Feminine Mystique* (New York: W. W. Norton, 1963). Also see bell hooks, *Feminist Theory: From Margin to Center* (Boston: South End Press, 1984).

24. Hamer, "'Nobody's Free Until Everybody's Free,'" 136.

25. Hamer, "It's in Your Hands," 612.

26. Hamer, "'America Is a Sick Place, and Man Is on the Critical List,'" 107.

27. Aldridge, "What Makes Fannie Lou Hamer Run?"

28. Mills, *This Little Light of Mine*, 270; Bracey, *Fannie Lou Hamer*, 149–52.

29. On Victorian ideals, see Martha Vicinus, ed., *Suffer and Be Still: Women in the Victorian Age* (Bloomington: Indiana University Press, 1972); Nancy Cott, *The Bonds of Womanhood: "Women's Sphere" in New England, 1780–1835* (New Haven, CT: Yale University Press, 1977); Glenna Matthews, *Just a Housewife: The Rise and Fall of Domesticity in American Society* (London: Oxford University Press, 1987).

30. Annette Samuels, "Fannie Lou Hamer," People Profiled, *New York Amsterdam News*, February 12, 1977. The article quotes from an earlier interview Hamer gave to the newspaper in the summer of 1976.

31. Samuels, "Fannie Lou Hamer."

32. Hamer, "'Is It Too Late?,'" 133.

33. Hamer, "'Is It Too Late?,'" 133.

34. Blain, *Set the World on Fire*, 85.

35. Shirley Chisholm, telephone interview by Kay Wright Mills, Williamsville, NY, January 19, 1990, quoted in Mills, *This Little Light of Mine*, 277.

36. Fannie Lou Hamer, "Fannie Lou Hamer Speaks Out," *Essence* 2, no. 6 (October 1971): 75.

37. Hamer, "Fannie Lou Hamer Speaks Out," 75.

38. Theoharis, *The Rebellious Life of Mrs. Rosa Parks*, 226.

39. "Nixon Intervenes: Senseless Killing Stirs Anger of Mississippi Blacks," *Call and Post*, June 5, 1971.

40. Mills, *This Little Light of Mine*, 282–84.

41. "Same Old Thing, Same Old Place; Murdered Girl Buried in Miss.," *Jet*, June 17, 1971, 12.

42. "Another Miss. Killing Brings Blacks Together," *New York Amsterdam News*, June 5, 1971.

43. "3 Arrested in Slaying of Black Girl," *Bay State Banner* (Boston), June 3, 1971.

44. "Nixon Intervenes: Senseless Killing Stirs Anger of Mississippi Blacks."

45. Lee, *For Freedom's Sake*, 169–70.

46. Hamer, "'Is It Too Late?,'" 133.

47. Mills, *This Little Light of Mine*, 282–83.

48. "Same Old Thing, Same Old Place; Murdered Girl Buried in Miss.," 14; Jo Etha Collier Building Fund to Bank of Ruleville, September 13, 1971, Box 1, Folder 2, "Correspondence, 1968, 1971 October," Fannie Lou Hamer Papers, Amistad Research Center at Tulane University, New Orleans.

49. "Same Old Thing, Same Old Place; Murdered Girl Buried in Miss.," 14.

50. Jo Etha Collier Building Fund to Bank of Ruleville, September 13, 1971, Box 1, Folder 2; David Bond to Hamer, September 3, 1971, Box 1, Folder 2, "Correspondence, 1968, 1971 October"; Lotta A. Hempel to Hamer, July 13, 1971, Box 10, Folder 3, "Correspondence, 1971"; Hamer to Robert S. Brown, August 23, 1971, Box 10, Folder 3, "Correspondence, 1971," Fannie Lou Hamer Papers, Amistad Research Center at Tulane University, New Orleans.

51. Check Made Out to Gussie Mae Love, November 1, 1972, Box 14, Folder 14, "Cancelled Checks, 1972"; Farm Operation Account, Freedom Farm Corporation (see "other expense" for Gussie Mae Love, Box 11, Folder 3, "Expense Statements"); David Bond to Hamer, September 3, 1971, Box 1, Folder 2, "Correspondence, 1968, 1971 October"; Lotta A. Hempel to Hamer, July 13, 1971, Box 10, Folder 3, "Correspondence, 1971," Fannie Lou Hamer Papers, Amistad Research Center at Tulane University, New Orleans.

52. Hamer, "'Nobody's Free Until Everybody's Free,'" 136.

53. Hamer, "'Nobody's Free Until Everybody's Free,'" 136.

54. "White Convicted in Slaying of Girl: Gets 20 Years in Shooting of Negro in Mississippi," *New York Times*, October 30, 1971.

55. Jason Berry, *Amazing Grace: With Charles Evers in Mississippi* (New York: Saturday Review Press, 1978), 292, quoted in Mills, *This Little Light of Mine*, 287.

56. Fitzgerald, *The Struggle Is Eternal*, 132.

57. Linda Gordon, *The Moral Property of Women: A History of Birth Control Politics in America*, rev. ed. (Urbana: University of Illinois Press, 2002) 160–62.

58. Sherie Randolph, *Florynce "Flo" Kennedy: The Life of a Black Feminist Radical* (Chapel Hill: University of North Carolina Press, 2018), 169.

59. Randolph, *Florynce "Flo" Kennedy*, 169.

60. Hamer, "'Nobody's Free Until Everybody's Free,'" 122.

61. Lee, *For Freedom's Sake*, 21–22, 172.

62. Samuel Yette, "Mrs. Fannie Lou Hamer Was Tough Fighter," *Baltimore Afro-American*, April 2, 1977.

63. Mills, *This Little Light of Mine*, 274. Also see Pamela Bridgewater, Lynn Roberts, Whitney Peoples, Erika Derkas, and Loretta Ross, eds.,

Radical Reproductive Justice: Foundation, Theory, Practice, Critique (New York: First Feminist Press, 2017).

64. Ethel L. Payne, "So This Is Washington," *Chicago Defender* (Daily Edition), December 18, 1969.
65. Payne, "So This Is Washington."
66. Hamer, "'Is It Too Late?,'" 133.
67. Simone M. Caron, "Birth Control and the Black Community in the 1960s: Genocide or Power Politics," *Journal of Social History* 31, no. 3 (Spring 1998): 545–69.
68. Hamer, "'Nobody's Free Until Everybody's Free,'" 122.
69. Caron, "Birth Control and the Black Community in the 1960s," 547–49; Nelson, *Women of Color and the Reproductive Rights Movement*, 106–7.
70. Combahee River Collective, *The Combahee River Collective Statement: Black Feminist Organizing in the Seventies and Eighties*, Freedom Organizing Series (Albany, NY: Kitchen Table/Women of Color Press, 1986). See also Keeanga-Yamahtta Taylor, *How We Get Free: Black Feminism and the Combahee River Collective* (Chicago: Haymarket, 2017).
71. Margaret Tarter, "150 Picket in Support of Abortion Funding," *Bay State Banner*, August 18, 1977, 1. On the Combahee River Collective, see Taylor, *How We Get Free*.
72. Mills, *This Little Light of Mine*, 273.
73. Hamer, "It's in Your Hands," 609.
74. Hamer, "It's in Your Hands," 610.
75. Hamer, "It's in Your Hands," 610.
76. Stephanie E. Jones-Rogers, *They Were Her Property: White Women as Slave Owners in the American South* (New Haven, CT: Yale University Press, 2019).
77. Hamer, "It's in Your Hands," 610.
78. Thavolia Glymph, *Out of the House of Bondage: The Transformation of the Plantation Household* (Cambridge: Cambridge University Press, 2012); and Rebecca Sharpless, *Cooking in Other Women's Kitchens: Domestic Workers in the South, 1865–1960* (Chapel Hill: University of North Carolina Press, 2010).
79. Hamer, "It's in Your Hands," 610.
80. Keisha N. Blain, "What Americans Still Owe Fannie Lou Hamer," CNN Opinion, August 26, 2020, https://www.cnn.com/2020/08/26/opinions/fannie-lou-hamer-legacy-voting-rights-blain/index.html. For more information on the founding of the NWPC, see "Early History," National Women's Political Caucus, https://www.nwpc.org/about.
81. Mills, *This Little Light of Mine*, 275.
82. Lee, *For Freedom's Sake*, 170.
83. Mills, *This Little Light of Mine*, 275; Ethel L. Payne, "Women Gird for Action," *Chicago Defender* (Daily Edition), July 15, 1971.
84. Peterson, "Fannie Lou Hamer: Mother of 'Black Women's Lib,'" 16.
85. Hamer, "'Nobody's Free Until Everybody's Free,'" 135.
86. Hamer, "'Nobody's Free Until Everybody's Free,'" 137.

87. Hamer, "'Nobody's Free Until Everybody's Free,'" 135.

88. Hamer, "'Nobody's Free Until Everybody's Free,'" 136.

89. On Combahee, see Taylor, *How We Get Free*. For an overview of the history of the Third World Women's Alliance, see Kimberly Springer, *Living for the Revolution: Black Feminist Organizations, 1968–1980* (Durham: Duke University Press, 2005). It is significant to note that the Third World Women's Alliance (TWWA) originally began as the Black Women's Liberation Committee (as part of SNCC) in December 1968. They adopted the name TWWA in 1970.

90. Hamer, "'Nobody's Free Until Everybody's Free,'" 136.

91. Payne, "Women Gird for Action."

92. For an overview on Chisholm's approach to politics in this era, see Anastasia Curwood, "Black Feminism on Capitol Hill: Shirley Chisholm and Movement Politics, 1968–1984," *Meridians: Feminism, Race, Transnationalism* 13, no. 1 (2015).

93. Curwood, "Black Feminism on Capitol Hill," 205.

94. Chisholm, interview by Mills, quoted in Mills, *This Little Light of Mine*, 277.

95. Chisholm, interview by Mills, quoted in Mills, *This Little Light of Mine*, 277.

96. Chisholm, interview by Mills, quoted in Mills, *This Little Light of Mine*, 277.

97. Lee, *For Freedom's Sake*, 170.

98. Ellen DuBois, *Feminism and Suffrage: The Emergence of an Independent Women's Movement in America, 1848–1869* (Ithaca, NY: Cornell University Press, 1978).

99. Eileen Shanahan, "Caucus to Seek Equal Number of Women Convention Delegates," *New York Times*, November 10, 1971.

100. "Cleveland NCNW Chapter to Host Regional," *Call and Post*, March 29, 1969.

101. Washington, "Freedom Fighter Still Seeking Human Right."

102. Lee, *For Freedom's Sake*, 172–73.

103. Mills, *This Little Light of Mine*, 286.

104. Mills, *This Little Light of Mine*, 285–86.

105. Mills, *This Little Light of Mine*, 287.

106. Fannie Lou Hamer, "Seconding Speech for the Nomination of Frances Farenthold," in *The Speeches of Fannie Lou Hamer*, 146.

107. Toni Anthony, "Black Women Map New Plans for Action," *Chicago Defender* (Daily Edition), January 11, 1972; Toni Anthony, "National Women's Confab in Chicago," *Chicago Defender* (Big Weekend Edition), January 8, 1972.

108. John H. Britton Jr., "Black Women in Politics: Do We Have a Future?" *Essence* 5, no. 11 (March 1975): 80–81, 90.

109. Britton, "Black Women in Politics," 80.

110. Britton, "Black Women in Politics," 81. Other reports cite 336 women. See, for example, Ethel Payne, "Women in Politics," *Call and Post*, November 3, 1973.

CHAPTER FIVE: AN EXPANSIVE VISION OF FREEDOM

1. Egerton, *A Mind to Stay Here*, 101.
2. Errol Nazareth, "Jermaine Carby Inquest Jury Makes 14 Recommendations Following 2014 Shooting Death," CBC News, May 26, 2016, https://www.cbc.ca/news/canada/toronto/jermaine-carby-inquest-1.3601734.
3. Keisha N. Blain, "On 'Transpacific Antiracism': An Interview with Yuichiro Onishi," Black Perspectives, African American Intellectual History Society, February 26, 2015, https://www.aaihs.org/on-transpacific-racism-an-interview-with-yuichiro-onishi-2.
4. Amien Essif, "How Black Lives Matter Has Spread into a Global Movement to End Racist Policing," *In These Times*, June 29, 2015, http://inthesetimes.com/article/18042/black-lives-matter-in-europe-too.
5. Judith Ohikuare, "Meet the Women Who Created #BlackLivesMatter," *Cosmopolitan*, October 17, 2015, https://www.cosmopolitan.com/entertainment/a47842/the-women-behind-blacklivesmatter.
6. Patrisse Cullors, Opal Tometi, and Alicia Garza, "Black Lives Matter Founders Describe 'Paradigm Shift' in the Movement," interview by Ari Shapiro, *All Things Considered*, NPR, July 14, 2016, https://www.wvpublic.org/post/we-still-have-jim-crow-hate-black-lives-matter-founders-reflect-3-years#stream/0.
7. Lilly Workneh, "Black Lives Matter Calls for Global Change at United Nations Assembly," Black Voices, *Huffington Post*, July 21, 2016, https://www.huffpost.com/entry/black-lives-matter-calls-for-global-change-at-united-nations-assembly_n_57911e16e4b00c9876cc96df.
8. Rhiannon Walker, "What We Know About the Alton Sterling Shooting," The Undefeated, July 6, 2016, https://theundefeated.com/features/what-we-know-about-the-alton-sterling-shooting/; German Lopez, "Philando Castile Minnesota Police Shooting: Officer Cleared of Manslaughter Charge," Vox, June 16, 2017, https://www.vox.com/2016/7/7/12116288/minnesota-police-shooting-philando-castile-falcon-heights-video?__c=1.
9. "UN Experts Urge US to Address Legacies of the Past, Police Impunity and 'Crisis of Racial Injustice,'" UN News, January 29, 2016, https://news.un.org/en/story/2016/01/521182-un-experts-urge-us-address-legacies-past-police-impunity-and-crisis-racial.
10. "UN Experts Urge US to Address Legacies of the Past, Police Impunity and 'Crisis of Racial Injustice.'"
11. Gerald Horne, *Black Revolutionary: William Patterson and the Globalization of the African American Freedom Struggle* (Urbana: University of Illinois Press, 2013); Carol Anderson, *Eyes Off The Prize: The United Nations and the African American Struggle for Human Rights, 1944–1955* (New York: Cambridge University Press, 2003).
12. Workneh, "Black Lives Matter Calls For Global Change."
13. Opal Tometi, "Address at the United Nations General Assembly—July 12, 2016," Archives of Women's Political Communication, Carrie Chapman Catt Center for Women and Politics, Iowa State University,

Ames, July 12, 2016, https://awpc.cattcenter.iastate.edu/2018/09/17
/address-at-the-united-nations-general-assembly-july-12-2016.

14. Tometi, "Address at the United Nations General Assembly."
15. Workneh, "Black Lives Matter Calls For Global Change."
16. On an expansive political agenda, see Ransby, *Ella Baker and the Black Freedom Movement*, 245.
17. Workneh, "Black Lives Matter Calls For Global Change."
18. W. E. B. Du Bois, "The Color Line Belts the World," in *W. E. B. Du Bois: A Reader*, ed. David Levering Lewis (New York: Holt, 1995), 42; on Du Bois and this vision of Black internationalism, see Robin D. G. Kelley, "'But a Local Phase of a World Problem': Black History's Global Vision, 1883–1950," *Journal of American History* 86 (1999): 1045–77. For a broader history of Black internationalism, see Michael O. West, William G. Martin, and Fanon Che Wilkins, eds., *From Toussaint to Tupac: The Black International Since the Age of Revolution* (Chapel Hill: University of North Carolina Press, 2009).
19. On the Black intellectual tradition, see Keisha N. Blain, Christopher Cameron, and Ashley D. Farmer, eds., *New Perspectives on the Black Intellectual Tradition* (Evanston, IL: Northwestern University Press, 2018); Mia Bay, Farah J. Griffin, Martha S. Jones, and Barbara D. Savage, eds., *Toward an Intellectual History of Black Women* (Chapel Hill: University of North Carolina Press, 2015); Brian D. Behnken, Gregory D. Smithers, and Simon Wendt, eds., *Black Intellectual Thought in Modern America: A Historical Perspective* (Jackson: University Press of Mississippi, 2017).
20. Hamer, "Nobody's Free Until Everybody's Free," 136.
21. Hamer, "'Nobody's Free Until Everybody's Free,'" 73.
22. Julia Erin Wood, "'What That Meant to Me': SNCC Women, the 1964 Guinea Trip, and Black Internationalism," in *To Turn the Whole World Over: Black Women and Internationalism*, eds. Keisha N. Blain and Tiffany M. Gill (Urbana: University of Illinois Press, 2019).
23. Doug McAdam, *Freedom Summer* (New York: Oxford University Press, 1988).
24. Carson, *In Struggle*, 134.
25. Harry Belafonte, "Postscript: 'A Trip to Africa,'" in *Voices of Freedom: An Oral History of the Civil Rights Movement from the 1950s through the 1980s*, eds. Henry Hampton and Steve Fayer (New York: Bantam Books, 1990), 204–6.
26. Elizabeth Schmidt, *Cold War and Decolonization in Guinea, 1946–1958* (Athens: Ohio University Press, 2007).
27. Kevin Gaines, *American Africans in Ghana: Black Expatriates and the Civil Rights Era* (Chapel Hill: University of North Carolina Press, 2006).
28. Joseph, *Stokely*, 217–18.
29. Joseph, *Stokely*, 277–318.
30. Wood, "'What That Meant to Me,'" 219.

31. John Lewis with Michael D'Orso, *Walking with the Wind: A Memoir of the Movement* (New York: Simon & Schuster, 1998), 293.

32. Wood, "'What That Meant to Me,'" 221.

33. Hamer, interview by McMillen, 11.

34. Hamer, interview by McMillen, 12.

35. Hamer, interview by McMillen, 12.

36. Wood, "'What That Meant to Me,'" 223.

37. Hamer, interview by McMillen, 12.

38. Hamer, *To Praise Our Bridges*, 21.

39. Brooks, *Fannie Lou Hamer*, 30.

40. Hamer, *To Praise Our Bridges*, 21.

41. Hamer, *To Praise Our Bridges*, 24.

42. Hamer, *To Praise Our Bridges*, 23.

43. Hamer, *To Praise Our Bridges*, 23.

44. Hamer, *To Praise Our Bridges*, 23.

45. Hamer, *To Praise Our Bridges*, 24.

46. Student Nonviolent Coordinating Committee, "Brief Report on Guinea," September 23, 1964, 3, Mss 577, Box 47, Folder 4, WIHVS3310-A, Social Action Vertical File-Student Nonviolent Coordinating Committee, Freedom Summer Digital Collection, Wisconsin Historical Society, Madison, http://content.wisconsinhistory.org/cdm/ref/collection/p15932coll2/id/64892.

47. Mohamed Saliou Camara, Thomas O'Toole, and Janice E. Baker, *Historical Dictionary of Guinea*, 5th ed. (Lanham, MD: Scarecrow Press, 2013), 110.

48. Student Nonviolent Coordinating Committee, "Brief Report on Guinea," 7.

49. Student Nonviolent Coordinating Committee, "Brief Report on Guinea," 3.

50. Student Nonviolent Coordinating Committee, "Brief Report on Guinea," 4.

51. For a discussion of how much the US State Department attempted to manage the image of the Jim Crow South during this period, see Anderson, *Eyes Off the Prize*; Penny Von Eschen, *Race Against Empire: Black Americans and Anticolonialism, 1937–1957* (Ithaca, NY: Cornell University Press, 1997); Mary Dudziak, *Cold War Civil Rights: Race and the Image of American Democracy* (Princeton, NJ: Princeton University Press, 2011).

52. Student Nonviolent Coordinating Committee, "Brief Report on Guinea," 3.

53. Student Nonviolent Coordinating Committee, "Brief Report on Guinea," 6.

54. Student Nonviolent Coordinating Committee, "Brief Report on Guinea," 5.

55. Student Nonviolent Coordinating Committee, "Brief Report on Guinea," 11.

56. Student Nonviolent Coordinating Committee, "Brief Report on Guinea," 11.
57. Belafonte, "Postscript: 'A Trip to Africa,'" 205.
58. Wood, "'What That Meant to Me,'" 229.
59. Wood, "'What That Meant to Me,'" 223–24.
60. Lee, *For Freedom's Sake*, 103.
61. Brooks, *A Voice That Could Stir an Army*, 130.
62. Wood, "'What That Meant to Me,'" 226.
63. Manning Marable, *Malcolm X: A Life of Reinvention* (New York: Viking, 2011); and Les Payne and Tamara Payne, *The Dead Are Arising: The Life of Malcolm X* (New York: Liveright, 2020).
64. Malcolm X, "Malcolm X's Speech at the Founding Rally of the Organization of Afro-American Unity," June 28, 1964, BlackPast, October 15, 2007, https://www.blackpast.org/african-american-history/speeches-african-american-history/1964-malcolm-x-s-speech-founding-rally-organization-afro-american-unity.
65. Carson, *In Struggle*, 135.
66. Brooks and Houck, eds., *The Speeches of Fannie Lou Hamer*, 57.
67. William W. Sales Jr., *From Civil Rights to Black Liberation: Malcolm X and the Organization of Afro-American Unity* (Boston: South End Press, 1994), 171.
68. Brooks and Houck, eds., *The Speeches of Fannie Lou Hamer*, 57.
69. Peniel Joseph, *Waiting 'Til the Midnight Hour: A Narrative History of Black Power in America* (New York: Henry Holt, 2013), 148.
70. Brooks and Houck, eds., *The Speeches of Fannie Lou Hamer*, 57.
71. Brooks and Houck, eds., *The Speeches of Fannie Lou Hamer*, 57.
72. Fannie Lou Hamer, "Oral History Interview with Fannie Lou Hamer, African-American, Woman, FDP: Member of Ex Com., 0491, Ruleville, Mississippi. 0491," interview by KZSU Project South Interviews, 1965, transcript, 6, Department of Special Collections and University Archives, Stanford University Libraries, Stanford, https://exhibits.stanford.edu/oral-history/catalog/zb317wv2717.
73. Hamer, "Oral History Interview with Fannie Lou Hamer . . .," 6.
74. Hamer, "'I'm Sick and Tired of Being Sick and Tired,'" 62.
75. William Pickens, "The American Congo: Burning of Henry Lowry," *The Nation*, March 23, 1921.
76. Nan Elizabeth Woodruff, *American Congo: The African American Freedom Struggle in the Delta* (Cambridge, MA: Harvard University Press, 2003).
77. Adam Hochschild, *King Leopold's Ghost: A Story of Greed, Terror, and Heroism in Colonial Africa* (Boston: Houghton Mifflin, 1999); and Georges Nzongola-Ntalaja, *The Congo from Leopold to Kabila: A People's History* (London and New York: Zed Books, 2002).
78. Brenda Gayle Plummer, *In Search of Power: African Americans in the Era of Decolonization, 1956–1974* (New York: Cambridge University Press, 2013), 89–91.

79. Stephen R. Weissman, *American Foreign Policy in the Congo, 1960–1964* (Ithaca, NY: Cornell University Press, 1974); Lise Namikas, *Battleground Africa: Cold War in the Congo, 1960–1965* (Stanford: Stanford University Press, 2013).

80. Piero Gleijeses, "Flee! The White Giants Are Coming: The United States, Mercenaries, and the Congo, 1964–1965," in *Empire and Revolution: The United States and the Third World Since 1945*, eds. Peter L. Hahn and Mary Ann Heiss (Columbus: Ohio State University Press, 2001).

81. Hamer, "'I'm Sick and Tired of Being Sick and Tired,'" 62.

82. Hamer, "'What Have We to Hail?,'" 80.

83. Hamer, "'What Have We to Hail?,'" 80.

84. Hamer, "'What Have We to Hail?,'" 80.

85. Hamer, "'What Have We to Hail?,'" 80.

86. Hamer, "'America Is a Sick Place, and Man Is on the Critical List,'" 117–18.

87. Hamer, "'We Haven't Arrived Yet,'" 183.

88. Hamer, interview by McMillen, 12–13.

89. Hamer, "'We Haven't Arrived Yet,'" 186.

90. Hamer, "'We Haven't Arrived Yet,'" 186.

91. Hamer, "'We Haven't Arrived Yet,'" 183.

92. Piero Gleijeses, *Conflicting Missions: Havana, Washington, and Africa, 1959–1976* (Chapel Hill: University of North Carolina Press, 2003).

93. Dennis Merrill, *Negotiating Paradise: U.S. Tourism and Empire in Twentieth Century Latin America* (Chapel Hill: University of North Carolina Press, 2009); and Daniel Immerwahr, *How to Hide an Empire: A History of the Greater United States* (New York: Farrar, Straus and Giroux, 2019).

94. Albert J. Raboteau, *American Prophets: Seven Religious Radicals and Their Struggle for Social and Political Justice* (Princeton, NJ: Princeton University Press, 2016), 190.

95. Raboteau, *American Prophets*, 190

96. John D'Emilio, *Lost Prophet: The Life and Times of Bayard Rustin* (New York: Free Press, 2003), 445–46.

97. Fannie Lou Hamer, "'To Make Democracy a Reality,' Speech Delivered at the Vietnam War Moratorium Rally, Berkeley, California, October 15, 1969," in *The Speeches of Fannie Lou Hamer*, 98.

98. Hamer, "'To Make Democracy a Reality,'" 98, 100.

99. Hamer, "'To Make Democracy a Reality,'" 101.

100. George Lipsitz, "The Possessive Investment in Whiteness," in *White Privilege: Essential Readings on the Other Side of Racism*, ed. Paula S. Rothenberg with Soniya Munshi, 5th ed. (New York: World Publishers, 2016), 71.

101. Lipsitz, "The Possessive Investment in Whiteness," 71.

102. Lipsitz, "The Possessive Investment in Whiteness," 71.

103. Lipsitz, "The Possessive Investment in Whiteness," 71.
104. O'Dell, "Life in Mississippi: An Interview with Fannie Lou Hamer," 242.
105. O'Dell, "Life in Mississippi: An Interview with Fannie Lou Hamer," 242.
106. O'Dell, "Life in Mississippi: An Interview with Fannie Lou Hamer," 233.
107. Hamer, "'To Make Democracy a Reality,'" 102.
108. Hamer, "'To Make Democracy a Reality,'" 100.
109. Hamer, "'To Tell It Like It Is,'" 90.
110. Sheryl Fitzgerald, "Black Leaders Urge Gulf Oil Boycott," *Norfolk Journal and Guide*, August 25, 1973.
111. Randall Robinson, Chris Nteta, and Brenda Robinson, Letter to Supporters of the Pan-African Liberation Committee, Fall 1973, Brookline Village, MA, Private Collection of David Wiley and Christine Root, African Activist Archive, East Lansing, MI, https://africanactivist.msu.edu/document_metadata.php?objectid=210-808-402. On the PALC and the broader support for African liberation movements during this period, see Plummer, *In Search of Power*, 277.
112. Robinson, Nteta, and Robinson, Letter to Supporters of the Pan-African Liberation Committee.
113. Hamer, "'To Make Democracy a Reality,'" 103.

CHAPTER SIX: TRY TO DO SOMETHING
1. Hamer, "'We're On Our Way,'" 53.
2. Sylvie Laurent, *King and the Other America: The Poor People's Campaign and the Quest for Economic Equality* (Oakland: University of California Press, 2018).
3. Laurent, *King and the Other America*, 191.
4. "About the Poor People's Campaign: A National Call for Moral Revival," Poor People's Campaign, https://www.poorpeoplescampaign.org/about, accessed October 15, 2020.
5. Rev. Dr. William Barber II and Rev. Dr. Liz Theoharis, "Introducing The Poor People's Moral Budget: Everybody's Got the Right to Live," in *Poor People's Moral Budget: Everybody Has the Right to Live*, eds. Shailly Gupta Barnes, Lindsay Koshgarian, and Ashik Siddique (Poor People's Campaign/Institute for Policy Studies, June 2019), https://www.poorpeoplescampaign.org/wp-content/uploads/2019/12/PPC-Moral-Budget-2019-report-FULL-FINAL-July.pdf; Katrina vanden Heuvel, "A New Poor People's Campaign Wants to Change How Society Defines Morality," *Washington Post*, December 5, 2017, https://www.washingtonpost.com/opinions/a-new-poor-peoples-campaign-wants-to-change-how-society-defines-morality/2017/12/05/d4524b68-d90d-11e7-b1a8–62589434a581_story.html.
6. "Current US Poverty Statistics," Kairos: The Center for Religions, Rights, and Social Justice, March 2018, https://kairoscenter.org/wp-content/uploads/2018/03/Poverty-Fact-sheet-March-2018.pdf.

7. "Current US Poverty Statistics," Kairos: The Center for Religions, Rights, and Social Justice, January 2017, https://kairoscenter.org/wp-content/uploads/2017/02/Poverty-Fact-sheet-Jan-2017.pdf.

8. Barber and Theoharis, "Introducing The Poor People's Moral Budget," 7.

9. Barber and Theoharis, "Introducing The Poor People's Moral Budget," 7.

10. Rev. Dr. William J. Barber and Rev. Dr. Liz Theoharis, "Introduction," in *The Souls of Poor Folk: Auditing America 50 Years After the Poor People's Campaign Challenged Racism, Poverty, the War Economy/Militarism and Our National Morality*, eds. Saurav Sarkar, Shailly Gupta Barnes, and Aaron Noffke (Poor People's Campaign/Institute for Policy Studies, April 2018), 17, https://www.poorpeoplescampaign.org/wp-content/uploads/2019/12/PPC-Audit-Full-410835a.pdf.

11. Barber and Theoharis, "Introducing the Poor People's Moral Budget."

12. Public Affairs, UC Berkeley, "Berkeley Talks Transcript: Rev. Dr. William J. Barber II: 'Forward Together, Not One Step Back,'" Berkeley News, April 14, 2019, https://news.berkeley.edu/2019/04/14/berkeley-talks-transcript-rev-dr-william-j-barber-ii.

13. Public Affairs, UC Berkeley, "Berkeley Talks Transcript: Rev. Dr. William J. Barber II."

14. Hamer, "'We're On Our Way,'" 53.

15. *The Life of Fannie Lou Hamer: Never Turn Back*, dir. Bill Buckley. (Emphasis added in text.)

16. It is significant to note that Mississippi was ranked the poorest state in the United States in 2019. See Liz Knueven, "The Typical American Household Earns $61,000 a Year. Here Are 15 States Where the Typical Resident Earns Even Less," *Business Insider*, August 19, 2019, https://www.businessinsider.com/personal-finance/poorest-states-in-the-us-by-median-household-income-2019–8#1-mississippi-15.

17. DeMuth, "Fannie Lou Hamer: Tired of Being Sick and Tired."

18. Hamer, "Fannie Lou Hamer Speaks Out," 53.

19. Payne, *I've Got the Light of Freedom*, 16.

20. Payne, *I've Got the Light of Freedom*, 17.

21. William Leuchtenburg, *Franklin D. Roosevelt and the New Deal, 1932–1940* (New York: Harper and Row, 1963).

22. Harvard Sitkoff, *A New Deal for Blacks: The Emergence of Civil Rights as a National Issue* (New York: Oxford University Press, 1978).

23. Bruce J. Schulman, *From Cotton Belt to Sunbelt: Federal Policy, Economic Development, and the Transformation of the South, 1938–1980* (Durham, NC: Duke University Press, 1994), 20.

24. National Sharecroppers Fund, *From the Mississippi Delta Comes a Challenge to All Americans . . .* (New York: National Sharecroppers Fund, 1964), https://www.crmvet.org/docs/nsf_brochure.pdf.

25. Dittmer, *Local People*, 125.

26. Dittmer, *Local People*, 125.

27. White, *Freedom Farmers*, 68.

28. White, *Freedom Farmers*, 68.

29. White, *Freedom Farmers*, 68.

30. Hamer, "'I Don't Mind My Light Shining,'" 5.
31. Hamer, "'The Only Thing We Can Do Is to Work Together,'" 71.
32. Hamer, "'I Don't Mind My Light Shining,'" 5.
33. Hamer, "'To Tell It Like It Is,'" 89.
34. Hamer, "'The Only Thing We Can Do Is to Work Together,'" 71–72. For information on the NCNW, see Rebecca Tuuri, *Strategic Sisterhood: The National Council of Negro Women in the Black Freedom Struggle* (Chapel Hill: University of North Carolina Press, 2018).
35. Hamer, "'The Only Thing We Can Do Is to Work Together,'" 72.
36. *The Life of Fannie Lou Hamer: Never Turn Back*, dir. Bill Buckley.
37. Hamer, "'To Tell It Like It Is,'" 91.
38. Hamer, "'To Tell It Like It Is,'" 92.
39. Hamer, "'I'm Sick and Tired of Being Sick and Tired'" and "'What Have We to Hail?,'" 57–64, 74–83, respectively.
40. White, *Freedom Farmers*, 69; Brooks, *Freedom Fighting Woman*, 142.
41. Hamer, "'I'm Sick and Tired of Being Sick and Tired,'" 63.
42. Asch, *The Senator and the Sharecropper*, 133.
43. Hamer, "'What Have We to Hail?,'" 75.
44. Asch, *The Senator and the Sharecropper*.
45. Tuuri, *Strategic Sisterhood*, 2.
46. Tuuri, *Strategic Sisterhood*, 186.
47. Hamer, "'The Only Thing We Can Do Is to Work Together,'" 72.
48. Hamer, "'The Only Thing We Can Do Is to Work Together,'" 73.
49. Hamer, "'To Tell It Like It Is,'" 92.
50. Hamer, "Testimony Before the Democratic Reform Committee, Jackson, Mississippi, May 22, 1969," 96.
51. Hamer, "'What Have We to Hail?,'" 74.
52. Robert Dallek, *Lyndon B. Johnson: Portrait of a President* (Oxford: Oxford University Press, 2004).
53. Dallek, *Lyndon B. Johnson*.
54. Ira Katznelson, "Was the Great Society a Lost Opportunity?," in *The Rise and Fall of the New Deal Order*, eds. Steve Fraser and Gary Gerstle (Princeton, NJ: Princeton University Press, 1989).
55. Hamer, "'What Have We to Hail?,'" 80.
56. Brooks, *Freedom Fighting Woman*, 123.
57. "A Short History of SNAP," US Department of Agriculture, Food and Nutrition Service, September 11, 2018, https://www.fns.usda.gov/snap/short-history-snap#1964.
58. Hamer, "'Until I Am Free, You Are Not Free Either,'" 126–27.
59. Brooks, *A Voice That Could Stir an Army*, 158.
60. Hamer, "'What Have We to Hail?,'" 82.
61. Hamer, "'What Have We to Hail?,'" 82.
62. Albert J. Raboteau, "Is This America? Fannie Lou Hamer and the Voices of Local People," in *American Prophets: Seven Religious Radicals and Their Struggle for Social and Political Justice* (Princeton: Princeton University Press, 2016).
63. Hamer, "'What Have We to Hail?,'" 83.

64. Peterson, "Fannie Lou Hamer: Mother of 'Black Women's Lib,'" 21.
65. Brooks, *Fannie Lou Hamer*, 144; Bracey, *Fannie Lou Hamer*, 138.
66. White, *Freedom Farmers*.
67. "Fannie Lou Hamer Founds Freedom Farm Cooperative," SNCC Digital Gateway, https://snccdigital.org/events/fannie-lou-hamer-founds -freedom-farm-cooperative.
68. White, *Freedom Farmers*, 76; Lea E. Williams, "Fannie Lou Hamer, Servant of the People," in *Focus on Leadership: Servant-Leadership for the Twenty-First Century*, eds. Larry C. Spears and Michele Lawrence (New York: J. Wiley & Sons, 2002), 75–76.
69. Hamer, *To Praise Our Bridges*, 18.
70. Hamer, "'Until I Am Free, You Are Not Free Either,'" 128.
71. Hamer, interview by McMillen, 23.
72. White, *Freedom Farmers*, 65.
73. Dorothy I. Height, *Open Wide the Freedom Gates: A Memoir* (New York: PublicAffairs, 2003), 188.
74. White, *Freedom Farmers*, 157.
75. White, *Freedom Farmers*, 68.
76. "Fannie Lou Hamer Founds Freedom Farm Cooperative," SNCC Digital Gateway; White, *Freedom Farmers*, 73.
77. White, *Freedom Farmers*, 79.
78. Hamer, interview by Neil McMillen, 25.
79. White, *Freedom Farmers*, 72–75.
80. Aldridge, "What Makes Fannie Lou Hamer Run?"
81. Hamer, "'Until I Am Free, You Are Not Free Either,'" 127.
82. Paule Marshall, "Fannie Lou Hamer: Hunger Has No Color Line," *Vogue* 155, no. 10 (June 1, 1970): 191; J. Todd Moye, *Let the People Decide: Black Freedom and White Resistance Movements in Sunflower County, Mississippi, 1945–1986* (Chapel Hill: University of North Carolina Press, 2004), 156.
83. White, *Freedom Farmers*, 73.
84. Hamer, "'We Haven't Arrived Yet,'" 191.
85. June Jordan, "Mississippi 'Black Home': A Sweet and Bitter Bluesong Mississippi,'" *New York Times Magazine*, October 11, 1970, 77.
86. Hamer, *To Praise Our Bridges*, 17.
87. Robert A. Hill, ed., *The Marcus Garvey and Universal Negro Improvement Association Papers, Vol. X: Africa for the Africans, 1923–1945* (Berkeley: University of California Press, 1983), 697.
88. Erik S. McDuffie, "A New Day Has Dawned for the UNIA: Garveyism, the Diasporic Midwest and West Africa, 1920–1980," *Journal of West African History* 2, no. 1 (Spring 2016): 73–114.
89. McDuffie, "A New Day Has Dawned for the UNIA," 89.
90. Hamer, "'Until I Am Free, You Are Not Free Either,'" 127.
91. Marshall, "Fannie Lou Hamer: 'Hunger Has No Color Line,'" 191.
92. Jordan, "Mississippi 'Black Home,'" 77.
93. Jordan, "Mississippi 'Black Home,'" 77.
94. Jordan, "Mississippi 'Black Home,'" 74–77.

95. White, *Freedom Farmers*, 76.
96. White, *Freedom Farmers*, 76.
97. White, *Freedom Farmers*, 76.
98. Crystal Sanders, *A Chance for Change: Head Start and Mississippi's Black Freedom Struggle* (Chapel Hill: University of North Carolina Press, 2016); Mills, *This Little Light of Mine*, 204–6.
99. Rust College Head Start State Training Office, "Overview," 1977, Box 11, Folder 24, "Proposals," Fannie Lou Hamer Papers, Amistad Research Center at Tulane University, New Orleans.
100. Sanders, *A Chance for Change*, 53.
101. Mills, *This Little Light of Mine*, 205.
102. Tuuri, *Strategic Sisterhood*, 147.
103. White, *Freedom Farmers*, 84–86.
104. The trip formed the basis for Jordan's children's biography of Hamer. See Jordan, *Fannie Lou Hamer*.
105. Jordan, "Mississippi 'Black Home,'" 74.
106. Jordan, "Mississippi 'Black Home,'" 77.
107. Hamer, "'We're On Our Way,'" 53.
108. John T. Edge, "The Hidden Radicalism of Southern Food," *New York Times*, May 6, 2017, https://www.nytimes.com/2017/05/06/opinion/sunday/the-hidden-radicalism-of-southern-food.html.

CONCLUSION: UNTIL ALL OF US ARE FREE
1. Brooks, *Fannie Lou Hamer*, 165. It is significant to note that Delta Health Center has gone by a number of names over the years and newspapers and other sources of the period reported different names for the hospital. These include the Tufts-Delta Health Center, the Delta Community Health Center, and the Mound Bayou Community Hospital.
2. Brooks, *Fannie Lou Hamer*, 165–66.
3. Brooks, *Fannie Lou Hamer*, 166.
4. Hamer, interview by McMillen, 30.
5. Brooks, *Fannie Lou Hamer*, 176; Lee, *For Freedom's Sake*, 176.
6. Lee, *For Freedom's Sake*, 176.
7. Lee, *For Freedom's Sake*, 174.
8. Fannie Lou Hamer to Reverend Marion Elaine Myles, August 23, 1976, University of Mississippi Archive—Fannie Lou Hamer.
9. Lee, *For Freedom's Sake*, 177.
10. Brooks, *Fannie Lou Hamer*, 176.
11. Annette Samuels, "People Profiled: Fannie Lou Hamer," *New York Amsterdam News*, February 12, 1977.
12. Samuels, "People Profiled: Fannie Lou Hamer."
13. Samuels, "People Profiled: Fannie Lou Hamer."
14. Samuels, "People Profiled: Fannie Lou Hamer."
15. Samuels, "People Profiled: Fannie Lou Hamer."
16. "Fannie Lou Hamer Paid Tribute by National Figures," *Atlanta Daily World*, March 22, 1977, 1.

17. Thomas A. Johnson, "Young Eulogizes Fannie L. Hamer, Mississippi Civil Rights Champion, *New York Times*, March 21, 1977, https://www.nytimes.com/1977/03/21/archives/young-eulogizes-fannie-l-hamer-mississippi-civil-rights-champion.html.
18. "Fannie Hamer's Funeral," *Los Angeles Sentinel*, April 7, 1977.
19. Johnson, "Young Eulogizes Fannie L. Hamer, Mississippi Civil Rights Champion."
20. "Fannie Lou Hamer Paid Tribute by National Figures."
21. "Fannie Lou Hamer Paid Tribute by National Figures."
22. Marcia Gillespie, "Getting Down," *Essence* 8, no. 1 (May 1977): 55.
23. Gillespie, "Getting Down," 55.
24. Jessica Bennett, "Overlooked No More: Before Kamala Harris, There Was Charlotta Bass," September 4, 2020, *New York Times*, https://www.nytimes.com/2020/09/04/obituaries/charlotta-bass-vice-president-overlooked.html.
25. Denise Lynn, "Charlotta Bass for Vice President: America's Two-Parties and the Black Vote," Black Perspectives (AAIHS), January 21, 2020, https://www.aaihs.org/charlotta-bass-for-vice-president-americas-two-parties-and-the-black-vote.
26. Bennett, "Overlooked No More: Before Kamala Harris, There Was Charlotta Bass."
27. Kamala Harris, "Transcript: Kamala Harris' DNC Speech," August 20, 2020, CNN, https://www.cnn.com/2020/08/19/politics/kamala-harris-speech-transcript/index.html.
28. Harris, "Transcript: Kamala Harris' DNC Speech."
29. Harris, "Transcript: Kamala Harris' DNC Speech."

INDEX

IMAGE CREDITS

ABOUT THE AUTHOR

Keisha N. Blain is associate professor of history at the University of Pittsburgh, president of the African American Intellectual History Society, and a columnist for MSNBC. She is the author of the multi-prize-winning book *Set the World on Fire: Black Nationalist Women and the Global Struggle for Freedom*. With Ibram X. Kendi, Dr. Blain co-edited the *New York Times* bestseller *Four Hundred Souls: A Community History of African America, 1619–2019*.